CORPUS PALLADIANUM

VOLUME VI

CENTRO INTERNAZIONALE DI STUDI DI ARCHITETTURA "ANDREA PALLADIO"

BOARD OF ADVISORS

RODOLFO PALLUCCHINI - Professor of the History of Modern Art, University of Padua - *Chairman*

GIULIO CARLO ARGAN - Professor of the History of Modern Art, University of Rome

SERGIO BETTINI - Professor of the History of Medieval Art, University of Padua

Sir ANTHONY BLUNT - Professor of the History of Art, University of London - Director, The Courtauld Institute of Art

ANDRÉ CHASTEL - Professor of the History of Art, the Sorbonne, Paris

† GIUSEPPE FIOCCO - Director, Institute of Art History, Cini Foundation, Venice

PIETRO GAZZOLA - Soprintendente ai Monumenti di Verona - Lecturer, Corso di Specializzazione in Restauro dei Monumenti, University of Rome - President, Conseil International des Monuments et des Sites

MARIO GUIOTTO - Lecturer on restoration of monuments at the Istituto di Architettura, Venice

LUDWIG HEYDENREICH - Director Emeritus, Zentralinstitut für Kunstgeschichte, Munich

WOLFGANG LOTZ - Director, Bibliotheca Hertziana, Rome

GUIDO PIOVENE - Accademico Olimpico

CAMILLO SEMENZATO - Professor of the History of Art, Facoltà di Magistero, Padua

† RUDOLF WITTKOWER - Institute for Advanced Study, Princeton University

BRUNO ZEVI - Professor of the History of Architecture, University of Rome

RENATO CEVESE - Secretary, Centro Internazionale di Studi di Architettura "Andrea Palladio"

CORPUS PALLADIANUM

Already published:

I THE ROTONDA, by Camillo Semenzato
II THE BASILICA, by Franco Barbieri
III THE CHIESA DEL REDENTORE, by Wladimir Timofiewitsch
IV THE LOGGIA DEL CAPITANIATO, by Arnaldo Venditti
V THE VILLA EMO AT FANZOLO, by Giampaolo Bordignon Favero
VI THE CONVENTO DELLA CARITÀ, by Elena Bassi

In course of publication:

THE VILLA BADOER AT FRATTA POLESINE, by Lionello Puppi
THE PALAZZO DA PORTO FESTA IN VICENZA, by Erik Forssman

In preparation:

THE PALAZZO ANTONINI IN UDINE, by Camillo Semenzato
THE PALAZZO CHIERICATI, by Franco Barbieri
THE PALAZZO THIENE IN VICENZA, by Renato Cevese
THE PALAZZO VALMARANA-BRAGA, by Nino Carboneri
THE VILLA BARBARO VOLPI AT MASER, by Giuseppe Mazzariol
THE VILLA CORNARO AT PIOMBINO DESE, by Douglas Lewis
THE VILLA MALCONTENTA AT MIRA, by Licisco Magagnato
THE VILLA PISANI AT BAGNOLO, by Marco Rosci
THE VILLA PISANI AT MONTAGNANA, by Carolyn Kolb Lewis and Francesco Cessi
THE VILLA SAREGO AT SANTA SOFIA DI PEDEMONTE, by Pietro Gazzola
THE TEATRO OLIMPICO, by Licisco Magagnato
THE PROJECTS OF PALLADIO, by Manfredo Tafuri

Editor of the Series: Renato Cevese
Assistant Editor: Abelardo Cappelletti

THE CONVENTO DELLA CARITÀ

Elena Bassi

THE CONVENTO DELLA CARITÀ

CORPUS PALLADIANUM

VOLUME VI

THE PENNSYLVANIA STATE UNIVERSITY PRESS
UNIVERSITY PARK & LONDON

THE PREPARATION OF THE MONOGRAPHS OF THE CORPUS PALLADIANUM HAS BEEN MADE POSSIBLE WITH THE AID OF THE CONSIGLIO NAZIONALE DELLE RICERCHE OF ITALY AND OF THE ENTI FONDATORI OF THE CENTRO INTERNAZIONALE DI STUDI DI ARCHITETTURA " ANDREA PALLADIO " IN VICENZA.

THE AUTHOR'S THANKS GO TO RODOLFO PALLUCCHINI, WHO WITH HIS CONSTANT SUPPORT HELPED GUIDE THIS WORK TO ITS COMPLETION; TO RENATO CEVESE FOR HIS KIND AND INTELLIGENT HELP; TO RUDOLF WITTKOWER AND WOLFGANG LOTZ, WHO HAVE ENCOURAGED ME WITH THEIR ADVICE; TO THE DIRECTOR AND STAFF OF THE ARCHIVIO DI STATO AND THE SOPRINTENDENZA ALLE GALLERIE ED AI MONUMENTI IN VENICE, WHO HAVE ASSISTED ME IN FINDING DOCUMENTS AND IN PROVING THEIR VALIDITY; TO THE CENTRO INTERNAZIONALE DI STUDI DI ARCHITETTURA " ANDREA PALLADIO " AND ITS SECRETARIAL STAFF; AND TO THE ARCHITECTS GILDA D'AGARO, VITTORIA PELZEL PALLUCCHINI, PIETRO PELZEL, AND ANDRZEJ PERESWIET-SOŁTAN.

E. B.

TRANSLATED BY C. W. WESTFALL
COPYRIGHT © 1973 BY THE CENTRO INTERNAZIONALE DI STUDI DI ARCHITETTURA " ANDREA PALLADIO "
PUBLISHED BY THE PENNSYLVANIA STATE UNIVERSITY PRESS
LIBRARY OF CONGRESS CATALOGUE CARD NUMBER 72-1140
STANDARD BOOK NUMBER 0-271-01155-6
ALL RIGHTS RESERVED
PRINTED IN ITALY
OTV STOCCHIERO S.p.A. - VICENZA

CONTENTS

CHAPTER I	The Monastery before Palladio		13
	Notes to Chapter I		21
CHAPTER II	Itinerarium Mentis		23
	Notes to Chapter II		36
CHAPTER III	Execution of the Project		39
	Notes to Chapter III		54
CHAPTER IV	The Interpretation of the Concept		55
	Notes to Chapter IV		73
CHAPTER V	The Monastery after the Fire		75
	Notes to Chapter V		81
CHAPTER VI	Visual and Literary Records		83
	Notes to Chapter VI		125
CHAPTER VII	Conclusion		127
Questo benedetto teatro			133
Comparative measurements of the projects and the executed building			136
Chronological Table			137
Documents			139
Manuscript Sources			151
Bibliography			153
Index of Persons and Places			155
List of Illustrations in the Text			161
List of Plates			165
List of Scale Drawings			167

THE CONVENTO DELLA CARITÀ

I
THE MONASTERY BEFORE PALLADIO

The origin and the early history of the complex of buildings within which Palladio worked at the Carità has been described by Gino Folgari, in a study based on documents and concentrating on the church. Although Folgari took his study only up to the sixteenth-century rebuilding of the monastery, it is still useful to recapitulate some of his conclusions.

In 1134 a number of regular canons of Santa Maria in Porto moved from Ravenna to Venice. They constructed their monastery with its cloister beside the Church of Santa Maria della Carità. In 1260 a Scuola dei Battuti, which was later called the Scuola della Carità, asked to be accommodated beside the monastery. It obtained a room near the dormitory, next to the entrance to the building. For many decades the scuola enjoyed considerable wealth, while the neighboring monastery remained in financial straits.[1] Poverty constrained the canons to sell some land situated along the rio della Carità, now the rio terra' della Carità, to the scuola on March 17, 1344. There the confraternity members constructed their Casa Grande, with a prospect over open space. The entrance, which was around the corner from the main façade, served both the Casa Grande and the monastery. It gave access to a first courtyard (fig. XCVII), which the two groups held in common after the sale. The members of the scuola assumed the responsibility for maintaining the well therein, which was ornamented with reliefs representing the confraternity members supporting the symbols of the scuola (fig. LXXXVI).

Some decades later the church and monastery needed restoration. The wall that enclosed the small cemetery of the monastery was lapped by the water of the Grand Canal and the rio di Sant'Agnese (now the rio terra' Foscarini); it threatened to collapse and carry the campanile with it. In 1384 the scuola lent the monastery 100 gold ducats for this work. In exchange, the scuola set up its own lodgings in the room it had fitted out in 1294. This had been its first site; it was against the wall of the contiguous monastery. Later, in November of 1411, the two institutions established a further agreement that allowed the members of the scuola to expand their lodgings along the wall of the church. In this way the complex assumed the proportions it has retained ever since.[2]

In 1431 the Venetian Gabriele Condulmer became Pope Eugenius IV, and the congregation of the Lateranensi began to reconstruct and enlarge their establishment. First, the church was rebuilt between 1441 and 1445 to make it grand and modern. In vain, the members of the scuola attempted to prevent incursions into their grounds. They were no longer able to enlarge their lodgings, which were their most important legacy; nor could they prevent others from laying hands on the tombs of their first members. But the

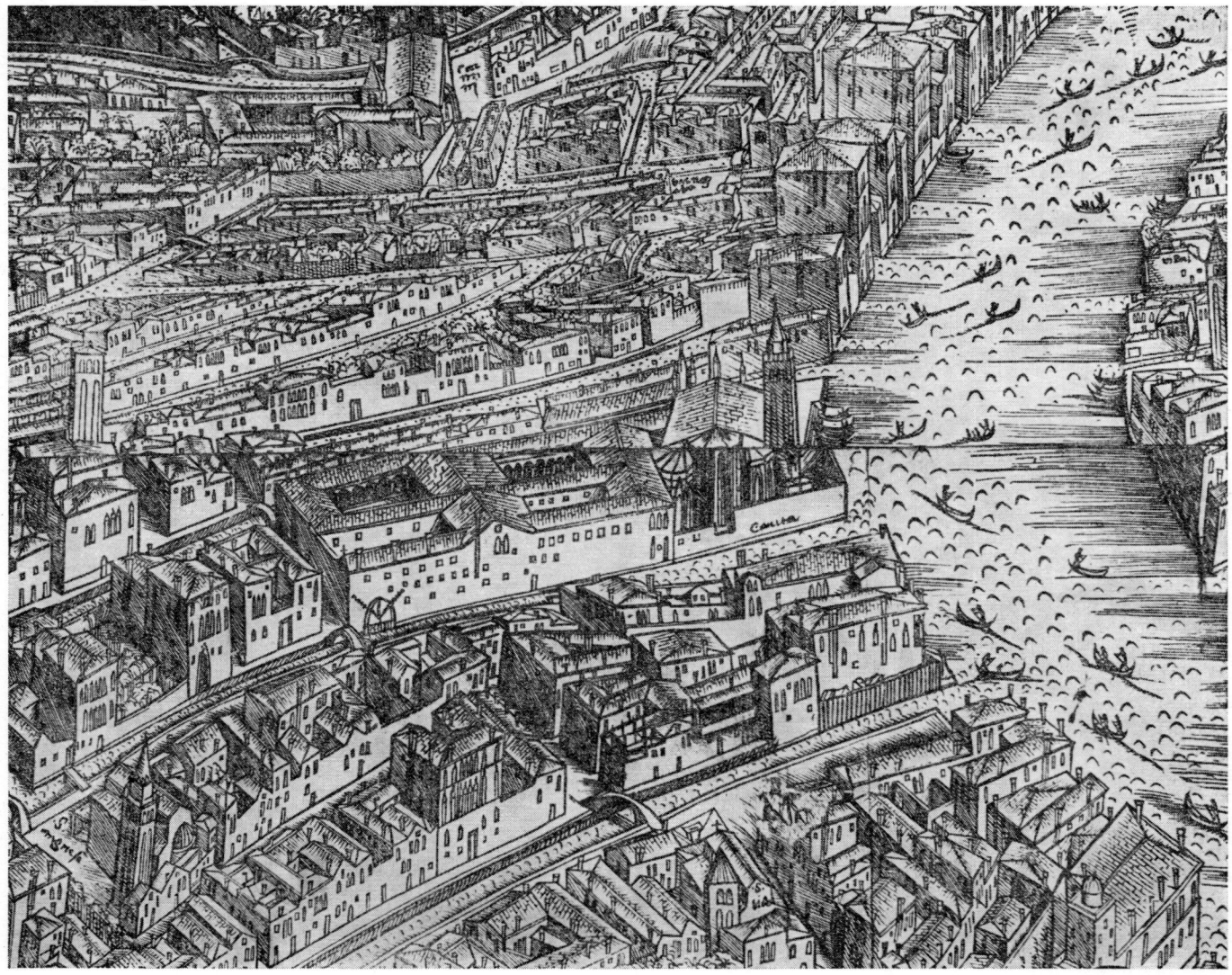

I - JACOPO DE' BARBARI, *Monastery and Church of the Carità* (from the plan of 1500)

scuola profitted nonetheless; the entrance atrium was rebuilt with elegant columns and well-carved beams, and this gave greater importance to the entire monastery precinct (fig. LXXXIX).

When the work was completed the monastery, church, and scuola had the appearance that can be seen rather clearly in the plan of Jacopo de' Barbari (fig. I). The new triple-apsed church is flanked by a tall campanile; an enclosing wall along the Grand Canal and the rio di Sant'Agnese defines the cemetery and abuts the old monastery, which extends in a long rectangular space, divided into four sections with courtyards and cloisters. Its appearance along the rio di Sant'Agnese is clear; it has windows arranged asymmetrically, the central part projects upward obliquely, and there is a wide water-gate. The two stretches that are visible toward the rio di Sant'Agnese seem unadorned; the others, toward the rio della Carità, encircled by arcades, resemble the cloisters of the contemporaneous Venetian monastery of Sant' Apollonia, which is still extant. The southernmost one possibly served as the hospital and as the priorate of the scuola. Also to the south a *calle* (called the calle del Dose) is visible. Eventually the canons would make various attempts to acquire it, because later, when Palladio set about to design the new monastery, land beyond it belonging to the canons would be proposed as the site for their refectory.[3] The impression here is of a fortified monastery;

II - Zuan Andrea Vavassori, called Vadagnino, *Monastery and Church of the Carità* (from the plan of 1517)

this is also evident in the Vavassori plan of 1517 (fig. II).

Some documents drafted at the end of the quattrocento make it clear that the canons also wanted to give new dignity to the monastery. In December, 1497, they obtained from Antonio Vitturi and the members of the Carità, their noble neighbors, permission to construct an overpass across the calle del Dose to give them access to their vineyard; on April 2, 1498, they obtained similar permission from the Maggior Consiglio and from the Magistrato al Piovego. The Maggior Consiglio, however, imposed the condition that, when building in their field, they had to remain a required distance from the house of the Memmo family. The Memmo, along with the Vitturi and the Bonzi, had property bordering on that of the canons. On April 4, 1503, the canons addressed a petition to the " Serenissimo Prencipe, ... per poter serrar una Cale qual discorre tra esso Monasterio, et una casa che fù da cha bonza per essi Reverendi Canonici acquistata per potersi allargar con ditto suo Monasterio." On April 7, in another petition, they clarified their position; they wished to close the *calle* that went " dal Canal de san Trovaso piccolo " (now the rio terra' della Carità) to the "Rio de santa gniese." They added that they had already had an affirmative " respondeat " from the judges of the Piovego.[4]

Testimony beginning in the 1530s suggests that substantial work was carried out subsequently. On February 18, 1538, the canons contracted for " miara 30. de piere

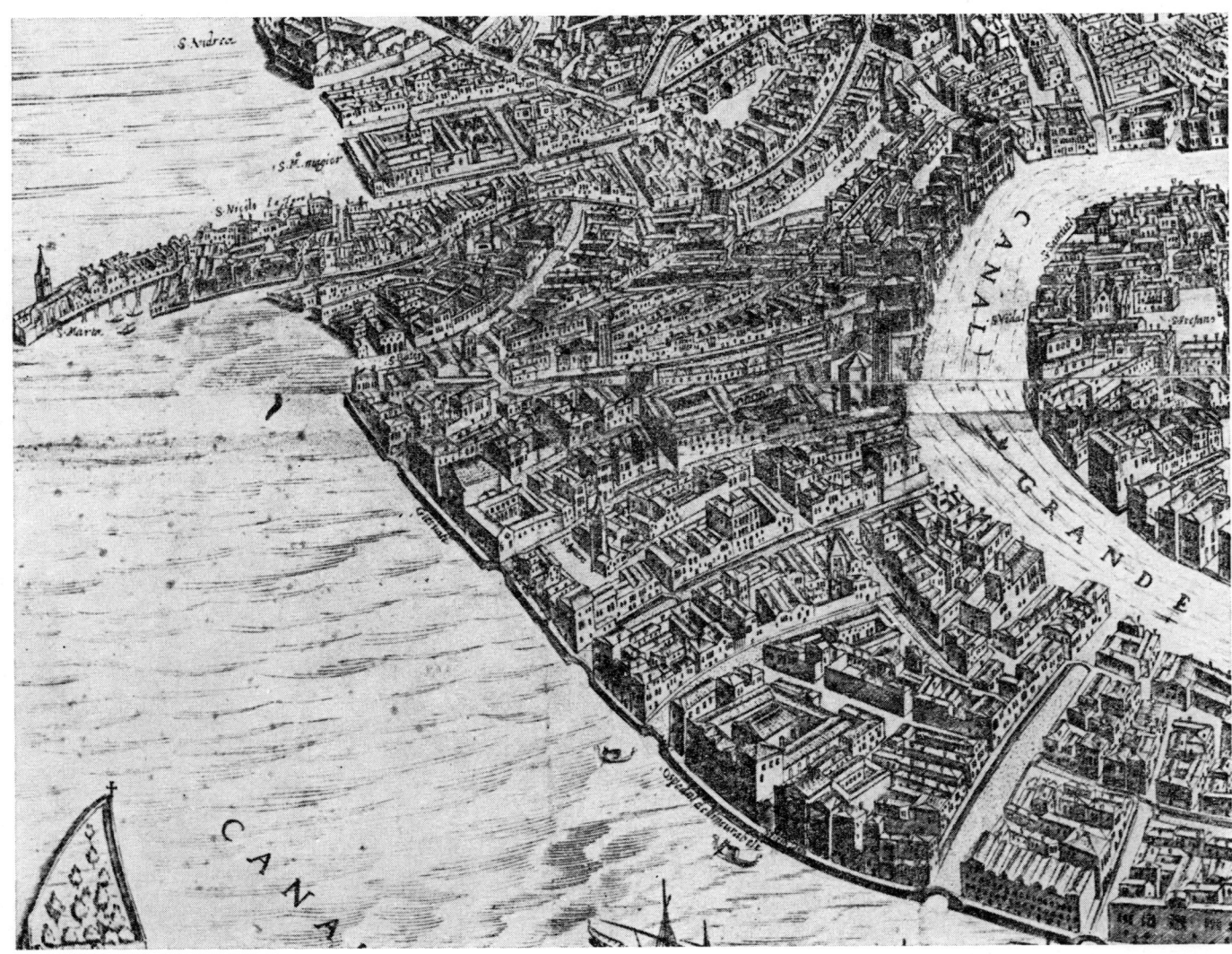

III - Pietro Merlo, *The Area of the Convento della Carità* (from the plan of 1696)

cotte." We do not know exactly what was done with the 30,000 bricks, or even what was planned for them; nor do we know what use was made of the "due partite di Zecca" that Gerolamo and Pietro Corner and Antonio Dandolo set up "in conto della fabrica del ... monastero" on April 26, 1541.[5] It appears probable that around 1540, when reconstruction of the church was being finished and a crypt and altar for the Mocenigo was completed,[6] renovation of the monastery was already being considered. The "partita di Zecca" of 1541 speaks explicitly of construction, and on August 24, 1543, the owner of the contiguous land, Anzolo Memmo, protested because the "finestre principiate à far in la proprietà et case di essi Canonici" had corbels that projected into a little courtyard of his; he did not intend to share its air with the reverend canons.[7] Although this brief seems to deal with construction in the monastery, it could be referring to something built beyond the calle del Dose in the Vineyard.[8] A document mentioned by Paoletti refers to "arche funerarie ch'erano nel Claustro, rimosse per fabbricare" in 1548.[9] And finally, on January 30, 1555, in the "Sommario delle Scritture" (see documents section, p. 142) there is another contract for "piere ben conditionate."[10] For various reasons one can suppose that by then Palladio himself had already conceived the splendid Corinthian atrium that he would be able to build with all that fine material.

The Lateran canons were strictly tied to their superiors in Rome, and they consid-

IV - CANALETTO, *Santa Maria della Carità*. London, The National Gallery

V - BENEDETTO CALIARI, *St. Augustine Giving the Rule of the Lateran Canons*. Altarpiece executed for the sacristy of the Church of the Carità. Venice, Gallerie

VI - *The rio terrà' Sant'Agnese on November 4, 1966.* From *Venezia fino a quando?*, 1967

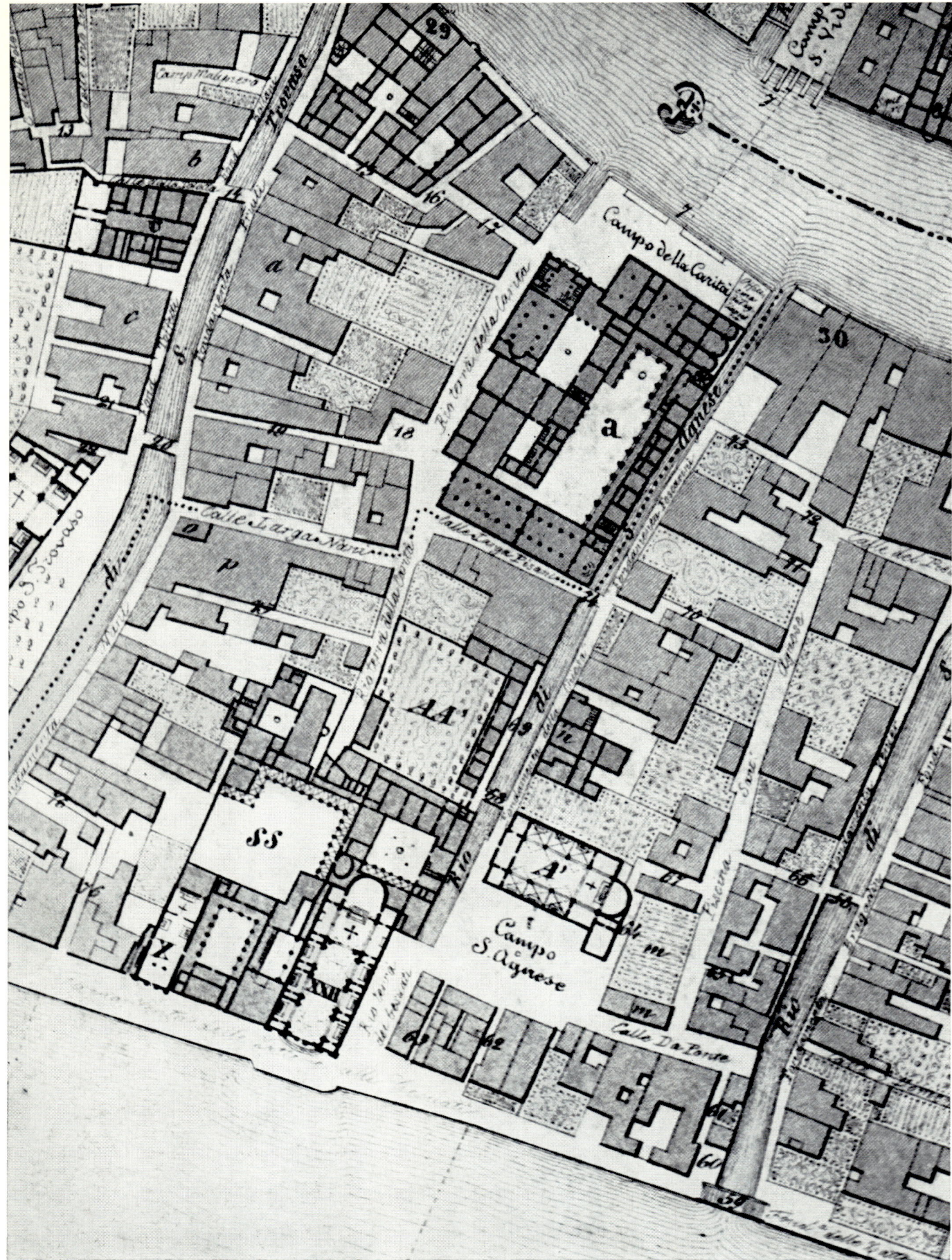

VII - *Convento della Carità adapted for use by the Accademia.* Engraving by Combatti (1847)

ered themselves to be Romans; their natural propensities, therefore, predisposed them to accept a classicizing project for their building. On March 5, 1555, Palladio had requested of the Vicentine authorities " licenza di andar in certi suoi servigi in servizio di alcuni signori veneziani." [11] In that year he had been consulted about the problem of selecting a model for the Scala d'Oro at the Doges' palace.[12] And, also in 1555, Doni had referred to him with great praise; he was that " honorato huomo ... venuto al Mondo per suscitare l'architettura." [13]

The concept of the Venetian monastery became concrete after a long period of maturation; it drew from the deepest roots of culture, experience, and practical sense. In it, Palladio evoked earlier projects and experiences that represented years of intense study. To him, the capital of the Venetian duchy—which was still as important as Rome in Euro-Asian politics—seemed prepared to accept a solemn building such as those of Michelangelo and the Sangallo. That the great monastery, constructed " ausu romano," would be placed among the humble buildings, the houses and small palaces, that gave a particular scale to the city did not concern him. In Venice, humble and grand buildings had always been mixed together. At a distance of 500 meters from the Carità as the crow flies stood the Ca' Grande dei Corner, which was just then being completed. It was built throughout in Istrian stone, and it was the highest and largest palace built in the city up to that time. Palladio would demonstrate that not only Sansovino, a Tuscan, but also he, a Vicentine, knew how to build on a grand scale; in Venice, he hoped, he could more easily accomplish that feat than he could in gentle Vicenza.

A well-known, enchanting painting by Canaletto (fig. IV) shows the campo della Carità as it was when Palladio began formulating his plans. The only parts of Palladio's building visible in it is a part of the roof and a chimney. Among the small palaces and houses rise the thin campanile and the spires of the scuola and of the church. On the side of the great church building, there are some corbelled arches and a portal. Two modest canons' houses look over the Grand Canal. Next to these is the wall of the monastic cemetery, crowded with trees. Behind it, on the rio Sant' Agnese, would rise Palladio's great monastery.

NOTES TO CHAPTER I

[1] A little after their arrival, in 1261, the members of the Confraternity of the Carità acquired from the canons a tomb next to the church, for interring their own members; in 1287 they acquired a second one in the wall inside the church, hemmed in by others that were later obliterated in the fifteenth-century rebuilding. On March 7, 1294, the scuola was able to construct its own room for itself, situated in part above the portico and in part above the entranceway through which one passed from the campo della Carità to the courtyard of the monastery.

From the scant surviving notices we can still deduce that the church had some external arches in the lateral wall looking into the small courtyard and that it was preceded by a narthex like those which survive today in the churches of San Nicolò dei Mendicoli and San Giacomo di Rialto in Venice.

[2] Later it was ornamented by Antonio Vivarini and Giovanni d'Alemagna's triptych (1446), by the sparkling, carved wooden ceiling (1496), and by Titian's *Presentation of the Virgin in the Temple* (1534). Furthermore, in November, 1411, the canons ceded to the scuola two little houses at the end of the common courtyard and a garden and another house situated along the rio della Carità. The confraternity members were obliged not to build either a church or any other building in which they would

be able to celebrate religious functions, but they equipped there a hospice for the poor and a lodging for the prior. In exchange for the houses the scuola loaned the monastery 2,000 ducats, which were non-transferable (document I, under the date 4 November 1411).

[3] The scuola is not clearly visible in the de'Barbari map, but its appearance is represented in a painting in the Gallerie dell'Accademia attributed to Mansueti (*The Meeting of Doge Ziani with Pope Alexander III in the Campo della Carità*), in another of the same subject by Benedetto and Carletto Caliari in the Sala del Maggior Consiglio in the Doges' Palace, in a print by Carlevarijs (fig. XCVII), and, finally, in a well-known canvas by Canaletto (London, National Gallery; fig. IV).

[4] Document I, under those dates, and document II.

[5] Document I, under that date.

[6] G. Fogolari, 1924, p. 91.

[7] Document III.

[8] Meanwhile, the canons—already prosperous—had acquired other funds in 1547, when they became the proprietors of rich lands around Senigaglia: "Probata est eiusmodi acquisitio per Paulum III Kal. Decemb. ann. sui Pont. XIV existenti Priore dictj Monasteri Ven. P. D. Gregorio Barbadico Nobili Veneto, qui novam Monasterij fabricam inchoavit, quam utinam illius successores perfecissent (G. Pennotto, 1624, p. 587; also in Corner, 1749, p. 171).

Already at the end of the fifteenth century the sumptuous tombs of the two Barbarigo doges had been installed in the Church of the Carità; their design is attributable to Codussi. Gregorio Barbarigo, son of the doge Marco, was perhaps involved in the appointment through which Palladio conceived the project for the Carità, just as later, in 1577, the *procuratore* Agostino Barbarigo favored the selection of Palladio's project for the Redentore.

[9] 1893, II, p. 271.

[10] Document I, under that date.

[11] A. Magrini, 1845, X.

[12] G. Lorenzi, *Monumenti per servire alla storia del Palazzo Ducale*, Venice, 1869, Document X.

[13] A. F. Doni, *Seconda Libraria*, Venice, 1555, p. 155. In the first edition of the work (1551), Palladio is not mentioned.

a - CANALETTO: *The Courtyard of the Convento della Carità.* Windsor Castle, Royal Collections

II
ITINERARIUM MENTIS

Work on the Basilica in Vicenza had been underway since 1546. Through his friendship with Trissino, Palladio had been introduced to the circle of Bembo and Alvise Cornaro. Daniele Barbaro, Patriarch of Aquileia, was able to open the door to the religious and to the Venetian patriciate for the architect. By 1555 Palladio was rather well known in that circle.

Palladio's first visits to Rome (1541, 1547, 1549, 1554) had permitted him to review the most admired works of architecture; they had also borne fruit in the edition of the *Antichità di Roma* (1554) and in the illustrations for the *Architettura* of Vitruvius (1556), for which Barbaro had been translating and preparing comments since 1547. These learned activities would eventually culminate in Palladio's own *Quattro Libri* (1570).

If we collate the biographical references of this period, we notice that while undertakings in Vicenza diminish, those in Venice increase. Zorzi, with good reason, suggested that Palladio's contact with Venice had already begun in 1548.[1] Later, on January 11, 1554, he competed for the office of *proto all'Uffizio del Sale*; had he been given it, he would have become the supervisor for the preservation and transformation of the Doge's Palace. The office went instead to Pietro Guberni, about whom we know little, but who was certainly well known among the citizens of the time.[2] Then, in 1556, Palladio was relieved of having to direct the works at the Basilica in Vicenza. In 1557 construction on the Palazzo Chiericati was interrupted. On January 7, 1558, the contract for the façade of San Pietro di Castello was drafted, and it was followed by a contract for the refectory of San Giorgio Maggiore on November 22, 1561.[3] Already in 1560, Marc'Antonio, the son of the architect, who had been inscribed among the sculptors in Vicenza and was also active at the Basilica, took employment with Vittoria in Venice. The next year Palladio was working with Vittoria and Marc'Antonio for Gian Francesco Priuli, cousin of the doge then in office.[4] In 1556 Girolamo had succeeded his brother Lorenzo as doge, and it was to Girolamo that Daniele Barbaro had addressed a congratulatory discourse.[5] Certainly both knew Palladio.

It seems that a project containing preliminary proposals for the reconstruction of the monastery, which for the most part survives in the Archivio di Stato in Venice, may safely be dated to around 1555.[6] Until now it has escaped the attention of scholars. The "ductus" of the drafting, the calligraphy, and, above all, the articulate character of the plan firmly establish it as Palladio's (figs. XVII-XIX).

Although somewhat schematic, the design has distinct analogies to the plan for the palace for Giacomo Angarano in Vicenza[7] and to one of the solutions proposed for the "casa degli antichi"—more precisely, with the casa dei Greci (fig. XXXVI).[8] It shows that in the mind of the architect, the Church of the Carità was to be integrated into the complex; after entering from a portal on the side, turned toward the Grand Canal, and then crossing the sacred area, the canons would have found themselves in an atrium (here called "corte") surrounded by columns on three sides, with the fourth occupied by a refectory. The refectory was perhaps already situated at that spot in the monastery as represented by de'Barbari; in the Palazzo Angarano the analogous zone would have been occupied by the great stairhall. Beyond the refectory is a cloister, which in the plan is called "horto"; it corresponds to the courtyard of the Palazzo Angarano. In the palace in Vicenza the area beyond this was reserved for services, while in the monastery, in the area beyond the calle del Dose—which is in part incorporated into the "horto"—are the granaries and woodsheds. In both the projects, there are few openings to the outside; perhaps the architect recalled that the house of antiquity was isolated, like a fortress.

The plan in the archives therefore suggests a monastery rather different from the one later decided upon. Its construction would have preserved part of what already existed. The area belonging to the scuola and the courtyard with the well are marked out from the plan with strong, straight lines; Palladio would not invade it. He was contented to place against it a pantry and other areas near the kitchen in a long, narrow, corridorlike row of rooms. The refectory, which was between the court and the "horto," is large; it measures 8.52 by 21.73 meters, with a height of 10.43 meters. The major chapter hall (*capitolo*) is 8.69 meters, with a mezzanine lodging for the doorkeeper below it and a cellar in a semi-basement level, as is learned from the inscriptions. All the other areas are 5.21 meters high. On one side of the refectory is a vestibule, a kitchen, and a pantry of the "bocali"; on the other side is the principal stair, a small chapter hall, and the sacristy, which, like the one that already existed, is certainly contiguous to the church (doc. IV).

Above the kitchen on the next story is the "camera del fuoco"; on the other side of the atrium, above the sacristy and the smaller chapter room, is a room labeled "camera," a library, and the sacristan's room. On the second and third floors on the side facing the orchard are the guest rooms, which include a "barbaria" and a cloakroom ("vestiario"). Above the "cavana," which opened to the canal, there is a mezzanine, taken up by lodging and a storage room; rooms such as these were to be found above the "cavana" in the executed project. The dormitories are on the third floor. In the area that projected behind the hospice of the scuola are the oven and laundry, flanked by a courtyard with a colonnaded loggia on three sides.

In substance, the plan is for a rather traditional monastery, but the atrium and its great cloister (28.51 by 23.12 meters) would have allowed so much light to enter that the earlier construction would have shown up rather poorly. We do not know what caused this project to flounder. It may have been the impossibility of expropriating the calle del Dose, which was public property; alternatively, it may be that upon further reflection Palladio thought that at the Carità he would be able to construct a full-blown "casa degli antichi," complete with tablina and an atrium with a true "impluvium." Thus, the second and definitive concept, which Palladio showed in the *Quattro Libri* as the "Atrio Corinthio" (figs. XI-XIV), was born.

It is clear that the atrium was at the

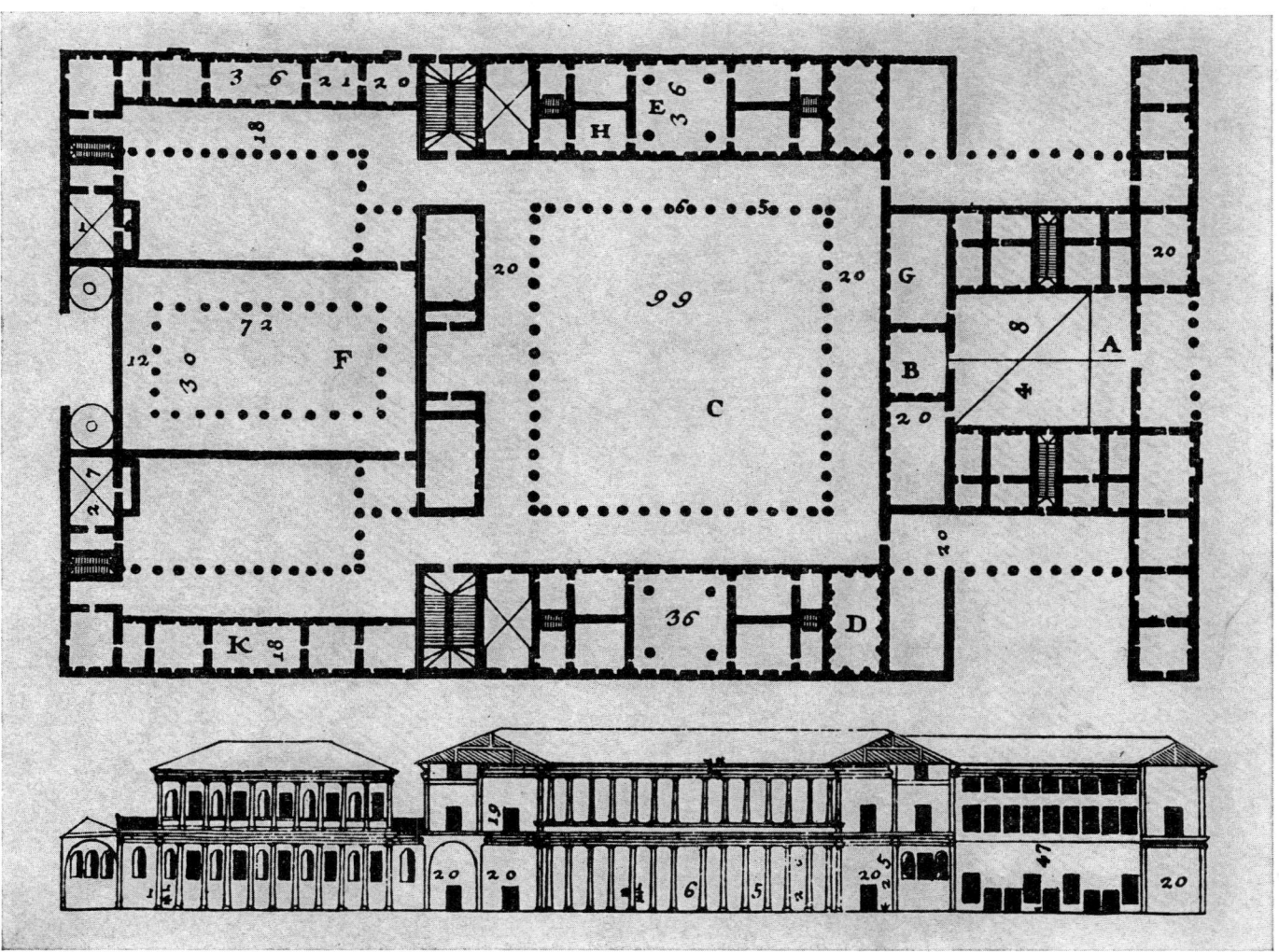

VIII - ANDREA PALLADIO, *The casa dei Romani*. From *I Quattro Libri dell'Architettura*, 1570, II, vii, p. 34

center of his interest. One instance of this is revealed in a sarcastic quatrain of the period: "Non va il Palladio per male a puttane / che se talvolta pur gli suole andare / lo fa perché le esorta a fabbricare / un atrio antico in mezzo Carampane."[9] The lively and irreverent verse shows that Temanza, the eighteenth-century architect who quoted it, took satisfaction in learning that new construction should contain motifs that were derived from classical architecture, but that were also revised. The malicious poet suggests that every community, be it of "canonici" or of "honorati cortigiane," was entitled to an "atrio antico." In Venice, in the area called Carampane, there still exists an elegant wing of a fifteenth-century courtyard with narrow, superimposed loggias, which we might imagine was a portion of a brothel that was famous for centuries; within that courtyard, it would have been possible to construct an atrium (fig. LXXXVII). Like the one at the Carità, the wing appears to have been inserted into a preexisting structure. Indeed, at the old monastery the plan remains unaltered, either because the new one was not allowed to extend beyond the boundaries of the old or because the new was never finished. The quatrain perhaps dates from the time of the second project, as one may suppose by its insistence on the atrium. It is perhaps not beside the point to mention that Pietro Aretino, who years before had become a Venetian, died of a heart attack in 1556. We would never attribute such stylistically slovenly verses to him, but in some way he might have been their inspiration.

The second, definitive project can with

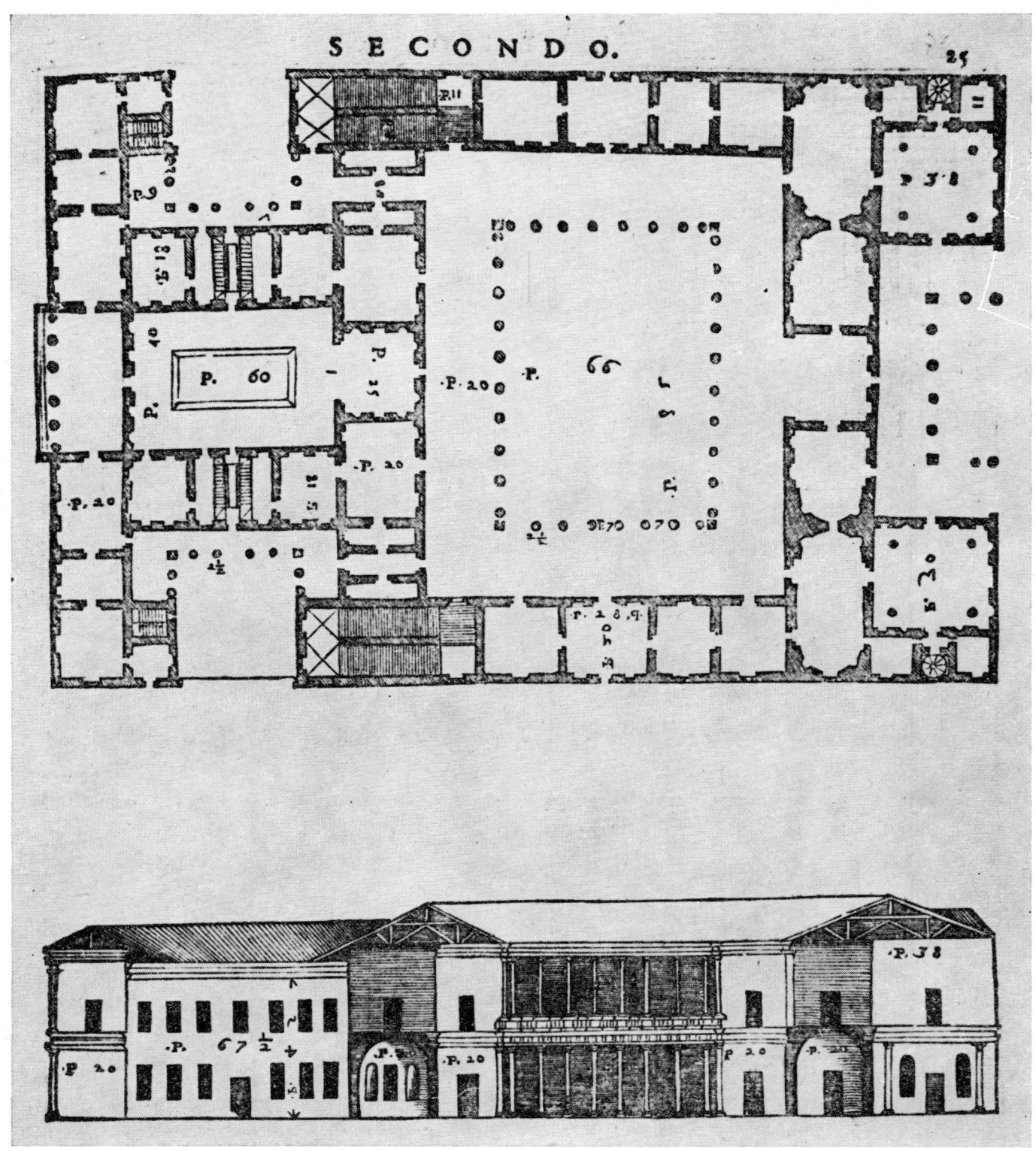

IX - ANDREA PALLADIO, *Tuscan atrium, in small-scale representation.*
From *I Quattro Libri dell'Architettura*, 1570, II, iv, p. 25

reason be placed in the years 1555-56. It is the one that the architect illustrated in the second book of the *Quattro Libri* in which, as he explained on the title page, "the Designs of Several Houses Ordered by [*sic*] him both within and out of the City are contained, and the Designs of the Antient Houses of the GREEKS and LATINS." This is the liveliest of the four books, because Palladio showed many of the works here in their finished state. As studies for the ancient houses, the author described the Tuscan atrium, the atrium with four columns, the Corinthian atrium, halls with four columns, Corinthian halls, and Egyptian halls; he then turned to the

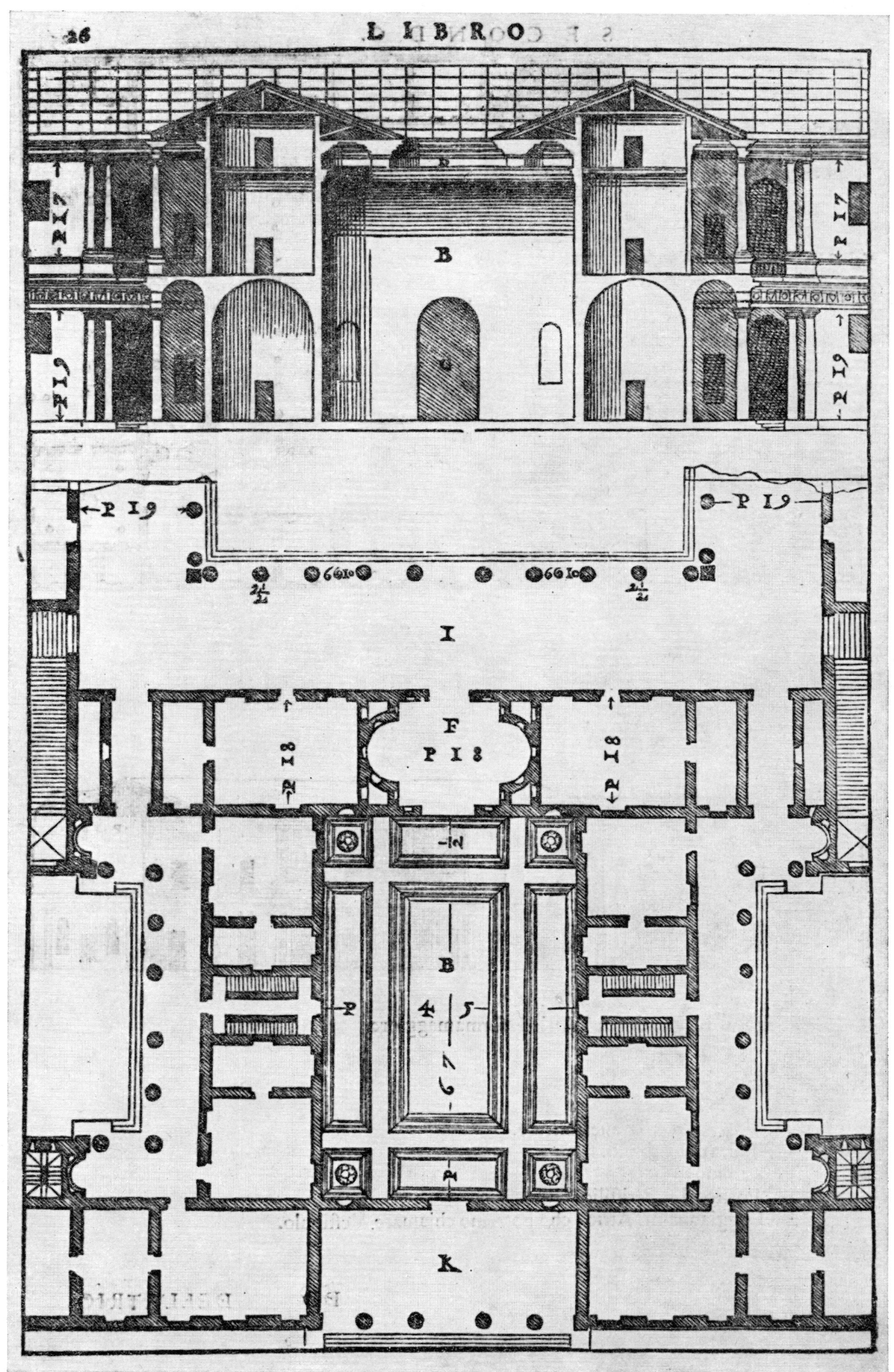

X - Andrea Palladio, *Tuscan atrium, in large-scale representation*.
From *I Quattro Libri dell'Architettura*, 1570, II, iv, p. 26

private houses of the Latins and Greeks, and, finally, to villas (figs. VIII-X; XXXVII-XXXVIII; XXXV-XXXVI). All the examples were theoretical, with the exception of that of the Corinthian atrium, for which, as he said himself, he adopted the composite order (figs. XI-XIV). The elevation of the "atrio di quattro colonne" (fig. XXXVII) is very similar to the elevation of the atrium of the Carità (fig. XII). Similarly, in the "sala di quattro colonne" (fig. XXXVIII) there are references to the tablinum-sacristy in the form and in the proportions of the niches and windows, in the module of the columns, in their placement in the space, and in their distance from the walls (scale drawings *h-i*).

Palladio gave the following description of his Venetian project:

" The following fabrick is of the convent *de la Carita* where are regular canons at Venice. I have endeavoured to make this house like those of the antients; and therefore I have made a Corinthian Atrio to it, whose length is the diagonal line of the square of its breadth. The wings are one part of three and a half, or two sevenths of its length. The columns are of the Composite order, three foot and a half thick, and five and thirty foot long. The uncovered part in the middle is the third part of the breadth of the Atrio. Over the columus [*sic*] there is an uncovered terrace level with the floors of the third order of the cloister where the Friar's cells are. The sacristy is on one side near the Atrio, incompassed with a Dorick cornice, which supports the vaults. The columns there seen, support that part of the wall in the cloister, which in the part above, divides the chambers or cells from the loggia's. This sacristy serves for a tablino (so they called the place where they lodged the images of their ancestors) tho' for conveniency, I have placed it on one side of the Atrio. On the other side is the place for the chapter, which answers to the sacristy. In the part near the church there is an oval stair-case, void in the middle, which is very convenient and pleasant. From the Atrio one enters into the cloister, which has three orders of columns, one over the other. The first is Dorick, and the columns project from the pilasters more than one half. The second is Ionick; the columns are one fifth part less than those of the first. The third is Corinthian, and the columns are a fifth part less than those of the second. In this order, instead of pilasters, there is the continued wall; and directly over the arches of the inferior orders, there are windows which give light to the entrance into the cells, the vaults of which are made with reeds, that they may not overcharge the walls. Opposite to the Atrio and cloister, beyond the stars, one finds the refectory, which is two squares long, and as high as the floor of the third order of the cloister: It has a loggia on each side, and underneath a cellar made in the same manner as cisterns are, that the water may not get in. At one end it has the kitchen, ovens, a yard for poultry, a place for wood, a place to wash clothes in, and a very agreeable garden; and at the other end, other kind of places.

There are in this fabrick, besides places for strangers, and others that serve for different purposes, forty - four rooms, and forty - six cells."[10]

In the chapter "Of stairs, and the various kinds of them, and of the number and size of the steps,"[11] he states: " Besides the usual manners of stairs, there was another sort of winding stair-case invented by the Clarissimo Signor Marc'Antonio Barbaro, a Venetian gentleman of a fine genius, which in very narrow places serves very well: it has no column in the middle; and because the steps are crooked, they are very long, and must be divided as the abovesaid.

The oval stair-cases are also divided in the very same manner as the round; they are very beautiful and agreeable to see, because all the windows and doors come to the head of the oval, and in the middle, and are sufficiently commodious.

I have made a stair-case void in the middle, in the monastery *de la Carità* in Venice which succeeds admirably" (fig. XV).

The architect describes with equal care both what had been built and what remained only a project. Some passages perhaps refer to technical difficulties that had been overcome. For example, in writing that the columns of the tablinum " support " the wall that in the " cloister " divides the cells from the " loggias," he is referring to having resolved an important technical problem with a felicitous solution (scale drawings *c, e*). Similarly, he notes that the " volti " of the cells on the third floor " sono fatti di canne " in order not to load the lower floors (figs. LXXI-LXXII). Such meticulous references to details of construction are not frequently found in the treatise. And we discover that supporting walls are of a considerable thickness, as was required in a solemn building (fig. LXXXIII).

The plates showing the Corinthian atrium are the only source for the appearance of that part of the monastery before the fire (figs. XI-XIV). Palladio does not show the exterior façade along the rio di Sant'Agnese; it would have followed directly from the plan and from the elevation's dimensions, and it would have had the sober appearance appropriate to a Venetian monastery constructed in the years in which one had to avoid costly ornamentation, as Eugenio Battisti has correctly noted.[12] The congregation of the Lateranensi canons was reformist, and for this reason, as well, their residence would not have been allowed a sumptuous appearance (plates 4-5). Nor does Palladio illustrate the section of either the tablinum or the stairs, although the stairs had been shown in the chapter "Of stairs..." (fig. XV). Thus, from both the plate and the text devoted to the Carità, it is clear that the architect had concentrated his efforts on the atrium.

For years Palladio had studied the houses of the ancients, in order to illustrate Vitruvius and to explain to himself what he had discovered when he explored ancient sites. Perhaps while touring the old area of the monastery and the extensive vineyard he had come to believe that the location was suitable for constructing the fruits of his research. At the Carità the similarity between the ancient and the contemporary is indefinite. We might believe that the architect desired to resolve the practical problems posed by certain sibylline phrases in Vitruvius and that he willingly exploited a commission in which he had ample space available.

Comparing the sections in the treatise on the house of the Romans with that of the Greeks and with the monastery of the Carità, we see that the first two are ill-resolved, while the Venetian building appears as a solid structure drawn from sound and immediate examples and not dependent only upon ancient texts and the learned arguments of Daniele Barbaro (figs. VIII, XXXV-XXXVI, XCV). Barbaro's Vitruvius dwells on the casa dei Romani, which is represented both in plan and in elevation.[13] The analogy to the monastery, however, is vague (fig. XXXV): the atrium is more spacious; the tablinum is small and is arranged, as the rules required, between the atrium and the peristyle, and it has two great exedrae, which characterize also the Carità's tablinum; the peristyle is arranged as a rectangle transverse relative to the atrium, while in the Venetian project it is disposed in the opposite sense; and at the top is the refectory, which, in a certain sense, substi-

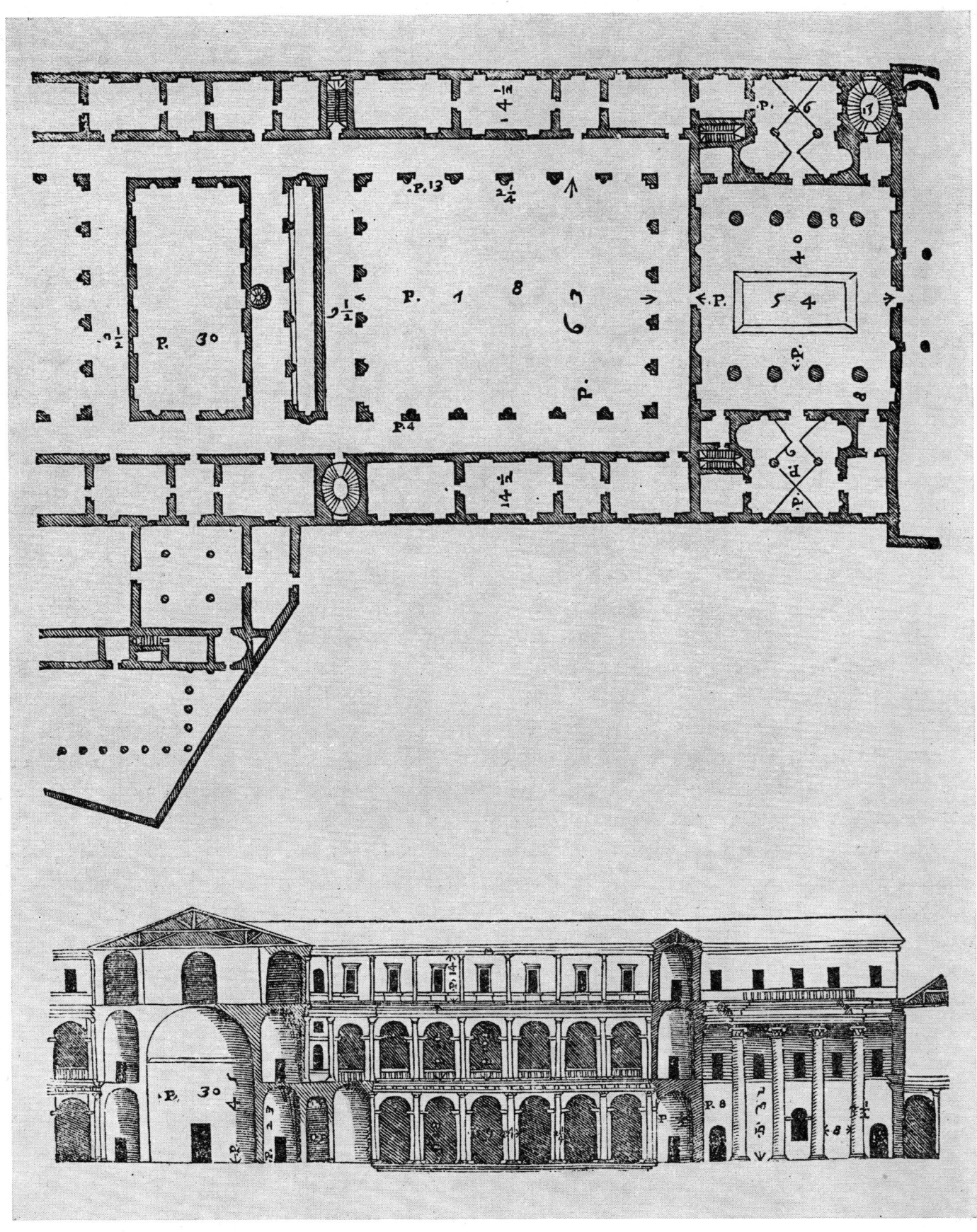

XI - Andrea Palladio, *Convento della Carità: plan and section.*
From *I Quattro Libri dell'Architettura*, 1570, II, vi, p. 30

tutes for the basilica in the ancient construction.

The *atrio testugginato* in the *Quattro Libri* is also illustrated by the plan of a Roman house (fig. VIII); it is interesting to note that in the scheme for its elevation the upper floor of the basilica is surrounded by a terrace. Such an element would have appeared at the Carità on the side of the refectory that is turned toward one of the peristyles; however, it was begun but not finished and was later removed in the nineteenth-century restorations.

The plates for the casa degli antichi, both in Barbaro's book and in the *Quattro Libri*, resulted from the rearranging of some basic themes that are also found at the Carità and that allow one to follow the " itinerarium mentis " of the Venetian monastery. But the monastery in front of which Palladio stood, the one in the view of de'Barbari, was to be transformed according to the project largely preserved in the archives. Palladio would have left in place many of the elements of the Romanesque monastery, while attempting to express himself with great elegance by settling the details and adjusting the parts. The classicizing character did not interfere with the functioning of the commodious, modern building. It still offered the canons ample space for moving around within the building and on the terraces and within the porticoes, loggias, open loggias, and long, broad corridors; they had for their use a beautiful sacristy, a chapter hall, and a spacious, high refectory.

The architect did not seek a stylish architecture; the canons were to be at their ease in a monastery that was very different from the one they had known earlier, with its meager porticoes and shadowy cells. Now they would have a healthy space of beautiful proportions; above the grand cloister a great rectangle of sky would allow them to watch the seasons change. In their spacious basement, constructed as an impermeable cistern, they would store the produce from the nearby orchards. In every way, Palladio's learned dream was subordinated to the requirements of a sixteenth-century monastic community.

When working for the Lateranensi Palladio faced and resolved problems posed by no other project. This was the single monastic building that he designed completely. Following custom, monastic complexes were built by the religious, which meant that in the treatises in vogue the theme was not dealt with in a complete or specific manner. His scheme did not contradict tradition; indeed, its cloister's elevation resembles that of Bramante's Santa Maria della Pace (and, even more, that of the courtyard of the Palazzo Farnese). Yet it clearly recalls a studied classicism, responding to a demand that was then widely diffused. Aretino, for example, had praised the buildings of Giulio Romano because they were " anticamente moderni e modernamente antichi." [14]

The final project is bolder than the first one. It derives from the " casa privata " published by Barbaro, but it is still closer to the invention of the Trissino brothers,[15] to the house of Iseppo de'Porti,[16] and to that of Ottavio Thiene,[17] in plan as well as in elevation.

The drawings executed in Rome of baths and imperial palaces had already been incorporated into the Palazzo de'Porti, with the great columns of the courtyard (36 *piedi* high and 3 ½ wide, the same as those of the Carità) and with the statues arranged across the top. Similarly, many niches had already been used to ornament the atrium of the Palazzo di Montagnana.

At the Carità the architect was able to appropriate everything, and he was freer than he had been at the monastery for the Benedictines at San Giorgio, where construction begun decades earlier by others

XII - Andrea Palladio, *Convento della Carità: atrium*, in large-scale representation.
From *I Quattro Libri dell'Architettura*, 1570, II, vi, p. 31

XIII - ANDREA PALLADIO, *Convento della Carità: atrium and cloister, in large-scale representation.*
Photomontage from *I Quattro Libri dell'Architettura*, 1570, II, vi, pp. 31-32

had been discontinued. When he was called in to complete it, the area of cells and a cloister were already finished, but the refectory was completed only to the height of the windows and had a basement and kitchens beneath. He urged the rebuilding of the church rather than the completing of that area.

Like the first project, the second covers a more extensive area than that which was eventually built on. Here, too, the calle del Dose is incorporated; it is transformed into a long underpass that projects through the monastery (fig. XI). The hospice of the Carità and the courtyard of the scuola are invaded by the second tablinum and by the wing of the monastery opposite the one

that was eventually built. The refectory (10.43 by 21.90 meters; 15.65 meters high) would have been beyond the *calle*, where the granary had been placed in the first project. The sacristy appears where it was in the first project, but because it now is in the guise of a tablinum, it has an elegant plan that derives from Palladio's investigations of Roman baths and suggests the transept of San Giorgio, with its motif of two great exedrae.

In the *Quattro Libri*, the monument is illustrated with three full-page plates and a rather extensive commentary. The woodcut devoted to the plan and section is printed in mirror image, because the architect, in preparing the block, gave no

XIV - Andrea Palladio, *Convento della Carità: cloister*, in large-scale representation. From *I Quattro Libri dell'Architettura*, 1570, II, vi, p. 32

importance to the fact that when printed it would emerge reversed (fig. XI). Some measurements also have their numbers reversed, which has distracted some scholars, who seem in addition to be only vaguely familiar with the topography of the area (figs. XL, XLIV-XLV); this reversal has led to a series of misinterpretations.

The designs of the Carità in a larger format and the plates with the elevations of the house in Barbaro's Vitruvius share a taste for ruins and a great refinement of execution; these are among the most beautiful woodcuts by Palladio. In the series of atria in the *Quattro Libri*, the large plates are more elegant than those smaller in format; at times, there is no correspondence in the proposals seen in the two sizes. For example, in the small plan of the Tuscan atrium the tablinum is very different from the one in the large plan, although this latter one is identical to that of the casa dei Romani in Barbaro (figs. IX, XXXV).[18]

That the ambitious project would have been built in its entirety must at once have appeared unlikely, but Palladio did live long enough to see the commodious and majestic stair completed, with the elegant monogram of the monastery at its top (plates 48-56), as well as the sinuous tablinum, the stupendous atrium, and a wing of the peristyle (plates 33-47; 8-30). And on the second floor, where one enters the Ionic loggia, he built a majestic portal inspired by that at the Temple of Vesta at Tivoli (plates 31-32; fig. XXVIII).

The design of the monastery belongs to the group of projects that dealt with constructing in a modern manner the houses of the ancients. This problem had interested the architect for some fifteen years; after he arrived at his solution, he offered variations of it to those who wanted villas and palaces, each time producing a building adapted to particular requirements, much as a sculptor or painter is able with the same *bozzetto* to produce either a Venus or a Magdalen. He made the scheme for the house of the ancients part of his formal patrimony; he allowed his artistic personality to develop around it for some years, and from it he obtained his design for the monastery, which was more grandiose than all his earlier projects. He then thought no more about the house of the ancients, but he passed on to other problems. Perhaps he had exhausted his interest in the arcane subject, or perhaps, as Ackerman has suggested, he believed that the antiquarian attitude was less in vogue in Venice than it was in Vicenza.[19]

NOTES TO CHAPTER II

[1] Zorzi, 1964, p. 36.
[2] G. B. Lorenzi, 1869, p. 281.
[3] Pane, 1961, p. 17.
[4] Zorzi, 1964, p. 305.
[5] Magrini, 1855, p. 70.
[6] Document IV.
[7] 1570, Libro II, p. 75.
[8] 1570, Libro II, p. 44.
[9] Temanza, 1778, p. 395.
[10] 1570, Libro II, p. 29; quoted from 1738, Book II, p. 43.
[11] 1570, Libro I, xxviii, p. 61; quoted from 1738, Book I, xxviii, p. 35.
[12] 1968, p. 127.
[13] D. Barbaro, 1556, p. 167.
[14] P. Aretino, *Lettere*, Venice, 1537, I, pp. 214-15.
[15] 1570, II, p. 74.
[16] 1570, II, p. 8.
[17] 1570, II, p. 13.
[18] "Voglio ... esortare gli Architetti, e Proti, che non vogliano applaudire, e assentire a padroni. Anzi, che gli dichino il vero, et gli consiglino bene, et amorevolmente, et che pensino bene prima, che gli facciano spendere i dinari, come altrove s'è detto, perché così facendo, veramente meritaranno laude, et nome conveniente alla loro professione," wrote Daniele Barbaro (D. Barbaro, 1556, p. 279), and, in response, Palladio wrote, " ... Commoda si deverà dire quella casa, la quale sarà conveniente alla qualità di chi l'haverà ad habitare, e le sue parti corrisponderanno al tutto, e fra se stesse. ... Si deverà dunque ... per quanto si possa, haver risguardo, et a quelli, che vogliono fabricare, e non tanto à quello, che essi possano, quanto di che qualità fabrica loro stia bene.... Ma spesse volte fa bisogno all'Architetto accomodarsi piu alla volontà di coloro, che spendono, che a quello, che si devrebbe osservare." Again: "Io mi rendo sicuro, che appresso coloro, che vederanno le sotto poste fabriche, e conoscono quanto sia difficil cosa lo introdurre una usanza nuova, massimamente di fabricare, della qual professione ciascuno si persuade saperne la parte sua; io sarò tenuto molto aventurato, havendo ritrovato gentil'huomini di così nobile, e generoso animo, et eccellente giudicio, c'habbiano creduto alle mie ragioni, e si siano partiti da quella invecchiata usanza di fabricare senza gratia, e senza bellezza alcuna; et in vero io non posso se non sommamente ringratiare Iddio ... che m'habbia prestato tanto del suo favore, ch'io habbia potuto praticare molte di quelle cose, le quali con mie grandissime fatiche per li lunghi viaggi c'ho fatto; e con molto studio ho apprese" (1570, II, pp. 3-4). Classical examples, therefore, are subordinate to modern "commodus"; the honest architect would have to persuade the patron to detach himself from long-standing and out-of-date habits.
[19] 1966, p. 156.

XV - Andrea Palladio, *"Delle scale."* From *I Quattro Libri dell'Architettura*, 1570, I, xxviii, p. 63. The example indicated with the letter "F" is the oval stair in the Convento della Carità

b - Convento della Carità: peristyle

III
EXECUTION OF THE PROJECT

Construction of the building was in full progress in 1561, as is shown by an autograph receipt (fig. XX) in which Palladio declares that he has been paid for the model, for a year of supervision of the work, and for the "stampi di piere."[1] The "stampi" had perhaps served in making the very beautiful and much discussed frieze, of which the architect, not forgetting his early experience as a sculptor, is presumed to have taken personal charge (plates 13-20). In the center of the frieze, along with the emblem of the monastery, appears the date 1561 (plate 16). Alternatively, "stampi" may refer to the template models for the bases, capitals, and other elements executed in stone. The word "piera," in the Venetian dialect, both then and now, could signify stone, brick, or terracotta; the soffits of the Doric and Ionic orders in the courtyard were executed in this material, so "stampi" could also refer to templates used for these elements (plates 25-26).

June 1, 1561, is the date of a contract made between the monastery and the mason Antonio Paleari, a native of Marcote in Alto Ticino and a frequent collaborator of Palladio's. He was at Palladio's side at the Carità from the beginning of the work, as we know from a contract that has not survived but that is cited in an appraisal of Paleari's work carried out in 1569.[2]

At a time when Palladio was occupied both at the Carità and at the refectory of San Giorgio Maggiore, the fathers of the Carità bought 100,000 Ferrarese stones (April 1, 1562). They were certainly the best obtainable, because while those acquired in 1538 cost five and a half lire per thousand, these were valued at nine lire and fifteen soldi. Shortly after, on June 24, a contract was made for "portar via il ruinazzo della fabbrica de santa Maria predetta, et condur terra." These two pieces of information indicate that demolition and reconstruction took place simultaneously.[3] Indeed, often the old materials were reemployed, as one may confirm by examining, for example, the quality of the bricks in the dividing walls in the guest rooms (fig. LXXXIII).

Following this period, we have few records of how the construction proceeded. On January 20, 1563, some work involving old stone was finished.[4] This is perhaps visible in the sill of a window and on the ledge of a niche in the stairs; in the first a bull has been carved, and in the second there is an inscription, which is indecipherable because it has been sliced in half. Both are of medieval execution (figs. LXVII-LXVIII). From the same document of 1573 we learn that on April 13, 1564, the acquisition of some lead had not been noted; this was perhaps to be used for the eaves, and thus it could indicate that by the spring of 1564 the building had already reached its full height.

In June, 1568, the "Sommario delle scritture" records that on three different dates the "fondamenta e i gradini sopra il rio di Sant'Agnese" had been measured to verify the bills of the mason and the stonecutter. The measurements were taken not only on the rio Sant'Agnese but also on the Grand Canal, and they totaled 2,872 feet (998.5944 meters). This was perhaps the length of the beds of Istrian stone used in the basement but later covered over when the canal was filled in.

The construction on the canal had certainly reached the corner at the calle del Dose, where a metope, which is among those still visible, is painted with the emblem of the monastery (plate 28); it perhaps indicates the extremity of the building, and the triglyph that follows would have been at the corner. Mezzanine rooms were placed above the great "cavana"; these were destroyed when the canal was filled and the "cavana" was rendered unnecessary, but on the wall, quite high with respect to the actual pavement of the area, there remain traces of a fireplace from the mezzanine story.

On November 30, 1569, five judges, some selected by the monastery and some by Paleari, appraised all of Paleari's outstanding receipts. They agreed that he should be satisfied with 2,949 ducats, subtracting sixteen ducats for " li muri che mancano à smaltar " (that is, which had yet to be " made white," or stuccoed) and some funds that he had already received on account.[5] Payment was completed on June 5, 1570, with 757 ducats, as appears from the same document, which cites a list of things that Paleari had not yet completed. This would perhaps reveal exactly what part of the work had been executed; nonetheless, if in June, 1570, it had been adjudged that only the " muri da smaltar " were incomplete, it is possible to conclude that the project had reached some sort of termination, if only a temporary one.

In the meantime, Palladio had worked at the refectory of San Giorgio, designed the theater for the Compagnia della Calza and the Church of San Giorgio (1565), undertaken the façade of San Francesco della Vigna (1568) and work on the Palazzo Barbaran in Vicenza, and finished the *Quattro Libri*.

He was therefore an established artist esteemed by the most significant people in the city; nevertheless, the reverend canons were not loath to call him to task on occasion (figs. XXI-XXII). On August 30, 1569, they made him agree to rebuild six coffers in the already completed atrium " che confinano con il foro di mezzo " because they were not perfectly waterproof. About a year later, on June 13, 1570, Palladio had to busy himself again in " disfar a tutte sue spese e danni li sei quadri del coperto della corte i quali sono de fuori dalle colonne." This perhaps deals with the coffers already cited in 1569, which had either not yet been remade or had been only poorly repaired, or perhaps with another six between the columns and the wall.[6] Zorzi and Magrini suppose that the second document refers to a restoration of the peristyle,[7] but in that space one would find neither " quadri del coperto " nor any " foro di mezzo." Furthermore, in sixteenth-century documents the peristyle was called the "claustro" or "inclaustro," and "corte" indicated a limited space, such as the atrium that was destroyed in the fire of 1630. For imagining the latter, the testimony of the architect Inigo Jones is extremely important. He was in Italy twice between 1597 and 1615, and he was therefore able to study the monastery when the work was not finished and was not being continued, as he himself wrote in his annotations to

XVI - *The Atrium of the Convento della Carità with the Project for Rebuilding the Terrace* (anonymous watercolor drawing). Venice, Archivio di Stato

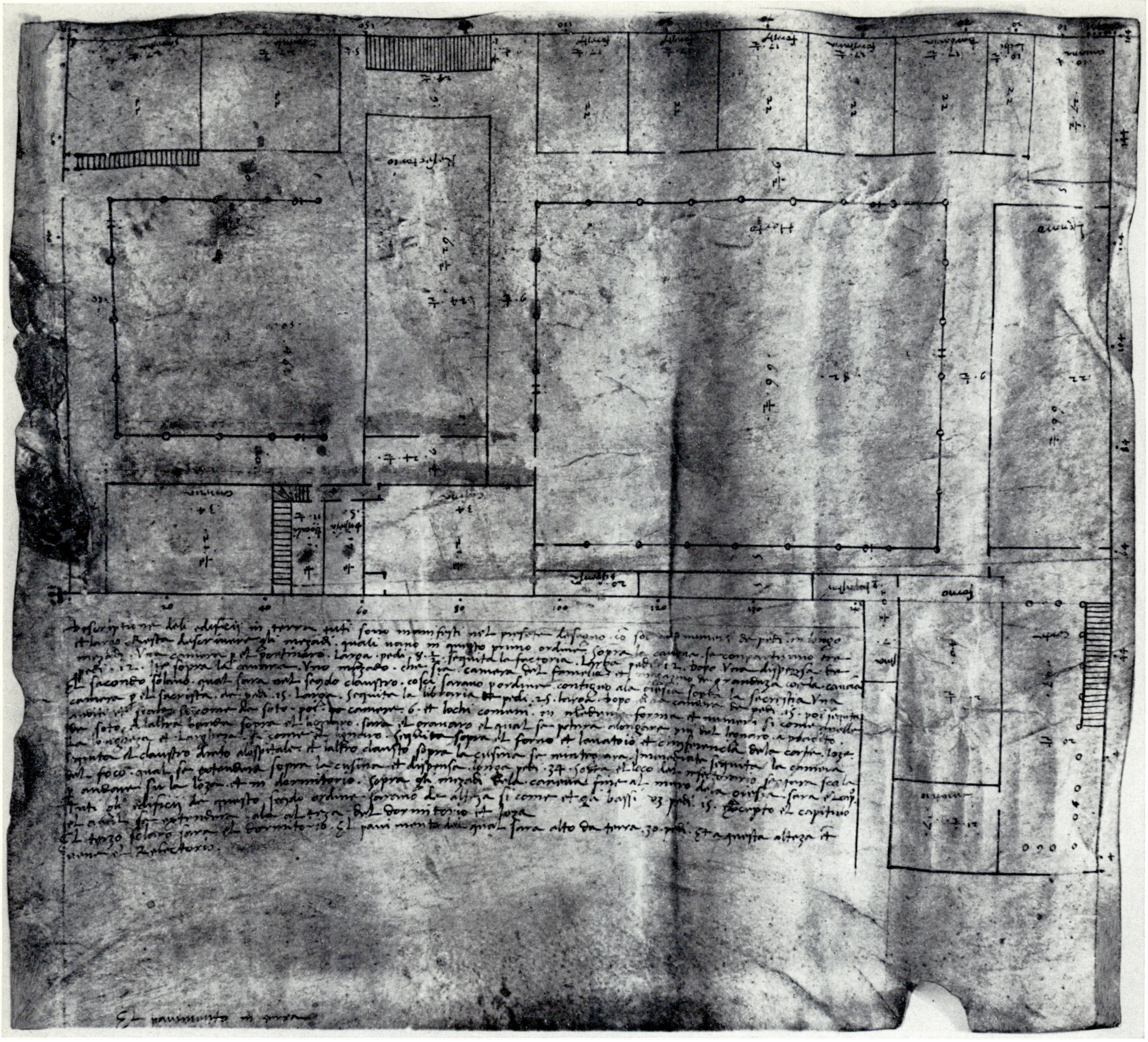

XVII - ANDREA PALLADIO, *Project for reconstructing the Convento della Carità: plan of the ground floor*. Venice, Archivio di Stato

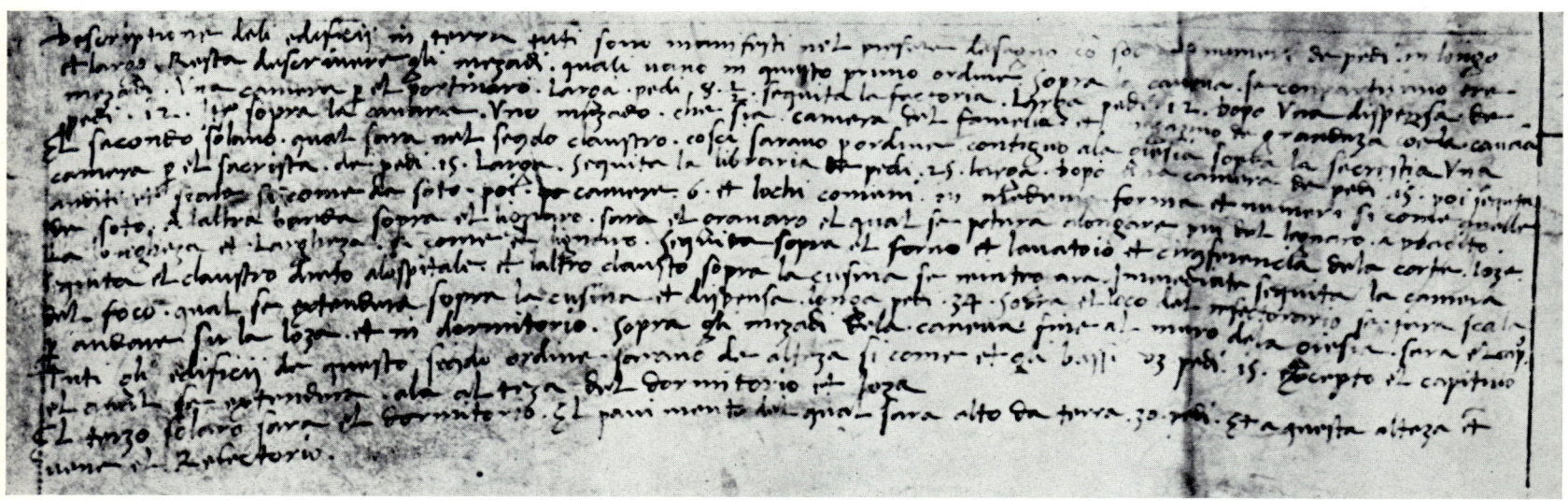

XVIII - ANDREA PALLADIO, *Legend illustrating the project for reconstruction* (detail of fig. XVII). Venice, Archivio di Stato

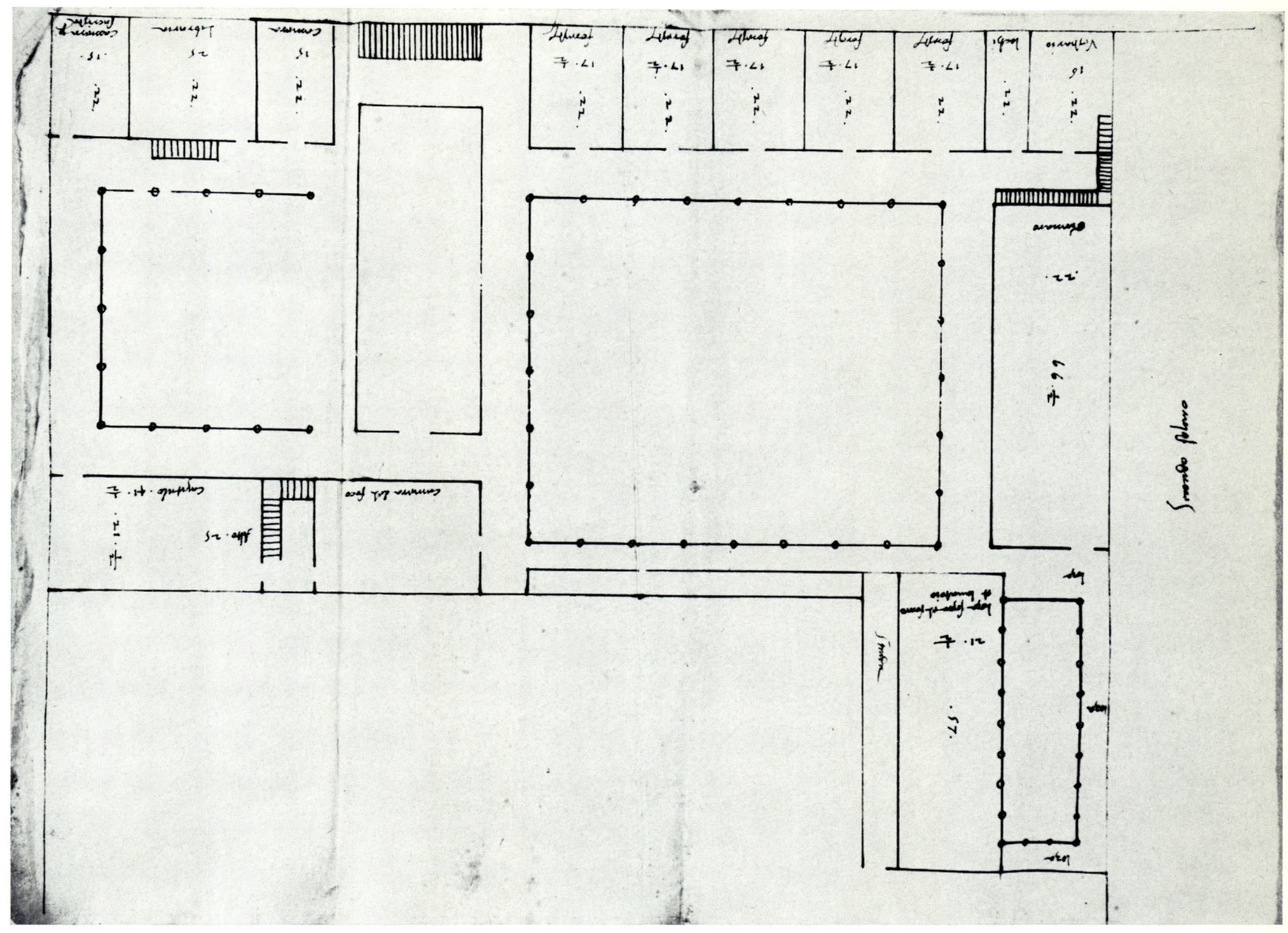
XIX - ANDREA PALLADIO, *Project for reconstructing the Convento della Carità: plan of the second floor.* Venice, Archivio di Stato

XX - Palladio's receipt for payment by the canons for the project of reconstructing the Convento della Carità and for beginning the work (June 1, 1562). Venice, Archivio di Stato

XXI-XXII - Instructions to Palladio for rebuilding "quadri nell'atrio" at the Convento della Carità
From the "Sommario delle scritture" of 1569 and 1570. Venice, Archivio di Stato

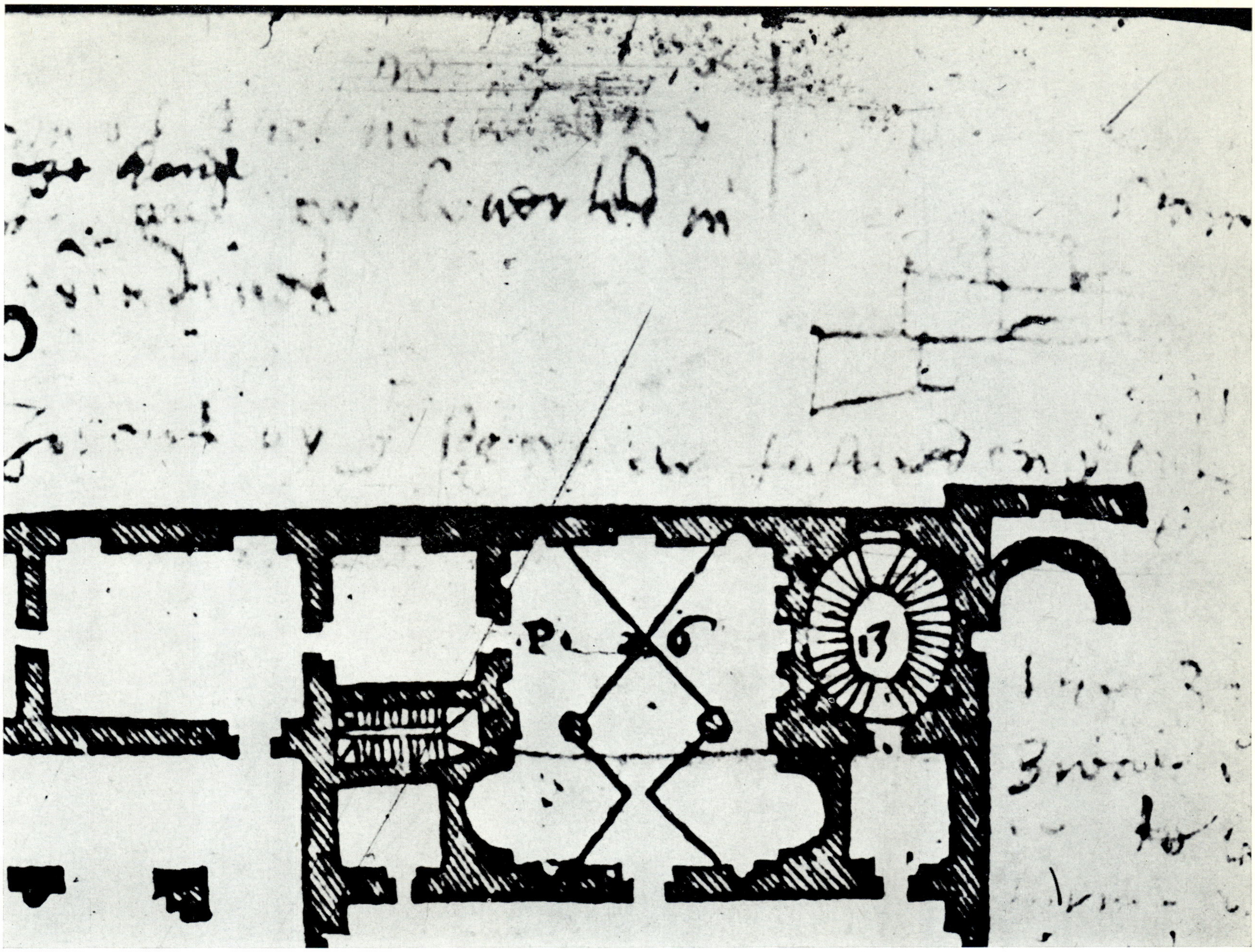

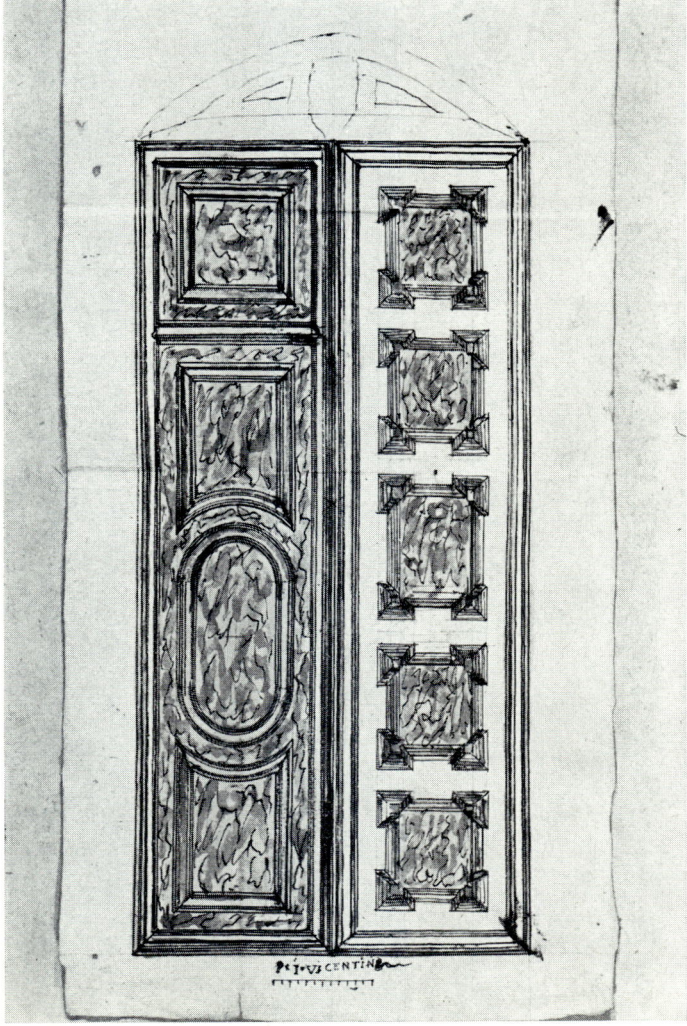

XXIII - INIGO JONES, *Sketch of the stairs in the Convento della Carità* (in the copy of Palladio's treatise belonging to Jones)

XXIV - *Anonymous designs for two doors proposed for the Convento della Carità*. Venice, Archivio di Stato

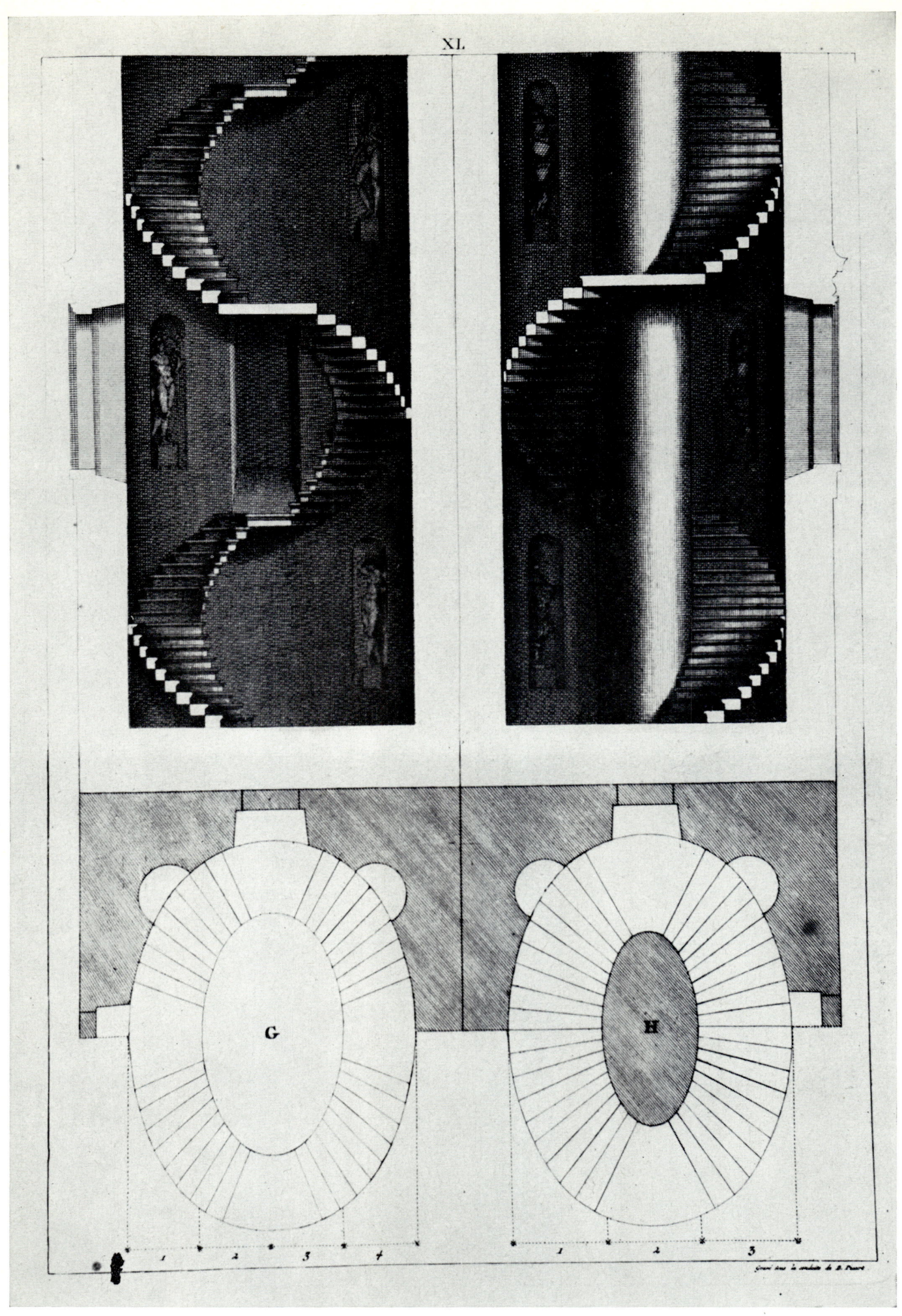

XXV - GIACOMO LEONI, *The stairs in the Convento della Carità (at left).*
From *The Architecture of A. Palladio in Four Books*, 1721, II, XL

XXVI - ANDREA PALLADIO, *Autograph design for the Palazzo of M. A. Thiene in Vicenza: detail of the façade along the via S. Stefano.* London, RIBA, XVII, 10

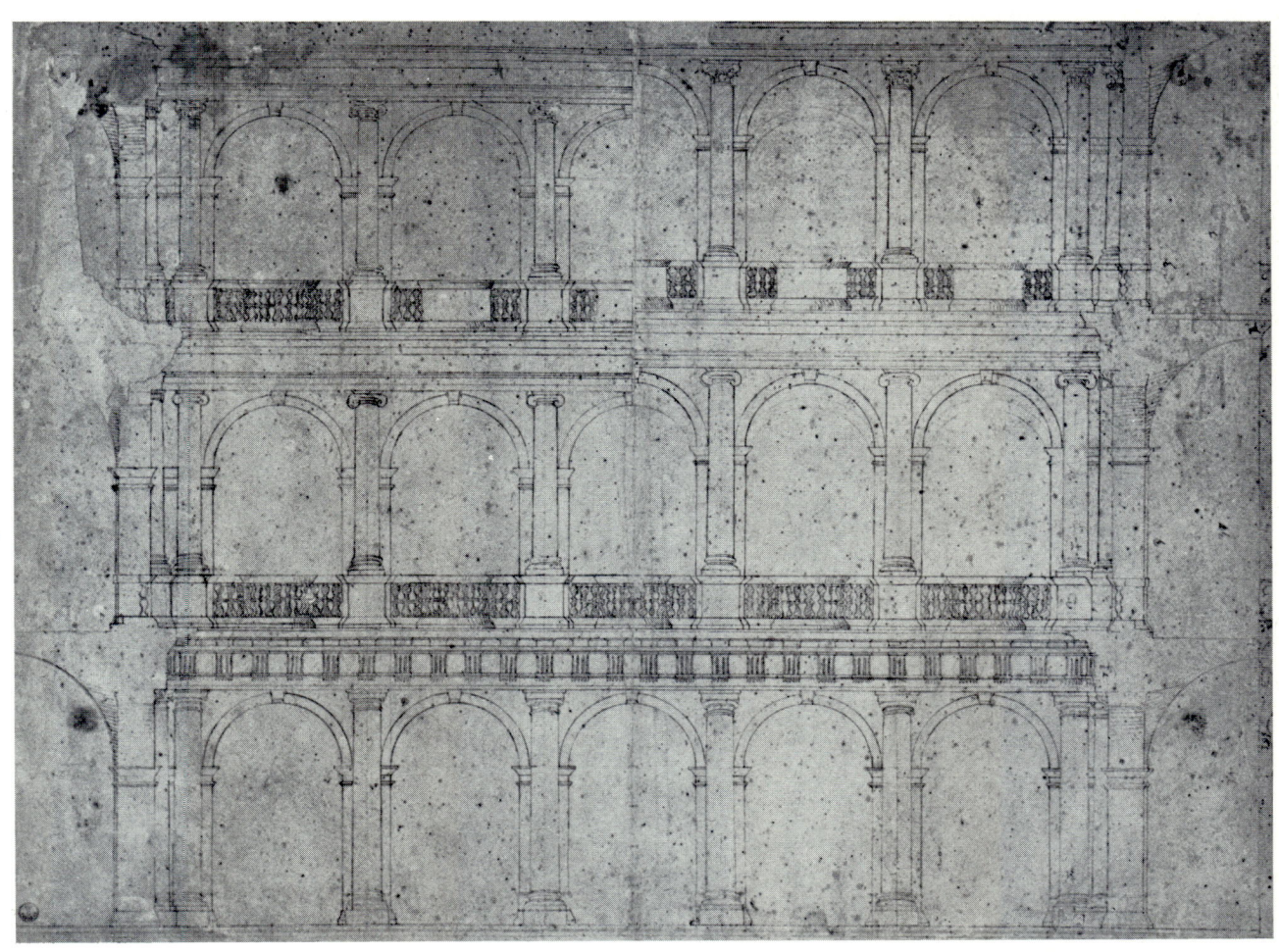

XXVII - ANTONIO DA SANGALLO THE YOUNGER, *Project for the courtyard of the Palazzo Farnese in Rome.* Florence, Uffizi, Gabinetto dei Disegni, 627A

XXVIII - Andrea Palladio, *Temple of Vesta at Tivoli: details.*
Vicenza, Museo Civico, D 4 v

his copy of the *Quattro Libri*.[8] The eight giant columns supported a covering of wood, on which rested a terrace paved with bricks (perhaps the usual squares of black and red found in so many Palladian buildings); because the rain filtered through, Jones tells us, the terrace had been covered. From that information we are able to deduce that the rebuilding requested of Palladio, if indeed it had been completed, did not correct the lamented defect.

Perhaps during construction the overhang had not been well worked out, or perhaps it had been executed quite low, as was common in Venice, and therefore the pavement of bricks above and the coffers of wood or stucco underneath turned out not to be waterproof.

In the Archivio di Stato there is an unpublished and unstudied design for the proposed covering mentioned by Jones (fig. XVI). The project is historically important and is not lacking in merit from the point of view of composition; it is designed rather well. However, it cannot be attributed to Palladio; the draughtsmanship, the use of wash, and the graphic symbols do not appear to be his. It would have been an absurdity for the architect, in constructing the most beloved part of his dream, using the Corinthian atrium as the fulcrum of the building, to have condescended to lay such a drastic hand to it as this. The change would have altered the significance and the function of the "impluvium"; it is not stylistically justifiable, and it deprives the top-story windows of light, although this can only be stated hypothetically. The execution of such a covering would require four columns on each side and two dormers with Serlian windows, as we see on the roofs of many dwellings in Venice. Two vaulted corridors would lead from one dormer to the other, so that, as Jones wrote, one would be able to walk under cover around the entire terrace.

The documents do not indicate when the superstructure was executed. The 1573 bill of lading for the stone does not speak of it—although perhaps it was not built of stone—and Jones saw it, presumably, in 1597. Thus we might suppose that it was executed within that period, most likely after the death of Palladio (1580). To future students of the problem, one may point out that in 1582, in the contiguous Church of the Carità, Vincenzo Scamozzi began the construction of the large cenotaph of the doge Nicolò Da Ponte, which was removed during the reconstructions of the nineteenth century; it is possible that in the monastery, as in other buildings, Scamozzi succeeded to Palladio's office.

Accompanying the study of the superstructure in the Archivio di Stato is a study for two alternatives for the doors of a portal, done in a scale measured in Vicentine feet. The design is attributable to the shop of Palladio, or, more likely, to that of Scamozzi; but its interest is only historical, because there remains no trace of a portal like it in the monastery (fig. XXIV).

The bill of lading for the stone, already referred to above, has not been studied by scholars. It is important, because it informs us of the extent of work and the quantity and value of the material used, both for what remains and for what no longer exists. Because it seems likely that the expenses were listed as they occurred in the course of laying up the stones in the work, what we probably have here is an indication of the order in which the work was undertaken.[9]

From the document we know that on the first of March, 1573, Master Antonio da Bissone, a mason from San Vitale—and therefore a Ticinese like Paleari—and Master Gerolamo Testagrossa presented the specifications for all the stones used in the fabric of the monastery. Their values were verified by four other masons, two of whom represented the contractor and two the patrons. The total value of the stone was judged to amount to 17,712 lire and four soldi (that is, about 2,857 ducats). The bill first records the stone for the basement of the building along the rio di Sant' Agnese, which the "Sommario" cited already in June of 1568.[10] Here one discovers that for the arch of the "cavana" fifteen stones were used, and that thirteen were needed for the portal near the ponte del Dose; these are still visible (plates 6-7). There were eight more stones on the corner toward the *calle*, which formed a rusticated bond. A similar quoin would also have been visible in the refectory beyond the *calle*; thus Palladio had given strength where required, while the other corner, which was toward the Grand Canal and was reinforced by the church, did not need such a bond.[11] These eight stones disappeared in the construction compaign of the nineteenth century; they were perhaps reused elsewhere.

The bill of lading then lists the stones used, floor by floor. It deals with the exterior toward the canal and then passes to the cloister, where nine Doric pilasters hold a socle "quale camina da un capo all'altro della fazada ... et volta sotto le due colonne che sono per testa." This indicates that there were eight arches, including the two return vaults in the corner. The filials, socles, architraves, bases, and capitals were in stone. The most costly were the bases and the capitals in the returns, which unfortunately were destroyed in the nineteenth century. No balusters are referred to; in fact, as we know also from Lazzari,[12] these were not executed. The nineteenth-century restorers obtained their number from the third plate of the *Quattro Libri* and took their form from the basement of the mud sill, where the lower portion of the half-column had been executed in stone, as is recorded with precision in the accounts of Antonio da Bissone. The form arrived at for these later balusters was similar to those of Sansovino, as Wittkower has observed,[13] but it is different from that suggested in the *Quattro Libri* for this place (plate 17; fig. XIV).

The bill of lading next lists the doors of the rooms and a vestments' wardrobe of which traces remain, as well as the doors of the church and the sacristy. Also supplied for this area were two columns "mandorlate," costing a good 955 lire (that is, 128 ducats), the bases and the capitals of the pilasters facing them, and, finally, the cornices and the architraves (plates 33-36).

Rather interesting is the subsequent notice concerning a window between the "Claustro grande et l'Atrio, sopra alla porta dela tramesera"; the mezzanine burned with the atrium, but if only the window and not the door was finished in stone, the work here had evidently not been completed.

After mentioning other doors and windows of the sacristy and the atrium, the bill deals with the second floor, where it lists the "scala a buovolo" and the door "che và sul Coridor" with two steps, and the pavement of the corridor "che và in coro." The expenses for the pavement were huge: 179 lire for "piane" and 116 lire for the eight corbels that held them. The pavement was apparently cantilevered, but the record is ambiguous. One might suppose that someone exiting from the stairs on the second story would have on the right a door entering the church's choir; the latter, as in the case of other "barchi" of Venetian churches, was about in the middle of the hall, and, to hazard a guess, at the level of the second floor of the monastery. There had to have been some way to enter the choir from that floor; otherwise, in order to reach it, the abbot and important guests would have had to follow a rather clumsy route, descending into the church and then climbing up to the "barco" (figs. XXXII-XXXIII). But the surface covered by the "piane" that the bill of lading cites is almost square (11.82 by 11.12 meters), and we may wonder where it was located. Certainly it was on the inside of the church; had the covering of the "barco" perhaps been rebuilt with the "piane" and the corbels? Scholars wishing to resolve the problem might note that the church is 16.80 meters wide.

The bill of lading next mentions the door of the abbot's room and four windows that look out into the atrium; there are five windows in all (fig. XI), but one appears in another part of the document in reference to the sacristy: "per una finestra nel canto dell'atrio nel muro della sagrestia con la feriata."

The imposing covering of the Doric order (plate 21), eighty-one feet long, costing 368 lire, is mentioned next, followed by the expenses for the Corinthian pilasters and for the doors and the service elements for the guest rooms, listed as if these were for the first order. This includes the covering of the Ionic order, which is longer than that of the Doric order (which runs only as far as the end of the terrace at the *calle*), the Corinthian pilasters (plate 22), the doors of the cells, the seven windows of the dormitory on the "claustro" (plate 21), and the windows on the atrium. The number of these windows, which are still extant (fig. LXII), is also given as four, but one served as the door to the terrace. The fifth window is visible in the plate; as was the case with the windows on the floor below, it is mentioned independently, in conjunction with the stairs. Perhaps when leaving the stairs for the corridors, one found a wall on one's left corresponding to a similar wall between the sacristy and the entrance to the sacristy on the ground floor, which made it possible to prevent the chill of the stairwell from entering the abbot's anteroom and the dormitory above. Next, the expenses are given for the door at the top of the stairs, for the rooms above the apse of the church, the eaves along the church, and the steps (plate 53; figs. LXI, LXIII). The stair, of course, was very costly. The ninety-six steps were valued at 1,200 lire, and the eight landings were 198 lire; thus the total for the stairs came to about 185 ducats (plate 54).

The façade toward the canal is the next item; here there were twelve windows on each floor, and once again the cost of the eaves is given (scale drawing *f*).

Last of all, the atrium is recorded. Here various stones were used for the lower bases of the columns, for five column bases, and for the eight abacuses of the capitals. The eight capitals are not mentioned; they were perhaps entrusted to skillful sculptors or executed by those who had furnished the three bases not mentioned in the documents. Finally, there are references to six fireplace breasts and four "pietre da fuogo" in the guest quarters, a "pila in barbaria per lavar la testa," the little window for the "roloio" (clock), and some stone that was not put in place. Other areas to the west of the atrium were not built; intended for the area where today we see a thick medieval wall built of good medieval brickwork, now blackened by the fire, were the second tablinum and the wing of the monastery symmetrical to that on the rio Sant'Agnese. There, facing the peristyle wing that was constructed, the other arcade was to be built on part of the reinforcing wall, which is more than a meter wide at the base (fig. LXXXII). The full extent of the project would have incorporated the scuola, which, when it was in full flower some decades earlier, had renovated the entrance from the campo della Carità and the courtyard with its new columns and elegant carved beams.

But the canons did not alter that area, as one can see by comparing the plan in the *Quattro Libri* and the plan of the actual construction (fig. XXXI).

Through superimposing the projected and actual plans, one discovers that the atrium had to be two meters narrower than it is shown in the treatise; indeed, Temanza and Bertotti Scamozzi noted the differences in the measurements. Furthermore, to construct the atrium according to the proportions of the *Quattro Libri*, it would have been necessary to demolish the medieval wall mentioned above and reconstruct it farther back. Instead, doors and windows, of which traces survive, were built (figs. LXXVIII-LXXX), although they were not placed where Palladio had planned. It is possible that in that area from earliest times were the chapter hall, refectory, kitchen, and cellar, and that this area, which was indispensable to a monastic community, had continued in service where it had originally been; at any rate, it is not known where else these facilities might have been located. A semi-subsurface opening, now walled up, perhaps led down into the cellar.

Following Temanza, scholars have believed that a second tablinum, which was used as a chapter house, and the side of the peristyle entered from the atrium had at one time been built and then destroyed in the fire. But the documents and the scale drawings measured "in situ" show clearly that only the eastern wing of the great project, along the rio di Sant'Agnese, was constructed; it included the atrium, the two bays of the Doric arcade that returned along the peristyle, and the small study in the short lower portico. The atrium was destroyed by the fire, the small study by Selva, and the two Doric bays by Lazzari.

Having settled their accounts in March, 1573, the canons considered further expenditures. On October 11, 1574, they entered into a 260-ducat contract with Antonio Murer (il Paleari), who, with his brother Battista (a mason of that name worked with il Paleari in the Sala delle Quattro Porte at the Palazzo Ducale), was to undertake the construction of the new refectory.[14] Unfortunately, the "Sommario" ends just after having given this suggestive indication of the canons' desire to continue the works, and no other document sheds light on this moment.

From Francesco Lazzari's memorandum on the " Edifizio palladiano,"[15] we discover that construction had been begun beyond the *calle*. Indeed, he wrote that in order to construct the foundations of the new building for use as a picture gallery, it was necessary to destroy a part of Palladio's arrangement to support the wall existing beyond the public street, a stretch 13.90 meters long. The dimension corresponds almost exactly to that of the neoclassical addition, and the total length, in turn, coincides with the projected extension in the first and second Palladian projects, which included the refectory (fig. XXXI). However, without excavations on that site we can have no exact knowledge about this important detail.

The succeeding years were difficult ones throughout the Venetian duchy; financial difficulties impeded the prosecution of the construction. The columns and the brick arches, which were both executed to very exacting standards, absorbed an enormous amount of money.

In about 1590 the commission for the altarpiece of the sacristy was given to Carletto Caliari (1570-1596); the altar was located in the exedra in front of the door that leads into the church (fig. V). The painting, now in the Gallerie dell'Accademia, represents St. Augustine giving the rules to the order of Lateran canons. The patrons of the architect—who was in charge of the entire altar—may be among the group of persons around the saint. The painting harmonized with the structure of the surrounding complex.

Later documents record long, frequent, and bitter altercations between the members of the scuola and the canons, which involved the area held in condominium or the boundaries of that area. These disputes could indicate that the canons still sought to complete the project that would intrude into the courtyard which lay next to their area. The hospice for the poor would have remained without light and would have been enclosed all round, and the calle del Dose, which was to be transformed into a long porticoed alley, could not have been freely used by the scuola.

A printed document of March, 1586, records in what places in the first courtyard the symbol of the scuola was visible.[16] In 1591 the canons reproached the members of the scuola for having constructed above their hospice two dormer windows, from which one could look into the monastery.[17] In November, 1595, the scuola protested because the canons had raised some construction above the face—that is, above the short lower portico that they had agreed to build along the *calle*—which was in contravention to the pact of 1497; at that time it had been agreed that in that spot the monastery would not be raised above a certain limit, which this construction exceeded, and thus it should be demolished. But the following January the canons obtained an adjudication from the judges of the Proprio that they were not in violation of the agreement.[18] Some years later, in 1601, the courtyard held in condominium and the position of the well within it were measured accurately.[19] One wonders if the canons were still thinking of completing the construction. A later document of 1610, which contains other measurements taken along the rio di Sant'Agnese, strengthens such a supposition.[20]

Furthermore, in a "strida" of 1628 the canons somewhat contemptuously reproached the members of the Carità for always loosing the litigations between them and the great monastery; among other things, they had had to agree to the construction of the "studietto della casa" above the calle del Dose.[21] The little study was in some manner the seed that would have eventually blossomed into the great refectory above the canons' vineyard. But the "strida" of 1628 permitted the fathers a satisfaction of brief duration, because on November 16, 1630, "si attaccò il foco nel convento della Carità et restò in buona parte incendiato."[22] The notices of this event are extremely laconic; those referring to it simply repeat the same information, without adding any details, and the few surviving papers in the archives of the monastery do not record the misfortune.

In the winter of 1630 the plague, which had not yet been conquered, offered a much more dramatic subject for the monastery's chronicle. The fire of November 16 had devastated a building by Palladio, but an action of the senate was of much more moment to the Venetians, for on October 22 it had decreed the construction of a votive church to Santa Maria della Salute. Caught up in litigation and exorbitant expenses, the architect's dream dissolved; the fire, the plague, and the decadence of the monastery would prevent further thought being given to the construction of the building.

Antonio Visentini, who knew the condition of the monastery in the first half of the eighteenth century, described it in a long exchange with a "Cavaliere Inglese";[23] after having observed that "i contanti / li mancò ai canonici incostanti," he affirmed that the building "cosi tronco e derelitto / Idea grande gli mostra in poco sitto." Here he left a vague record of the monastery as it existed before its remodeling into its present state.

NOTES TO CHAPTER III

[1] Document V.
[2] Document VI.
[3] Document I, under that date.
[4] Document VIII, p. 7.
[5] Document VII.
[6] Document I, under that date.
[7] ZORZI, 1964, p. 243; MAGRINI, 1845, p. 50.
[8] Chapter 6, n. 3.
[9] Document VIII.
[10] Document I, under that date.
[11] He wrote that the "angoli, perché partecipano di due lati, e sono per tenerli diritti, e congiunti insieme, devono essere fermissimi, e con lunghe e dure pietre come braccia tenuti" (1570, I).
[12] 1835, p. 16.
[13] 1968, p. 341.
[14] Document I, under that date.
[15] 1835, p. 22.
[16] Document IX.
[17] Document X.
[18] Documents XIII, XIV, XV.
[19] Document XVI.
[20] Document XVII.
[21] Document XVIII.
[22] Document XIX.
[23] Venice, Museo Civico Correr, Cod. Cic. 1967; document XX.

c - Convento della Carità: peristyle

IV
THE INTERPRETATION OF THE CONCEPT

"E se nella fabbrica anderanno adornamenti di colonne e di pilastri si potranno fare la base, i capitelli, e gli architravi di pietra, e l'altre parti di pietra cotta," Palladio had written in his treatise.[1] In the Venetian monastery he limited himself to the use of stone only where it was indispensable, but he executed the parts in brick with a workmanship so refined that the expenses were prodigious, because the brick had to be of the very finest quality. The monastery would not have seemed foreign to the canons, who were accustomed to passing their lives enclosed by the bricks of the church and of those old buildings of which we still see some broken remains. The architect had experimented with a technique which was not in use at that time; he developed it from the variety of experiences he had had in many fields of art. Indeed, the bricks were worked in the round with such an accuracy in the many profiles required for the eight giant columns in the atrium and for the Doric and Ionic half-columns in the peristyle that connoisseurs have been amazed.

Among all Palladio's Venetian works, Ambassador Henry Wooton noted only the Corinthian atrium, expressing lively admiration for the perfect execution of the columns.[2] Jones, Temanza, and Lazzari also wrote of the workmanship of the bricks; Jones believed that they were dressed in red stucco, Temanza thought they had a very subtle plaster covering, and Lazzari said that they were covered not "del solito intonaco, ma soltanto da una sottilissima cartellina rossiccia, ormai pressoché consunta."[3] Lazzari later indicated that he had had to rediscover the system of sixteenth-century workmanship when building the new arches, executing the curved bricks, and completing the frieze in terra cotta.

An inexpensive material that Palladio turned to good account was stucco. In the tablinum the dripstone is all in stucco, but so exact is the workmanship that it seems to be in *pietra serena* (plates 40-42). In the atrium, all the ornaments of the roof and under the terrace, and the coffers that the records show Palladio was called back to remake, are in stucco, wood, or terra cotta.

Only minimal use was made of marble; just the two columns of the tablinum (plate 46) and some fireplace breasts in the guest rooms—no longer extant *in situ*—were of that precious material. The fireplace breasts here were perhaps designed by Palladio; in various other buildings he gave meticulous attention to them.

Lazzari gives precise information about the polychrome pavement in the sacristy and about the manner used to attempt to protect it from humidity (fig. LVII; color plate *d*). In the tablinum, bricks of three tones produced a design worked out in a manner that emphasized the details of the plan; only an experienced artisan would

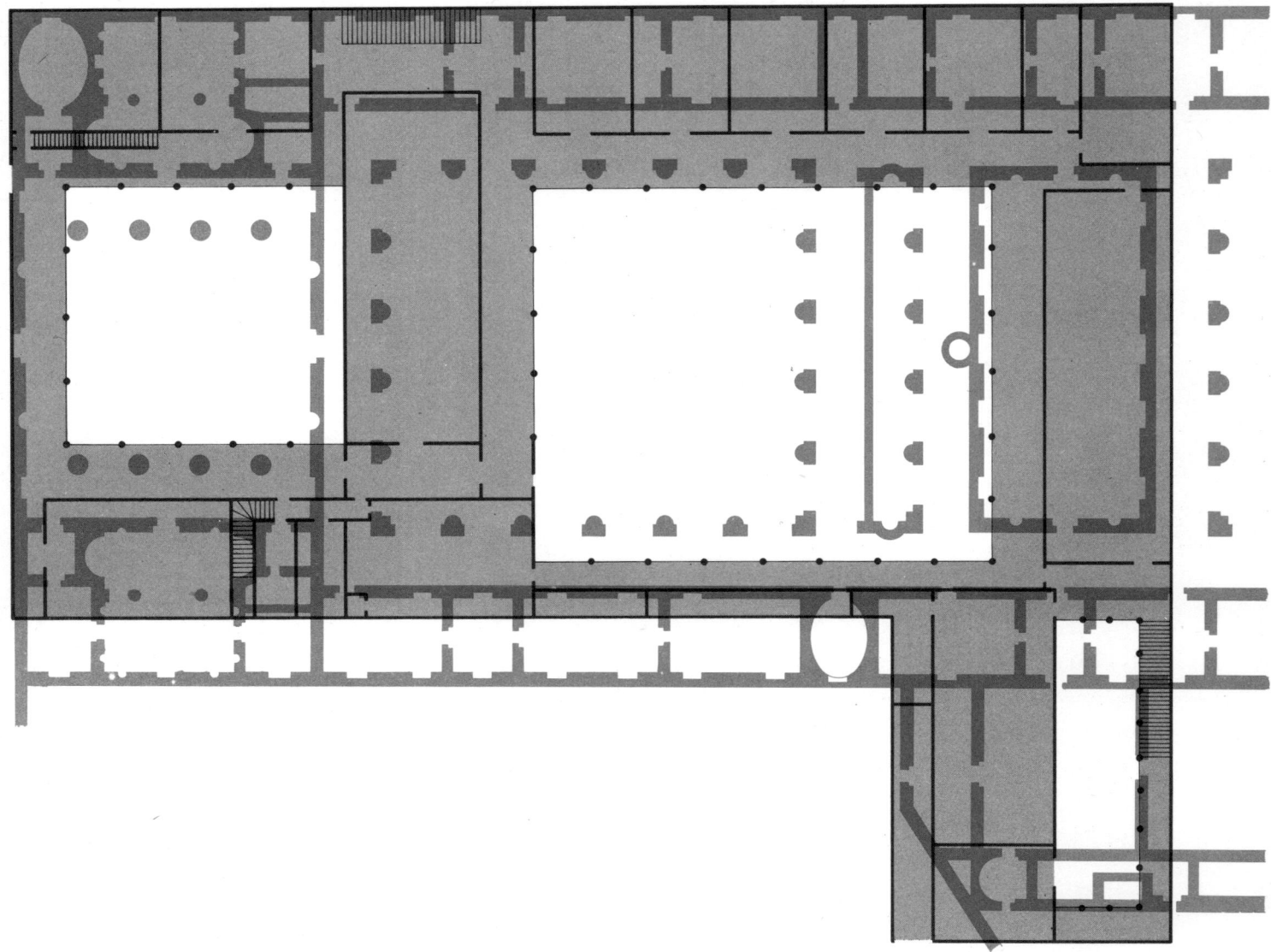

XXIX - *Comparison of the preliminary project and the project in the treatise for the ground floor of the Convento della Carità*

have been able to complete the work with precision.[4]

The continuous frieze above the Doric order in the peristyle was also executed in terra cotta (plates 13-17); its frieze zone was different from the traditional one, and critics and historians have written a great deal to justify or to condemn Palladio for its design. In the *Quattro Libri* he says nothing about it, but in the plate the continuous frieze is shown very clearly (fig. XIV).[5] The soffits of the Ionic and Doric cornices are also in terra cotta (plates 25-26). Traditional rosettes are used in the Ionic one, while in the Doric a canonic motif of lozenge and stud alternates with a paganizing attribute of Zeus's thunderbolt and wings conjoined with the flame of the Carità.

The decorative motif in the frieze of the Carità is perhaps an interpretation with coloristic refinement of a correggesque motif; in the Camera della Badessa, which was painted between 1518 and 1519, Correggio had invented something similar: rams' heads that carry pieces of fabric arranged as festoons. Critics have preferred to go back to the classical examples of the Ionic temple of Fortuna Virilis and to the Corinthian temples of Vesta at Rome and Tivoli, which are ornamented with a motif of bucrania and putti interlaced with garlands and which are exactly reproduced in the *Quattro Libri*. Bucrania and

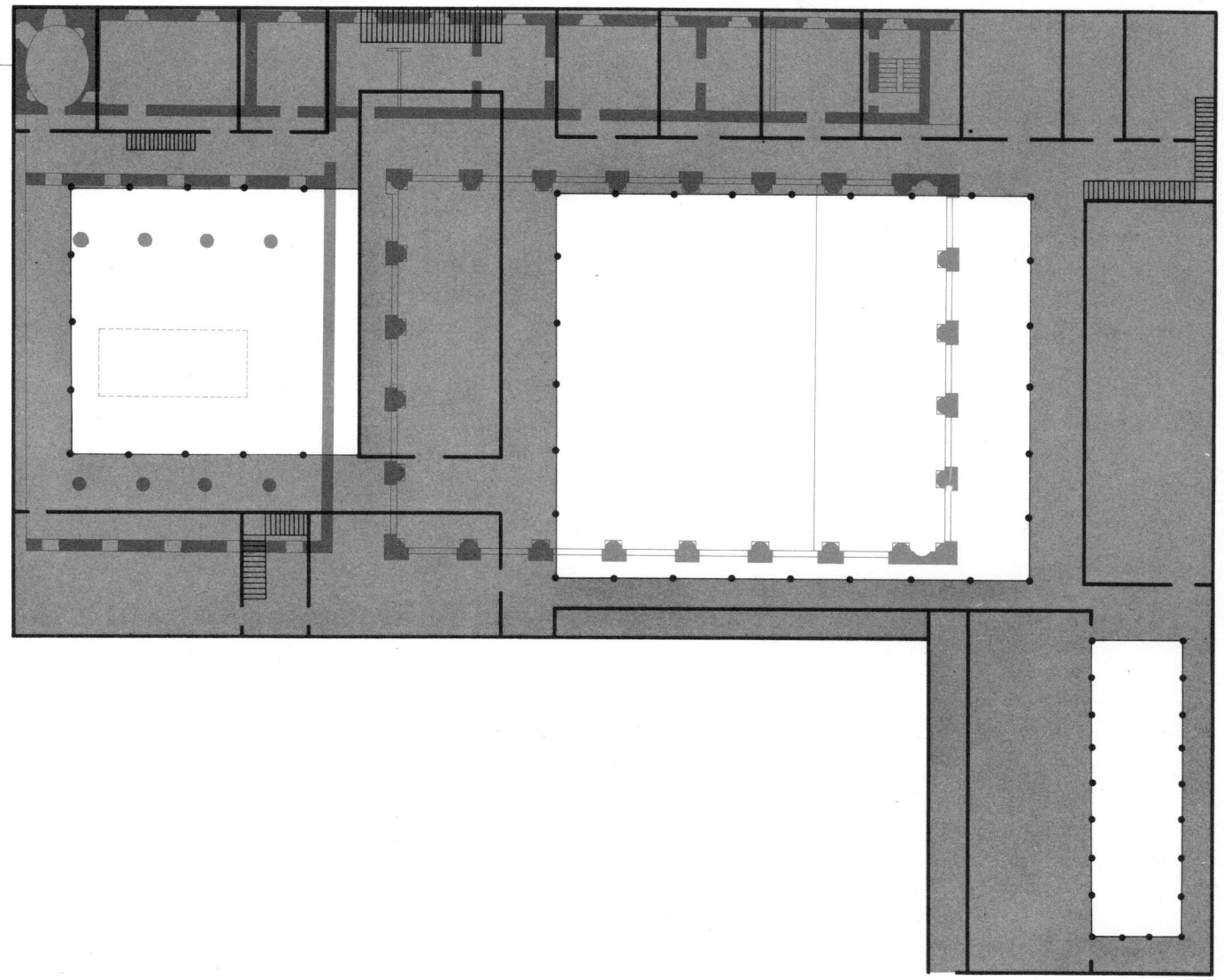

XXX - *Comparison of the preliminary project and the project in the treatise for the second floor of the Convento della Carità*

paterae are also found in Serlio,[6] but there they alternate with triglyphs. Palladio had designed such a frieze in one of the proposals of about 1550 for the façade of the Palazzo Thiene in Vicenza (fig. XXVI). This Vicentine decoration would also have been in terra cotta, but because its rhythm was interrupted by the Corinthian capitals of the pilasters, it would have had a different significance than that of the Venetian example. The recent Romans had used similar friezes above the Ionic and Corinthian orders; in Venice, Palladio found it worked well in the Doric order, and experts of the eighteenth century, classicists to a fault, were perplexed when passing judgment on such an unorthodox solution.

Muttoni seemed dismayed; he wrote that Palladio had proposed the frieze for reasons known only to himself, and he also advanced the hypothesis that it was a caprice of some other artisan active during Palladio's absence.[7] Visentini hesitantly affirmed " che l'ingegno sil basta per far bene / Unindo le cose sempre che conviene / Disponendole in forma ch'apparire / Di perfetto saper, e comparisce / L'ordine presto, e in buona semitria." Temanza proposed that the deed was justifiable because the area behind the frieze was not carried on beams but was vaulted, an aspect that Palladio wanted to reveal by putting a continuous frieze there.[8] Milizia accepted this opinion, but his Enlightenment convictions forced him to add the comment: " La sua filosofia fu a mezzo, se fosse andato colla ragione più avanti avrebbe visto che quel suo fregio tutto metopa sarebbe stato tutto un vano incapace di sostenersi, e perciò un fregio insignificante, e posto unicamente per adornare."[9] That, one might believe, is how Palladio might have thought about it. Bertotti Scamozzi, accepting the reasoning of Temanza, thought that the architect had wanted to arrange the Basilica in Vicenza in this way; there he had been the subject of criticism because the metopes were not square.[10] Selva picked up the reasoning of Bertotti, affirming that at the Carità it was not possible to make the metopes square, and therefore the orthodox decoration could not be used; otherwise, if Palladio had thought that he was justified because there were no beams behind the frieze, he would have repeated the same frieze along the canal, where one finds regular metopes and triglyphs instead.[11] Lazzari agreed neither with his master, Selva, nor with Selva's master, Temanza; he justified the original author of the frieze, thinking that he had wanted to use "una nuova maniera d'ornamenti, che a dir vero risulta molto leggiadra," avoiding the difficulty of making square metopes.[12]

Magrini, referring to the opinions of his predecessors, affirmed that the frieze becomes "molto leggiadro per l'introduzione di quei panni che graziosamente attaccati ai teschi servono quasi di sostegno alle patere a quelli interposti."[13]

Pane takes Magrini's position and believes that the frieze originated from a desire to create a continuity that avoided the rigidity of a triglyph frieze.[14]

Zorzi observed that such a frieze, which had been designed earlier for the Palazzo Thiene and was later executed in Venice, evidently pleased the architect, who did not worry himself with traditon.[15]

For us, it seems obvious that Palladio was stimulated above all else by aesthetic considerations. One tries to imagine a frieze of metopes and triglyphs repeated along the four sides of the cloister; the rhythmic caesuras would have abolished the "continuum" derived from the recurrence of the shaded, curved lines of the terra cotta's chiaroscuro quality, and the rigor of an orthodox frieze would have required solid stone. The ascension of the soft half-columns would have been interrupted, while the motif selected unifies the cloister —which, unfortunately, was completed only in the imagination of the artist—both horizontally and vertically. The festoons and bucrania, which were executed with refinement, give a subtle shading to the material the architect had selected. Palladio was no slave to measurement, even though he knew the rules to perfection, as is demonstrated by the orthodoxy of the bases, the capitals, and the trabeation (plates 29-30, 47; fig. LX). Still, the dripstones, which are also in terra cotta, only inadequately match the rigor of the Doric and the Ionic orders and are not aligned with the friezes below with the exactness that the architect himself had taught in his book (plate 26).

In 1573, defending himself in the famous impiety trial, Paolo Veronese admitted that at times artists profit from "licenze che si pigliano i poeti et i matti"; the architect as well, when drawing from and rearranging both ancient and modern parts, has taken the same sort of license in the Lateranense monastery. Here, knowledge and art made him an exquisite poet.

The wedge of stone inserted between the bricks of the architrave is an invention that gave great surprise to, for example, Lazzari (plate 13); its purpose is to prevent confusion from appearing within the neatness of the arcade and its trabeation.[16] It is perhaps a reference to Sangallo and to the courtyard of the Palazzo Farnese in Rome. The stone is always worked in an exemplary manner; the neatness and exactness of the bases, capitals, and elements in stone inserted both inside and outside the peristyle are notable. In the top floor the stone bases of the Ionic pilasters rest on two courses of little bricks, which make the entire height of the stone element visible from ground level (plates 21-22).

Lazzarri's information about the system used for the foundations of the great cloister is also of great interest. He made some soundings under the pilasters to discover how they were executed and discovered that the steps shown in the design had not been installed, and only the continuous socle recorded in the bill of lading for the stone had been. The neoclassic architect also established that piles had not been sunk, because the ground was compact; he did find traces of a caisson, which had perhaps been built in order to keep the construction dry during execution. Inside it were large, uniform pieces of stone. Above that were materials discarded from the project, then a decking of larch, and finally a foundation wall the depth of which corresponded to about a sixth of the height of the building, built as is prescribed in the *Quattro Libri*.[17]

Although we admire the construction for its elegance, proportions, commodity, and essential sobriety, we are still surprised at the nonchalance with which, for example, a window in the stairs is cut in half by a step and is not at the same level as others, disturbing the harmonious order of the exterior (plates 49, 5). The three windows facing the Grand Canal are also disturbing, but they are required because the stair needs light, and they were opened only in order to satisfy that function (plate 5); however, they are gracefully resolved on the interior, being placed in deep, asymmetrical, splayed openings (fig. XCII). The snail-plan stair, so elegantly inserted into the plan, seems to have been constructed with an unresolved elevation. The stair becomes an anomaly in the context of the exterior, provoking a tawdry asymmetry in the levels and dislocation of the windows (scale drawing *f*).

Palladio intended that this helicoidal spiral be compared with that of Bramante in the Belvedere, but the stair in the Carità has its own recent history as well. It was born from the desire that developed in the later sixteenth century, when there was a clamoring for novelty in Venice, to give importance and monumental development to an impulse for scenographic effects. Only a few decades earlier, after all, Venetians were still building modest exterior stairs in order not to rob enclosed areas of any space (scale drawings *g - h, j*).

Palladio must have considered himself again to be a sculptor when at the Carità he built the flight of suspended marble slabs lacking supports along the inner side; the trapezoidal steps and landings are inserted into the walls as if issuing effortlessly from them, even though they are heavy monoliths (plates 48-54). They made an impression on Inigo Jones, who made a minute sketch (fig. XXIII) and called the stairs "excellent" for the manner of their execution. They inspired him to execute the Tulip Staircase in the Queen's House in Greenwich (1616-29), which is also a snail-plan stair with no internal support (fig. XC). The stair is also referred to in the analogous and even more grand example in the Ospedaletto in Venice (1664-66) by Sardi and Longhena (fig. XCI). This one, however, does not have the charming, unadorned niches, filled with shadow, which are so attractive (plate 49). But Palladio's niches perhaps were meant to be filled with statues, as seen in Leoni,[18] as Palladio himself shows them in the plate dedicated to the sala a quattro colonne

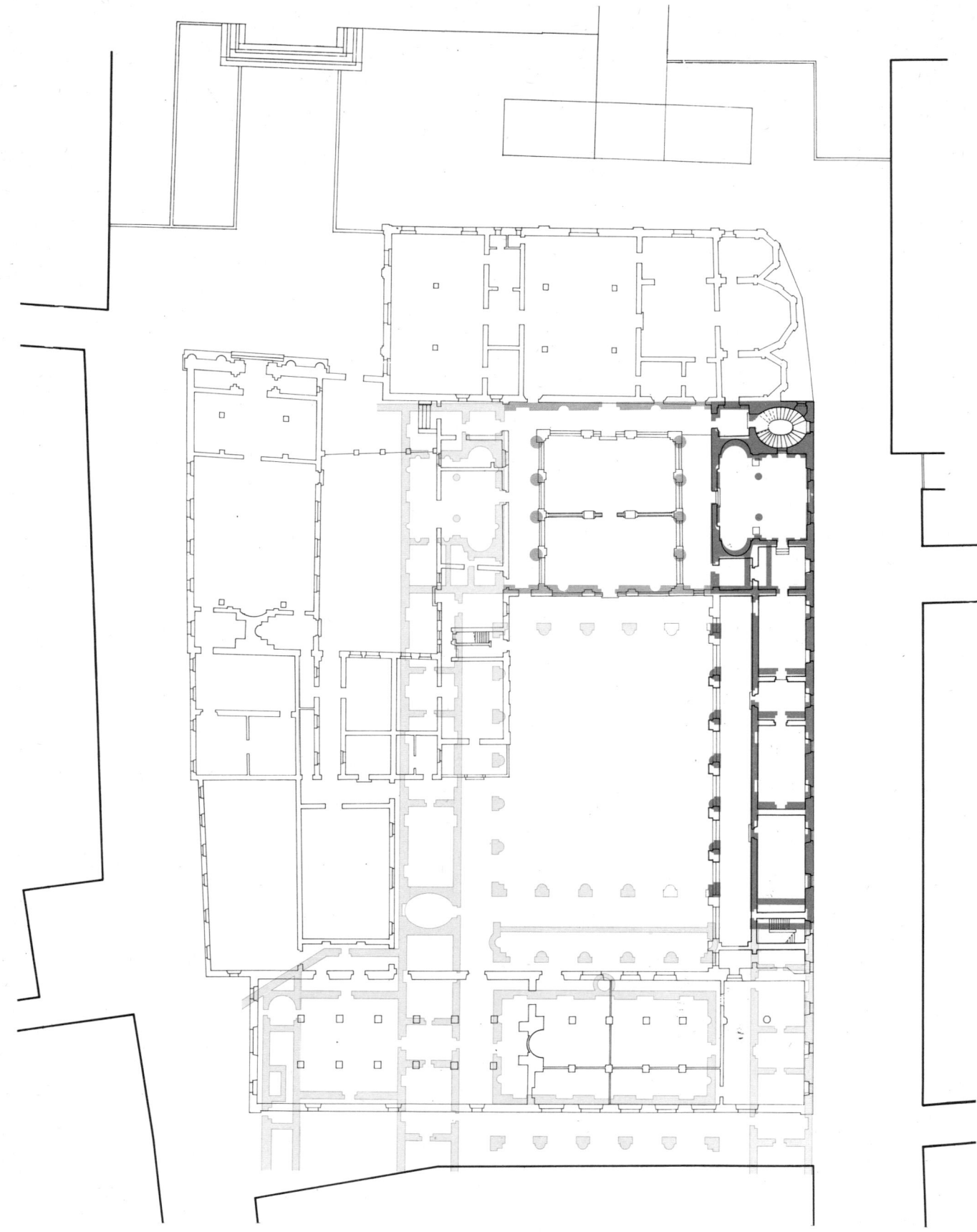

- ■ EXISTING STRUCTURE FROM DESIGN IN THE QUATTRO LIBRI
- ▨ STRUCTURE DESTROYED IN THE FIRE
- ☐ STRUCTURE DESTROYED BY LAZZARI
- ☐ SECTIONS OF PLAN NEVER CONSTRUCTED

XXXI - *Plan of the ground floor of the complex of the Convento della Carità (present condition) with the design in the Quattro Libri, containing indications of the parts that exist, those destroyed in the fire, and those destroyed by Lazzari, superimposed*

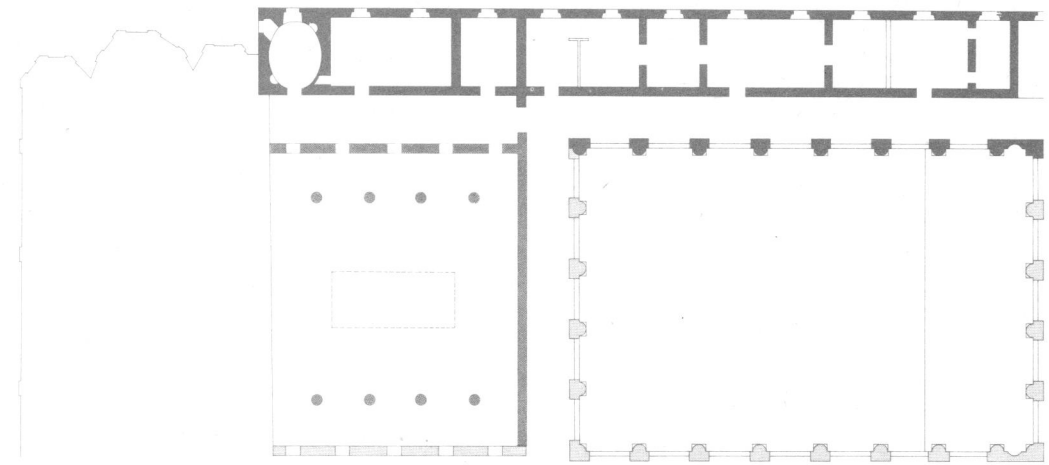

XXXII - *Convento della Carità: plan of the east wing of the second floor derived from the design in the* Quattro Libri, *with indications of the extant parts and of those destroyed in the fire*

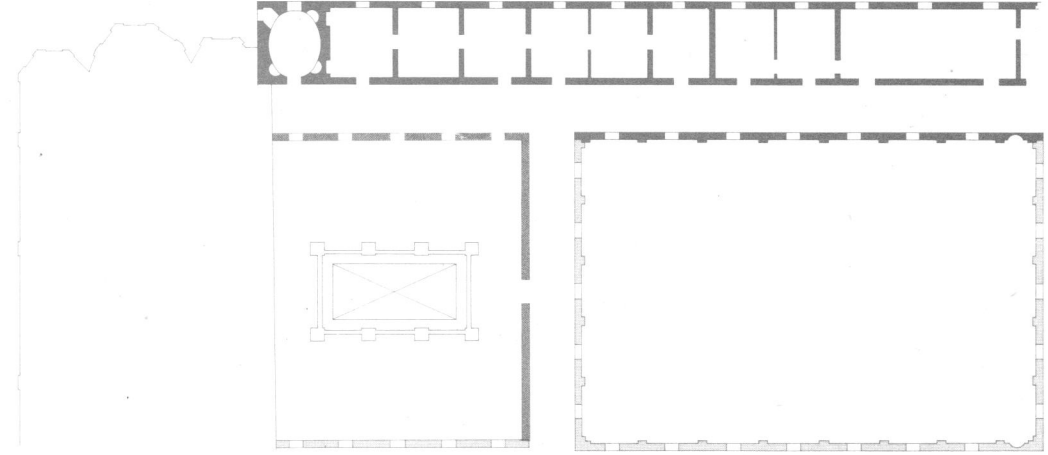

XXXIII - *Convento della Carità: plan of the east wing of the third floor derived from the designs in the* Quattro Libri, *with indications of the extant part and of that destroyed in the fire*

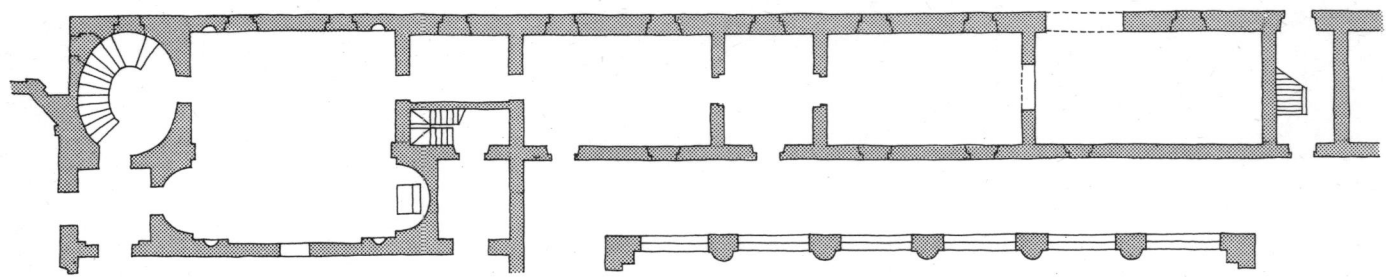

XXXIV - *Convento della Carità: the east wing of the ground floor (still extant) as it was built and used during the architect's lifetime*

(figs. XXV, XXXVIII), and as appears in the stairs at Chambord.[19]

The niches, which are not functional but decorative, recall those of Bramante. They are carved out of the wall and lighten it; perhaps to diminish the substance and the weight of the wall, the architect put two of them near and above one another where the stair terminates (plate 53). Cleanly cut, without mouldings, they become a melodic pause and augment the harmony of the architectonic experience. Goethe, after climbing them a few times, affirmed that "a person never grows weary of going up and down such a stair."[20] Here, as elsewhere, the architect has built with modernity and poetry.[21]

One may consider the oval stairs an essay in departure from the orthodox classicism found during the early sixteenth century and a prelude to the liberty and dynamism of the seventeenth century. The harmonious play of chiaroscuro effects in the niches and the rose color of the stairs and of the two great columns would have fused the two experiences of the stairs and the tablinum (plate 34; fig. XCIII). Perhaps in the architect's conception the dry proportions of the sacristy were redeemed by the narrowness of the stair-tower, which, being constrained between the two ample sacred spaces, somehow evokes the function of a campanile (scale drawing *g*). The white plaster also gave unity to the interior; it extends uniformly along the walls of the stairs, tablinum, guest rooms, and cells; today at the ground-floor level in the area used by the scuola, the original conception has been ignored by leaving the bricks visible (fig. LXXVII). But on the exterior parts of the courtyard there are warm colors; in the atrium, peristyle, and—had they been constructed—along the outside walls of the refectory, the striking two-toned effect of white stones and rosy bricks, covered by the most subtle stucco that leaves the joints just barely perceptible, would have been prevalent.

Palladio did not bother much with views connected with the building, but in the inside, where the conventual life was conducted, he resolved the gradation of light and colors of the area and of the cloisters with loving attention. From the well-lit street one could enter the dark church (this was also the case in the second project, which devolved from the casa degli antichi, where the church took the form of a loggia in front of the atrium[22]). From the sacred area one passes to the other tranquil oasis; here are the court, with the little piece of sky reflected in the "impluvium," the eight important reddish columns, and the square coffert analogous to those in the atrium of the Palazzo Chiericati. Then, crossing the arcade, one exits into the solemn peristyle, luminous, collected and serene, as if one has arrived in the piazza of a small walled town.

The correspondence between the design

in the *Quattro Libri* and that which was built is not exact. In some cases, functional solutions that were not justified by aesthetic considerations were imposed in the course of the work. For example, in the minuscule entrance to the sacristy, four doors were opened; these led, respectively, to the atrium, the church, the side stairs, and the sacristy (figs. XXXI, XXXIV). This last opening was carved out of the exedra of the tablinum and resembles the door cut into the apse of the chapel at the Redentore.[23]

In the side stairs the three windows opening toward the Grand Canal constitute an awkward interpolation (plate 5). The architect did not preoccupy himself with harmonizing the confrontation of the new edifice with what already existed; in fact, the monastery abuts the church with complete disgregard and extends above the left apse. On this apse, two little rooms that reach the height of the major apse were constructed, marring the aesthetic significance of the Gothic building on that side (fig. LXI). The church, although constructed only a hundred years earlier, was not considered an untouchable work of art; besides, some years later Palladio would propose the modern reconstruction of the Palazzo Ducale. The anomalous windows and rooms are recorded in the bill of lading for the stone in 1573, which shows that they were certainly executed while the architect was alive.

In the *Quattro Libri* the plan of the sacristy shows a door opening to the atrium in the middle of the wall between the two exedrae (fig. XI); in the elevation that door has become the window that was actually opened. This detail supports the thesis that the plan predates the elevation; the elevation reflects modifications made in the course of execution. But this explanation does not hold for other differences. According to the plan, in the tablinum there was to have been a single window toward the canal, and it would have been flanked by two niches; other pairs of niches appear on the lateral walls toward the stairs and the guest rooms. These were never executed; instead, two windows that were required for the harmonius arrangement of the exterior were opened toward the canal, and at the side of each is a niche (scale drawings *g-i*).

The door between the sacristy and the stairs, which was executed and is still visible in front of the one that leads to the guest rooms, does not appear in the projected plan; instead, two doors are shown in the second, unexecuted tablinum. And, again, the project shows a door flanked by two columns between the atrium and the church; so far as we know, it was never opened.

The small rectangular stairway between the sacristy and the monastery certainly existed; traces that survived the nineteenth-century transformation remain today (fig. LXX). Another little stairway, this one on the side of the rio di Sant'Agnese, leads now, as it did originally, all the way to the top floor. The single portal independent of the school that the plans show would have been opened in the asymmetrical zone onto the calle del Dose, where we might suppose the "giardino assai bello" was planned. This area was not built, because to do so required the destruction of the hospice; thus, the canons continued, as always, to enter the convent by crossing the church or by using the courtyard that they held in common with the scuola (figs. LXXXVI-LXXXIX).

If the project had been completed, when entering that courtyard one would have seen on the right the flank of the scuola with the stupendous Gothic portal that still exists (which would later be flanked by one executed on the designs of Scamozzi);

to the left would have been the flank of the monastery, aligned with the façade of the church and identical to that on the rio di Sant'Agnese. From the courtyard, if the hospice had been destroyed, one would have seen in front of him and beyond the calle del Dose the portal of the monastery; this would have led into a hall of four columns, similar to the atria of so many villas, and from there one would have been able to enter into all the areas inhabited by the religious—to the peristyle, refectory, workrooms, and bakery, which were already envisaged in the first project, and to the "giardino assai bello."

The analysis of the site destined for the refectory and for the enclosed areas there leaves various perplexities. For a long stretch of almost twenty-two meters, the calle del Dose would have become a "tunnel" rather than a lower portico with a terrace above it, as is indicated in the plan; in the section from the *Quattro Libri*, on the level of the Ionic order and of the terrace, the bases of the half-columns are contiguous to the high part of the refectory and linked to the niches at the extremities; as was noted, only one such end bay was executed and remains. Because the *calle* was inviolable, the two arcades on the ground floor parallel to the two canals—della Carità and di Sant'Agnese—could not be built with an odd number of arches as was canonic; but in the second and third orders the norm could have been respected, because above the porticoed *calle* a seventh bay could have been added to the six on the ground floor. In the elevation of the *Quattro Libri* that final bay seems to project a little relative to the other arches.

Under the refectory a cellar was envisaged, made in the same manner that cisterns are, so that water might not enter.[24] Considering the particular difficulties of the site, it would be interesting to know how it would be built in the place where its large walls and floor were to be lower than the usual level of the water. Perhaps the architect would have made use of the experience gained by others in the Convent of San Giorgio Maggiore, where the refectory, begun by others but completed by Palladio, had been built in a similar manner.

It is not easy to understand how the forty-four rooms that are indicated in the treatise were to be disposed. The forty-six cells are arranged on the top floor, with the "volti fatti di canne" in order not to overload the wall; the outer curvatures of those vaults are visible in the attic (fig. LXIX). One might presume that sixteen of the cells were to be placed along the rio di Sant'Agnese; four of these would have been above the refectory, but because it was not built, only eleven finally appeared on that side. Another sixteen would have been on the side toward the scuola and the common courtyard. Two rows of seven each would have been along the great room that was planned above the refectory, which would have been lit by dormer windows. The illumination of the refectory and of the room above it would have been somewhat scarce, as Roberto Pane has observed, if the work had been built as it was designed.[25] If, however, we recall how the architect resolved the problems in the refectory of San Giorgio, where he was not able to change the dimensions of the construction already in place, and where he succeeded in optically diminishing the extraordinary length by dividing the ceiling into three neat parts, we might suppose that, when faced with illuminating the refectory of the Carità, Palladio would have found an appropriate, harmonious solution on the construction site.

In the elevation, the pilasters of the cloistered area are shown resting on steps,

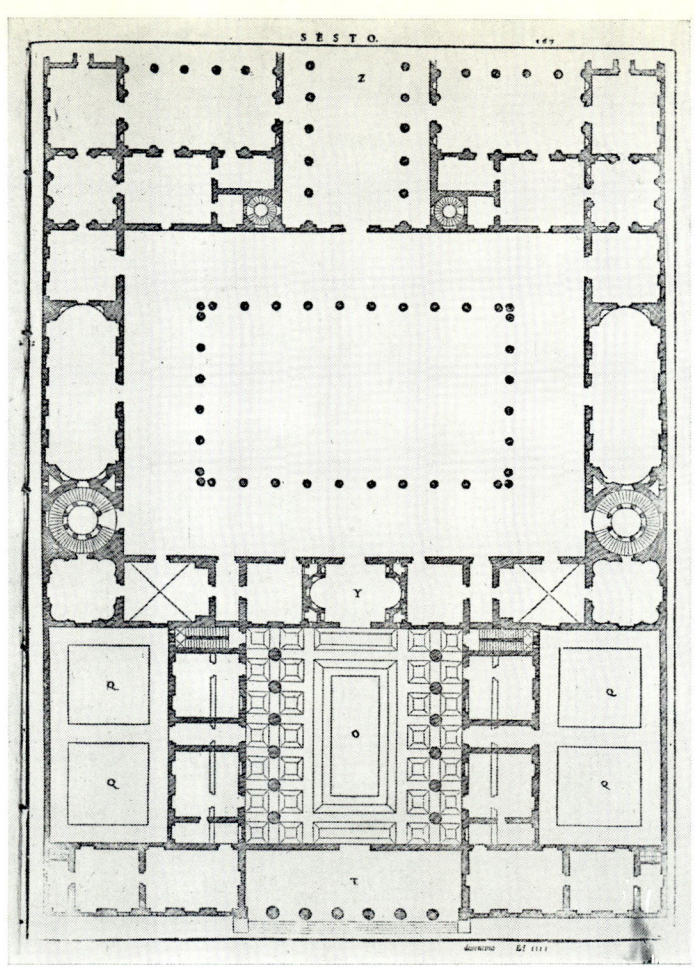

XXXV - DANIELE BARBARO, *The Casa dei Romani*. From *I Dieci Libri dell'Architettura di M.V. Vitruvio...*, 1556, VI, p. 167

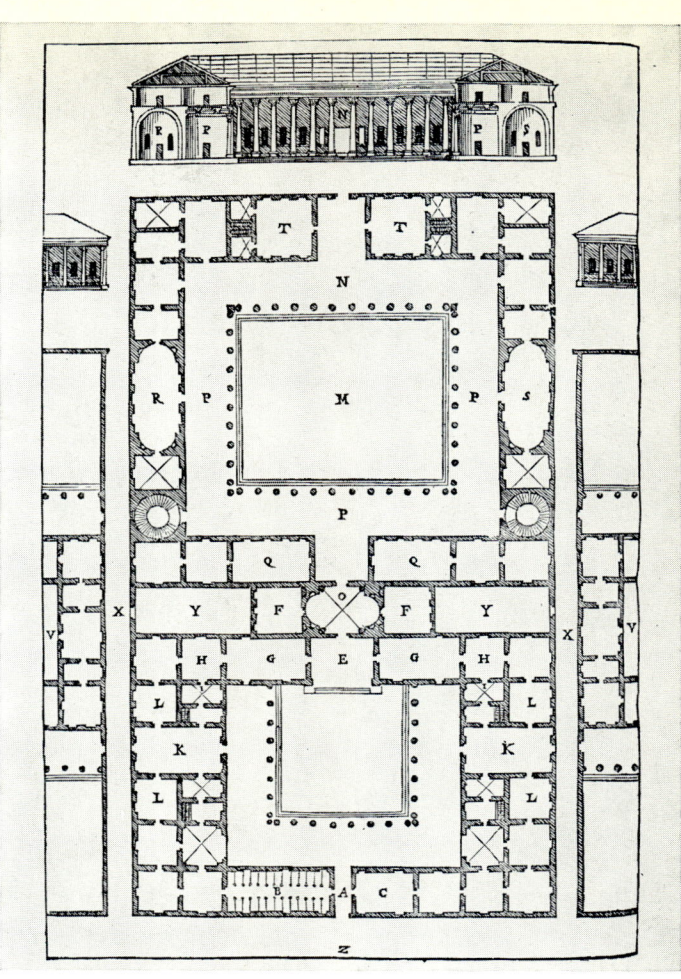

XXXVI - ANDREA PALLADIO, *The casa dei Greci*. From *I Quattro Libri dell'Architettura*, 1570, II, XI, p. 44

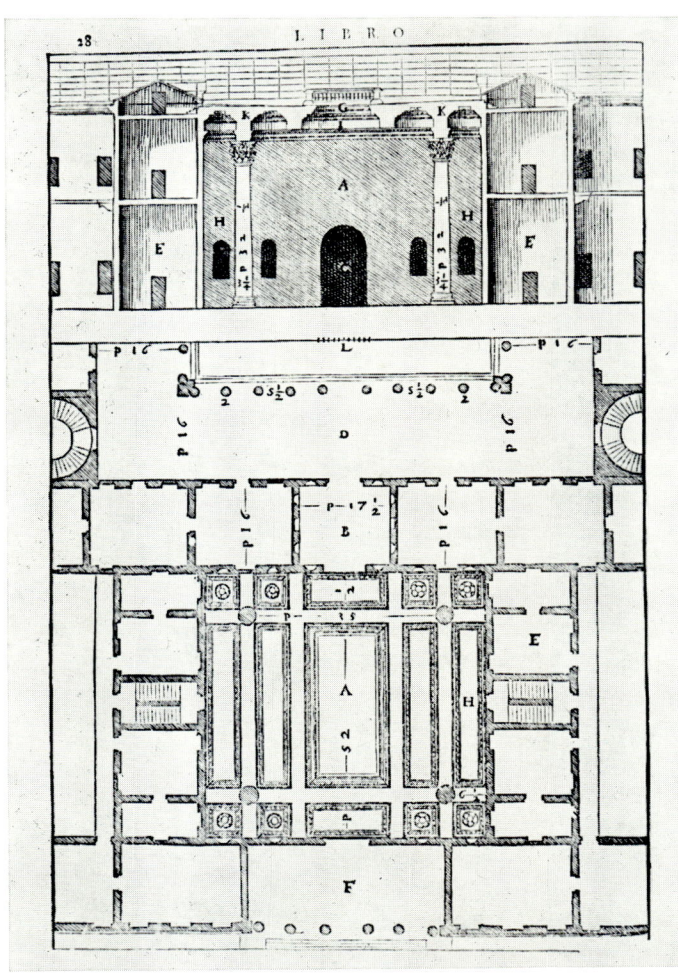

XXXVII - ANDREA PALLADIO, *L'atrio di quattro colonne*. From *I Quattro Libri dell'Architettura*, 1570, II, V, p. 28

XXXVIII - ANDREA PALLADIO, *Sala di quattro colonne*. From *I Quattro Libri dell'Architettura*, 1570, II, VIII, p. 37

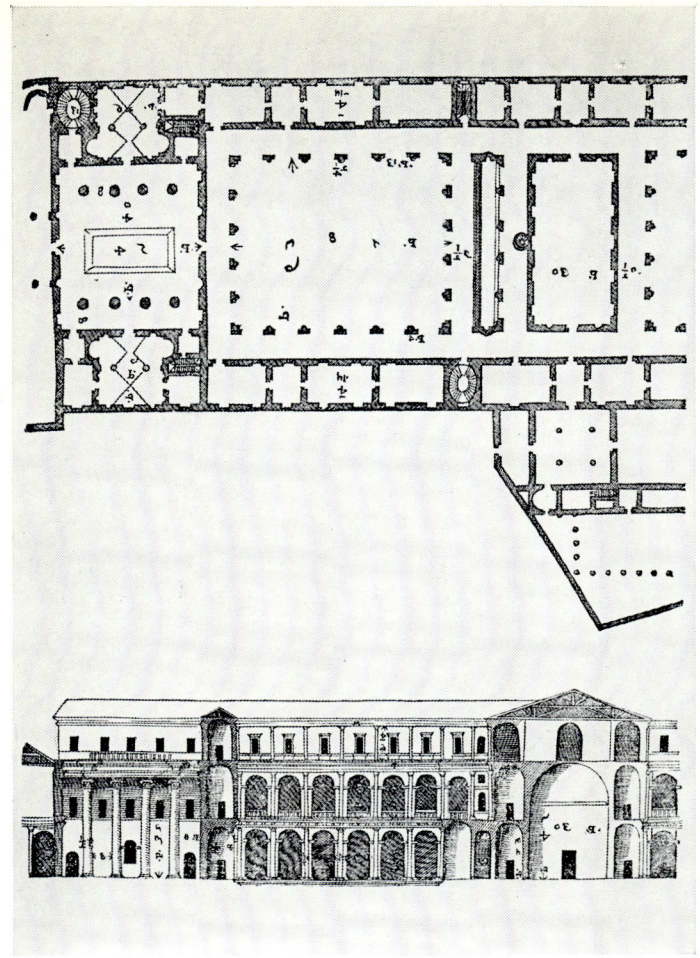

XXXIX - Andrea Palladio, *Plan and section of the Convento della Carità with the proter orientation.* From *I Quattro Libri dell'Architettura*, 1570, II, VI

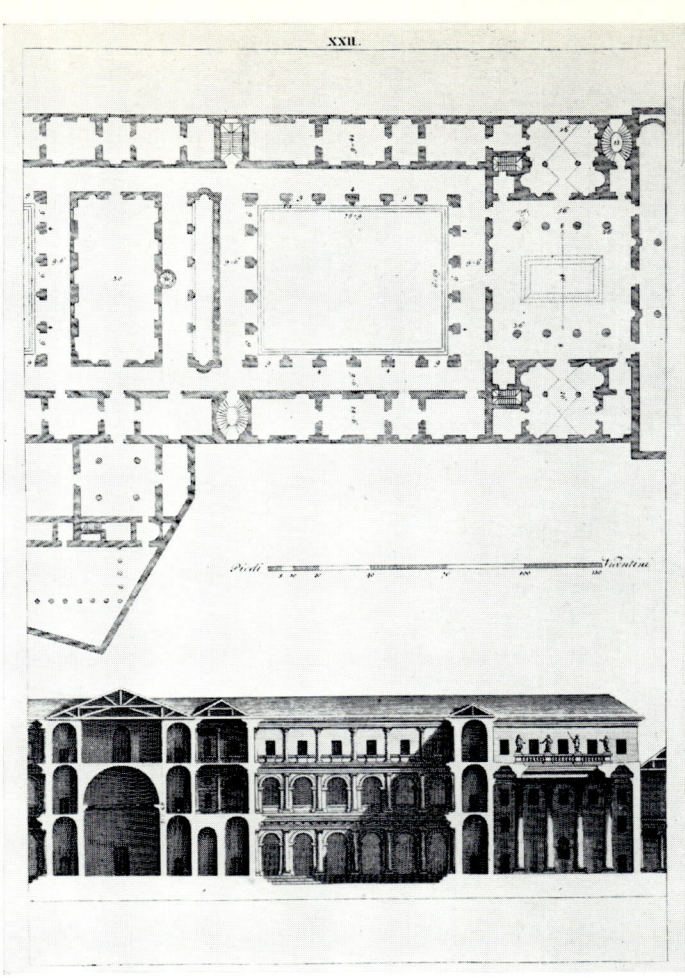

XL - Giacomo Leoni, *Plan and section of the Convento della Carità.* From the *Architecture of A. Palladio in Four Books*, 1721, II, pl. XXII

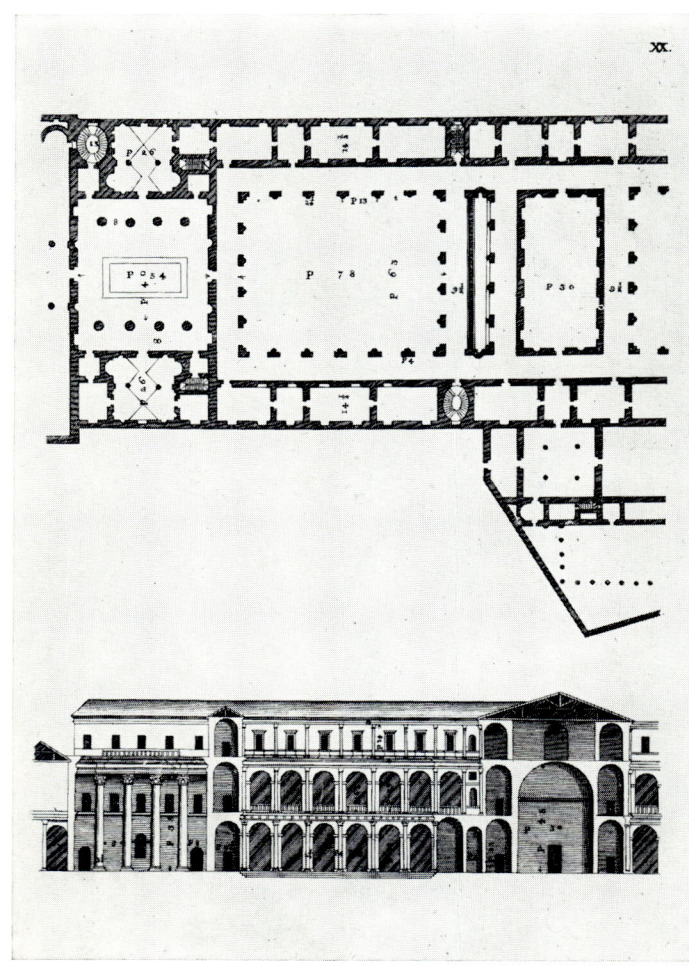

XLI - Isaac Ware, *Plan and section of the Convento della Carità.* From *The Four Books of Andrea Palladio's Architecture*, 1738, II, pl. XX

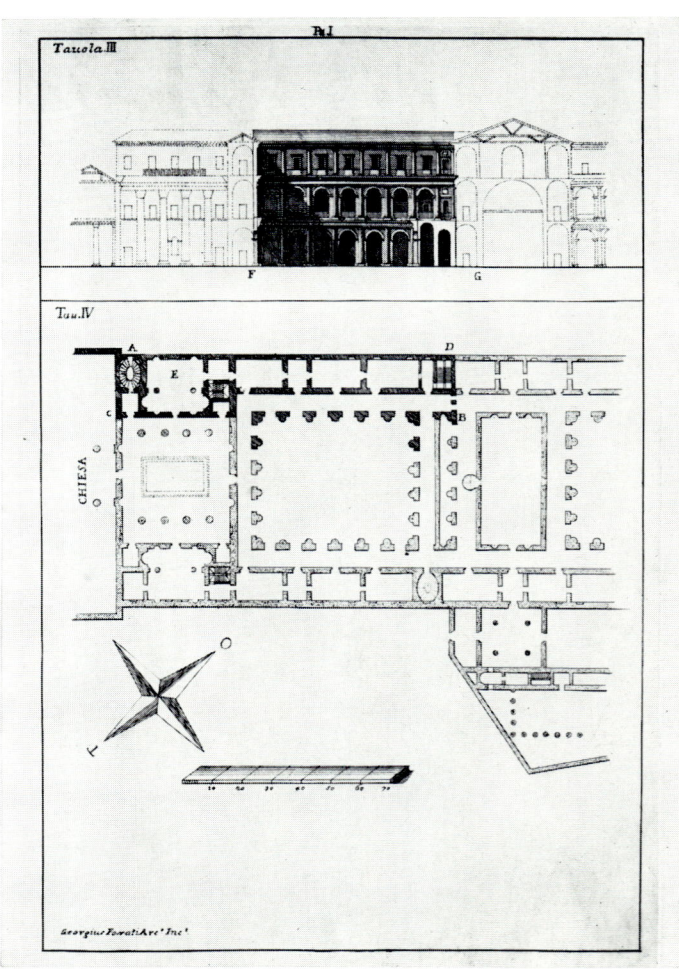

XLII - Francesco Muttoni, *Section and plan of the Convento della Carità.* From *Architettura di Andrea Palladio Vicentino*, I, pt. I, 1740, pls. III-IV

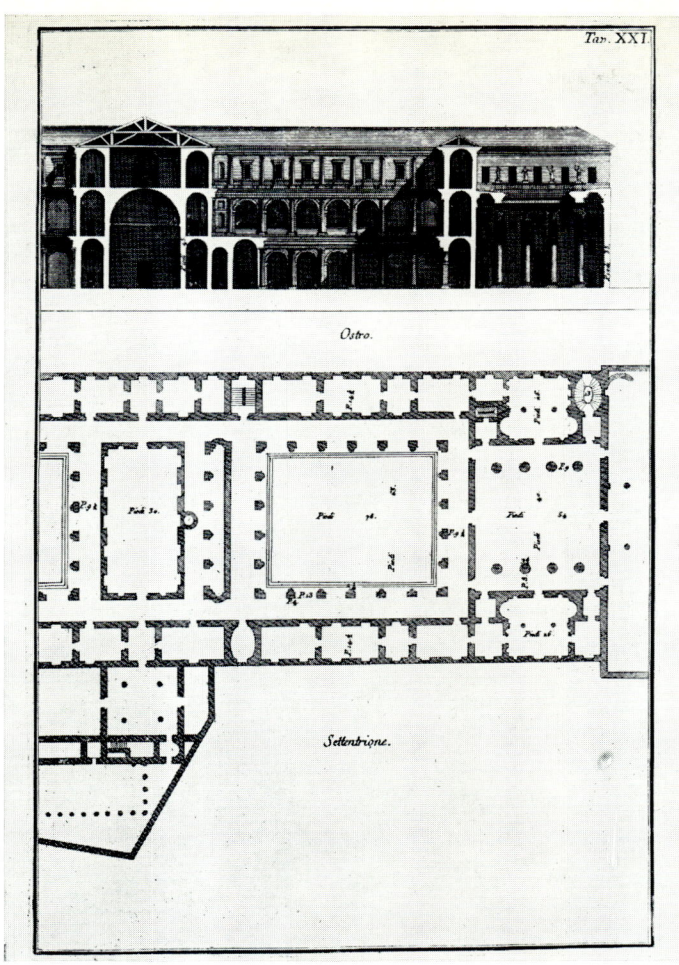

XLIII - Francesco Muttoni, *Section and plan of the Convento della Carità.* From *Architettura di Andrea Palladio Vicentino*, V, 1744, pl. XXI

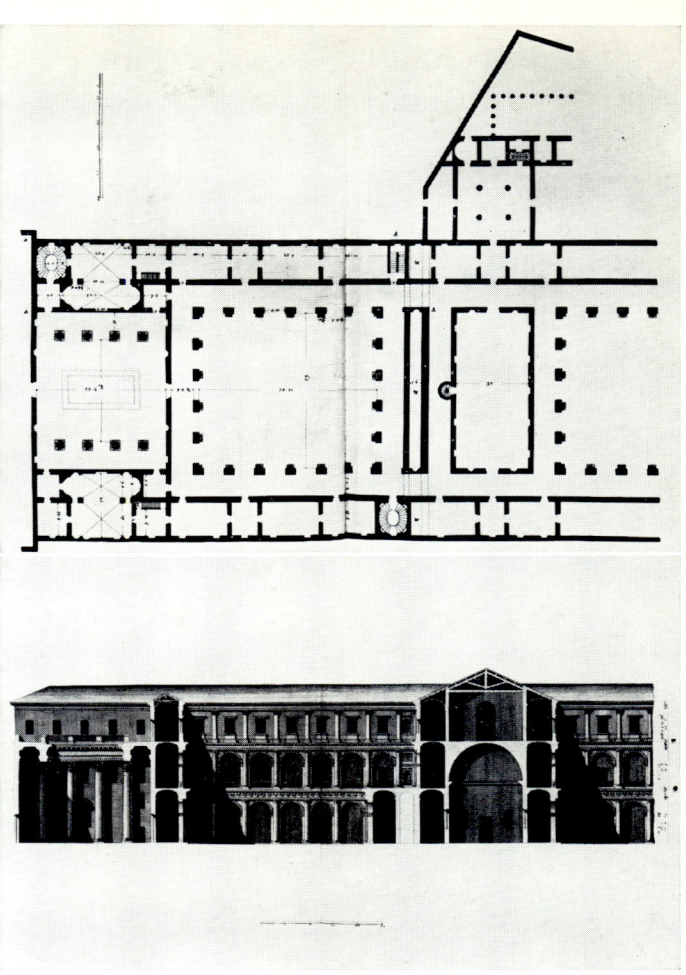

XLIV - Ottavio Bertotti Scamozzi, *Plan and section of the Convento della Carità.* From *Le Fabbriche e i Disegni di Andrea Palladio*, IV, 1783, pls. XXIV, XXVI

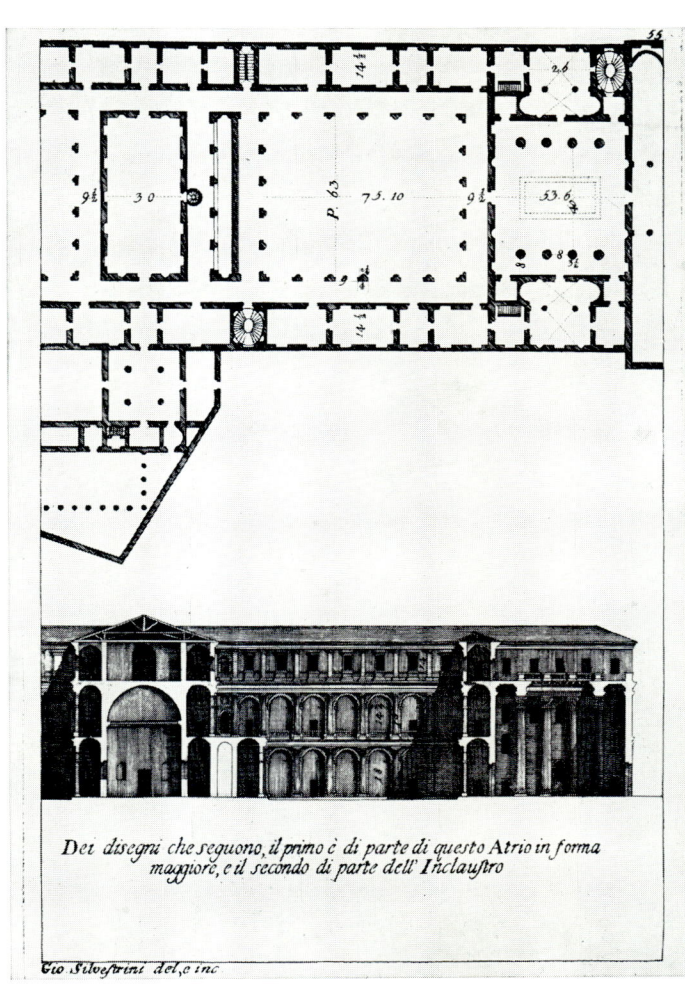

XLV - Alessandro Mucci, *Plan and section of the Convento della Carità.* From *I Quattro Libri dell'Architettura di Andrea Palladio*, 1791, II, p. 55

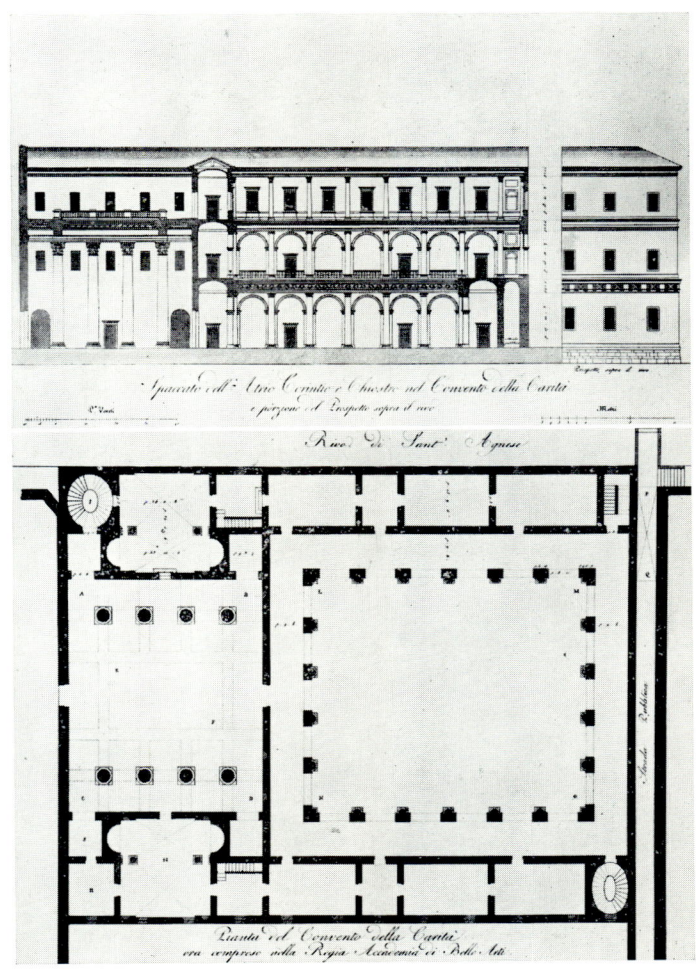

XLVI - Cicognara, Diedo, Selva, *Section and plan of the Convento della Carità.* From *Le Fabbriche e i monumenti cospicui di Venezia...*, 1858, pls. 207, 211

XLVII - ISAAC WARE, *Cloister of the Convento della Carità, in large-scale representation.* From *The Four Books of Andrea Palladio's Architecture*, 1738, II, pl. XXII

XLVIII - ISAAC WARE, *Atrium of the Convento della Carità, in large-scale representation.* From *The Four Books of Andrea Palladio's Architecture*, 1738, II, pl. XXI

IL - FRANCESCO MUTTONI, *Cloister of the Convento della Carità, in large-scale representation.* From *Architettura di Andrea Palladio Vicentino*, I, pt. I, 1740, pl. VI

L - FRANCESCO MUTTONI, *Cloister in the Convento della Carità.* From *Architettura di Andrea Palladio Vicentino*, I, pt. I, 1740, pl. V

LI - FRANCESCO MUTTONI, *Cloister in the Convento della Carità, in large-scale representation.* From *Architettura di Andrea Palladio Vicentino*, V, 1744, pl. XXIII

LII - FRANCESCO MUTTONI, *Atrium in the Convento della Carità, in large-scale representation.* From *Architettura di Andrea Palladio Vicentino*, V, 1744, pl. XXII

LIII - ALESSANDRO MUCCI, *Cloister of the Convento della Carità, in large-scale representation.* From *I Quattro Libri dell'Architettura di Andrea Palladio*, 1791, II, p. 59

LIV - ALESSANDRO MUCCI, *Atrium of the Convento della Carità, in large-scale representation.* From *I Quattro Libri dell'Architettura di Andrea Palladio*, 1791, II, p. 57

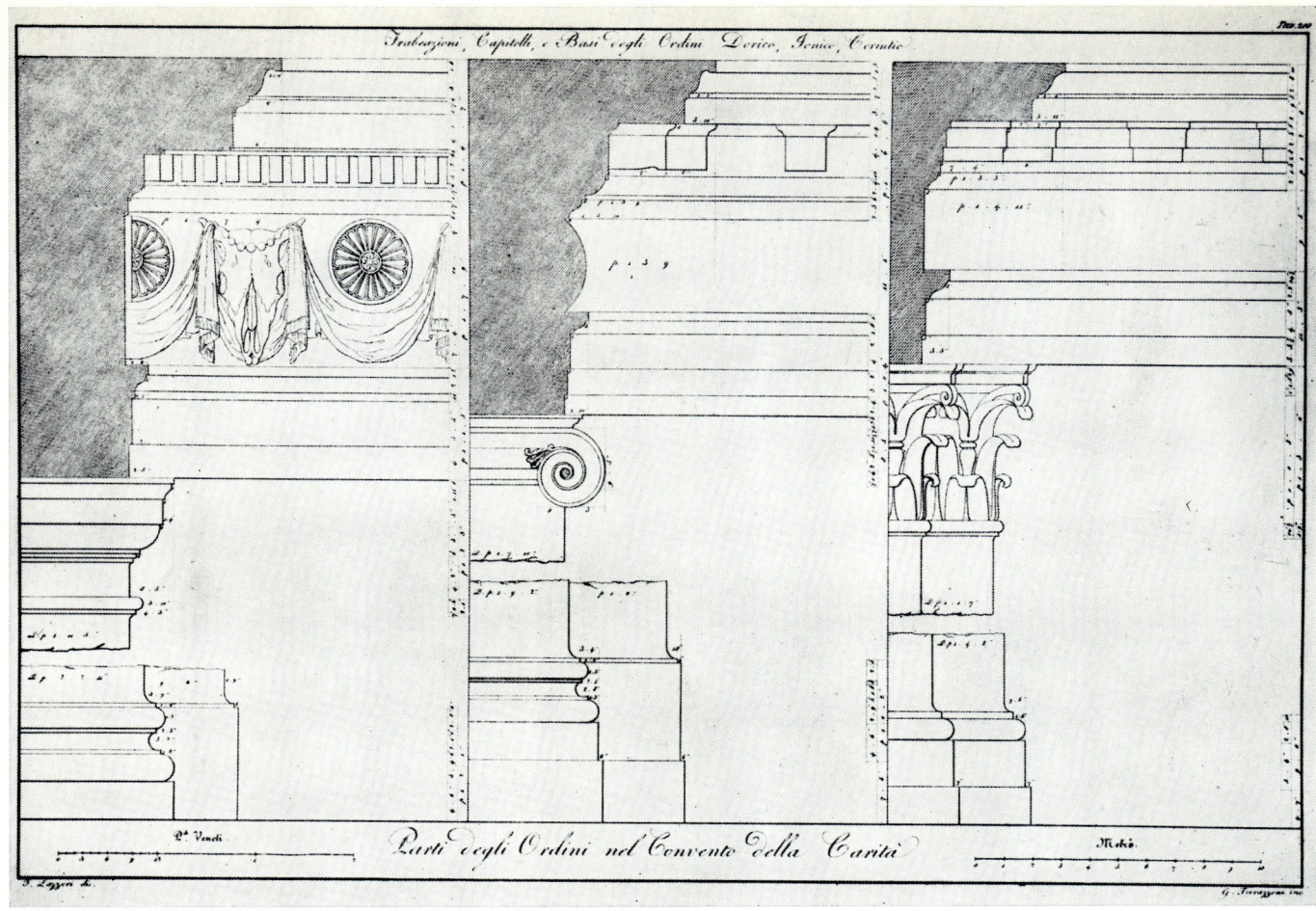

LV - Cicognara, Diedo, Selva, *Parts of the orders of the Convento della Carità.*
From *Le Fabbriche e i monumenti cospicui di Venezia...*, 1858, II, pl. 210

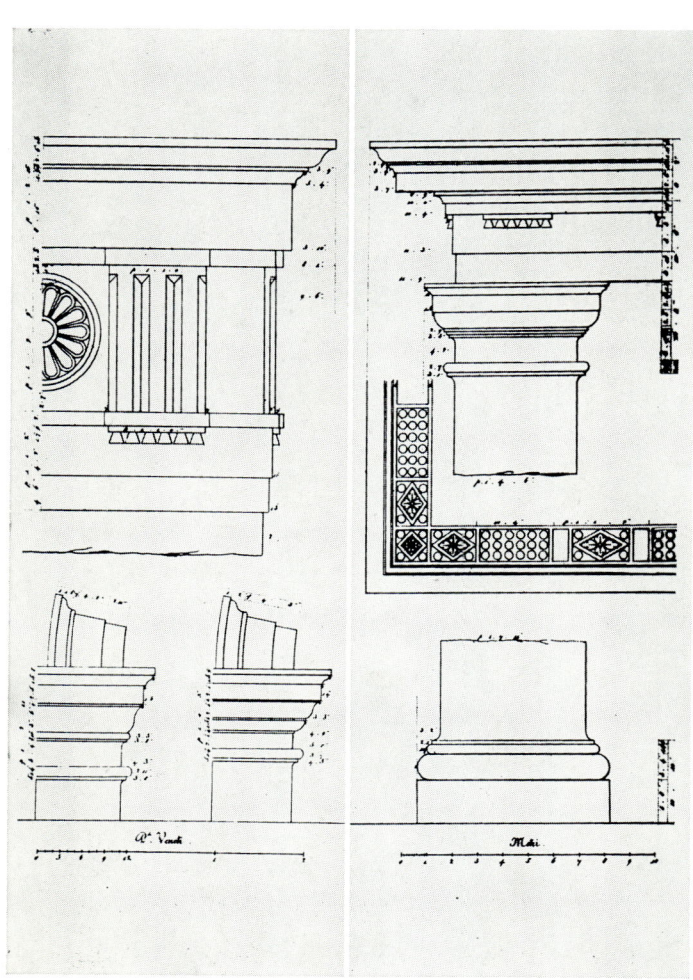

LVI - Cicognara, Diedo, Selva, *Parts of the orders of the Convento della Carità.* From *Le Fabbriche e i monumenti cospicui di Venezia*, 1858, II, pl. 209.

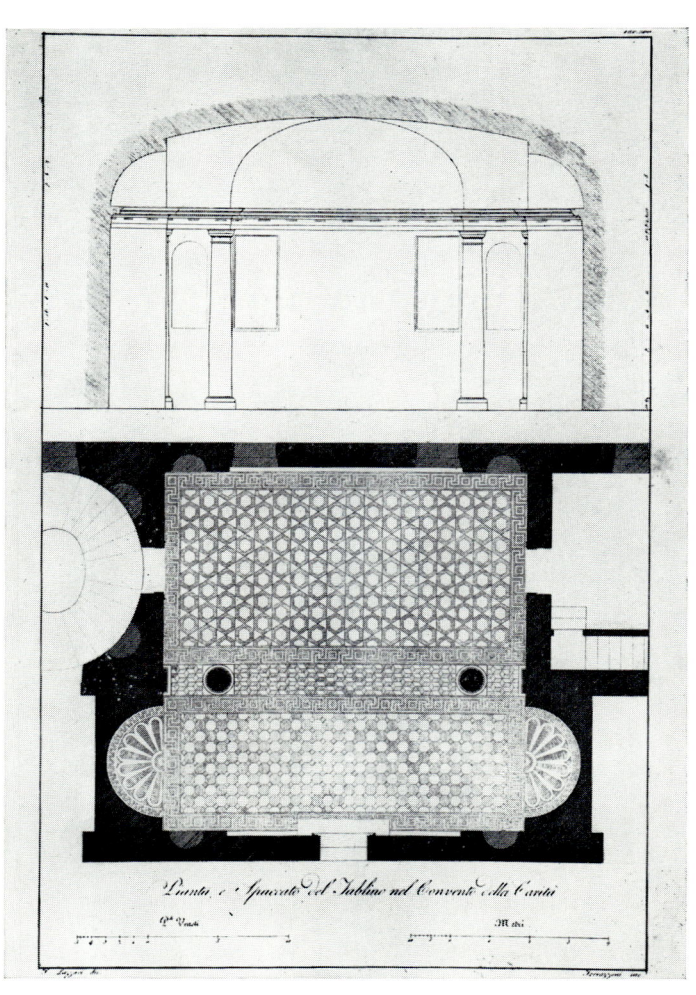

LVII - Cicognara, Diedo, Selva, *Section and plan of the tablinum of the Convento della Carità.* From *Le Fabbriche e i monumenti cospicui di Venezia*, 1858, II, pl. 208

LVIII - Ottavio Bertotti Scamozzi, *Section of the atrium of the Convento della Carità.*
From *Le Fabbriche e i Disegni di Andrea Palladio*, IV, 1783, pl. XXV

LIX - Cicognara, Diedo, Selva, *Peristyle of the Convento della Carità after the nineteenth-century restoration.*
From *Le Fabbriche e i monumenti cospicui di Venezia ...*, 1858, II, pl. 212

LX - *Convento della Carità: detail from the Ionic loggia on the second floor*

which were not executed and which do not appear in the coresponding plan. The nineteenth-century restoration exposed the entire height of the pilasters, but revealed no trace of these steps.

These observations allow one to conclude that, as usual, Palladio made a beautiful design and then brought it under control in the course of execution, as various opportunities presented themselves.

NOTES TO CHAPTER IV

[1] 1570, I, p. 22.

[2] 1649, p. 13; cf. ch. VI.

[3] 1835, p. 13.

[4] Palladio, in his first book, had written: "I pavimenti di pietre cotte, perché le pietre si possono fare di diverse forme e di diversi colori, per la diversità delle crete, riusciranno molto belli e vaghi all'occhio per la varietà dei colori (1570, I, p. 53). Concerning this argument, it is interesting to refer also to the different attitude found in the autograph fragment of the *Quattro Libri* preserved in the Museo Correr: "I pavimenti di pietre cotte perché le pietre si possono fare di diverse forme, e di diversi colori per la diversità di crete, riusciranno molto vaghi e belli disponendo le pietre in modi diversi, e commettendole talmente insieme che per la diversità de i colori rasembrino il rilievo"; but this addition follows: "A me non piace che parino di rilievo perché la vista se inganna et questa inganna il piede, et il pavimento deve essere eguale et parere eguale" (ZORZI, 1959, p. 173). We are able to ascertain that in the tablinum the *trompe d'oeil* is minimal.

[5] Concerning the temple of Castor and Pollux in Naples—of which now only a little remains but which Palladio reproduced as it was in the Cinquecento, elegant and solemn—after having treated the Corinthian capitals, the architect affirmed: "Sono intagliati a foglie di olivo, e sono lavorati diligentissimamente. È molto bella la inventione dei caulicoli, che sono sotto la rosa; i quali si legano insieme, e par che nascano fuori dalle foglie che vestono nella parte di sopra gli altri caulicoli le quali sostengono le corna dei capitelli. Onde così da questo, come da molti altri esempi sparsi per questo libro si conosce che non è vietato, all' Architetto partirsi alcuna volta dall' uso comune, pur che tal variatione sia gratiosa, et habbia del naturale" (1570, IV, p. 95).

With this consideration Palladio implicitly justified also the Ionic frieze on the Doric order in the Carità; besides, Sansovino had also contradicted tradition in the Libreria Marciana when he had placed metopes instead of the usual triglyphs at the corners and had thus provoked arguments still alive in the eighteenth century.

[6] 1537, p. 139v.

[7] 1740, p. 3.

[8] 1778, p. 207.

[9] 1785, p. 37.

[10] IV, 1796, p. 43 n. b.

[11] II, 1838, p. 107.

[12] 1835, p. 14.

[13] 1845, p. 50.

[14] 1961, p. 294.

[15] 1954, p. 245, n. 34.

[16] 1835, n. 15.

[17] "Si fanno le fondamenta a scarpa; cioè che tanto più decrescano, quanto più s'inalzano..." (1570, I, p. 53).

Concerning foundations, moreover, Palladio had observed: "Sono assai lodevoli nelle fabbriche grandi alcuni spiragli per la grossezza del muro delle fondamenta fino al tetto, perciocché danno a' venti, che meno diano noia alla fabbrica, scemano la spesa, e sono di non piccola commodità, se in quelli si faranno scale a lumaca, le quali portano dal fondamento sino al sommo dell'edificio"; and of that he had experience at the monastery, constructing the most masterful of his stairs in an oval form. He had written about this in his treatise, as has been cited above, p. 28; taking it up again, he added the words "molto commoda e vaga" (1570, II, p. 29).

[18] 1715, XL, G.

[19] 1570, II, VIII and I, XXVIII.

[20] 1957 (1786), p. 130.

[21] In fact, a similar structure cannot be inserted in the house of the ancients, although Palladio suggested the example in the three stairs in the plan of the Cripta Balbi and recorded the Porticoes of Pompey where there were "tre scale a lumaca di molto laudabile inventione; perciocché essendo esse poste nel mezo, onde non potevano haver lume se non di sopra; erano fatte su colonne acciocché il lume si spargesse ugualmente per tutto" (1570, I, p. 64).

[22] 1570, II, p. 34.

[23] Above this was suspended Briamonte's urn, ornamented with two reliefs, now in the Ca' d'Oro, executed by the brother Vittore Gambello; these represent combats of nudes, the compositions of which derive from the prints of Pollaiuolo and Mantegna. According to the notice recorded by Paoletti (1893, II, p. 271), the urn, executed in 1539, originally was in the cloister and was removed because of construction before 1548; Sansovino, however, mentions it still in the cloister (1581, p. 96v) and considered Briamonte "capitano illustre"; this error was perpetuated until it was corrected by Tassini (Tassini, 1877).

[24] 1570, II, p. 29.

[25] 1961, p. 293.

V
THE MONASTERY AFTER THE FIRE

Documents postdating 1630 concerning the extent of the fire are sparse; in addition, because we do not know exactly the form and extent of the monastery before the disaster, we can here only dissipate some false assertions, in part logical, which, by the authority of those who put them forth, have always been accepted by students by virtue of their "ipse dixit." Palladio's design had been built up to the point indicated by the bill of lading for the stone in March, 1573; in 1574 only the refectory beyond the *calle pubblica* was begun. After the fire, when improvements to the monastery were made, no more reconstruction of the atrium was undertaken. The only part of the original material of the atrium still visible is a series of semi-calcified little bricks on a terrace at the height of the third order (figs. LXII, LXVI): these must in some way have been part of the terrace that was around the "impluvium."

Temanza attributed the restoration of the area formerly occupied by the atrium to the abbot Gozzi, about whom we have no information at all. Pilasters with attached half-columns, whose height corresponded to that of the first order, were raised on the bases of the eight giant columns that were destroyed (fig. LXXVIII). In some manner they continued the motif of the arches of the peristyle (fig. LXXVII) and were carried around three sides of the space. The earliest visual evidence we have for this area dates from the nineteenth century (fig. CIII). Visentini, believing that Palladio himself had been driven to this modest solution because of a lack of funds, wrote, "Le arcate son quattro in ogni lato." In the plans of Ughi (1729) and Viero (1798) the two spaces are divided, but we do not know how reliable these plans are. Only excavations would be able to clarify many questions concerning what now remains of the original atrium.

The abbot Gozzi, as Temanza testified, wanted to construct an "atria lapidea," that is, the atrium, then extant and visible in Moschini's guide (fig. CIII); it had four arches in the long side and three along the short one. In 1938 it was covered, in which form it may now be seen, along with another part of the reconstruction that renovated the passage between the atrium and cloister that Palladio had planned. In the seventeenth-century renovation the two return arches, one on each side of the peristyle, were respected and are visible in the print cited above. In the patching of the atrium the curved bricks of the great columns were reused here and there.

We cannot be certain how the passage from the destroyed atrium to the peristyle was resolved in the reconstruction. There is no visual record, and the written sources are both unclear and contradictory. The neoclassical conversion of the building into the Accademia was done with haste, and, until then, there was no great flourishing of plans revealing the condition before that transformation. Only in Combatti's plan of 1847 do we have any very exact record of the rebuilding undertaken by Lazzari (fig. VII).

After the fire the Convento della Carità had been forgotten; as a work of architecture it is ignored in the guides of the later seventeenth and early eighteenth century, which, at most, name the paintings conserved in the sacristy and refectory.

The conventual family was no longer important; in 1666 Doglioni[1] recorded that only thirty religious lived at the Carità (at the Frari, in the same period, there were 106 brothers). The decline coincided with the flowering of the contiguous convent of the Dominicans, who, taking possession of the building left empty by the Gesuati at the Zattere when that order was suppressed (1668), had added to their property little by little, buying various private houses and also a part of the vineyard of the Lateran canons, with the intention of arranging the refectory and other buildings. This is known from a plan conserved in the Archivio, which is undated but which belongs to the early eighteenth century. At that time the Dominicans executed some construction along the rio di Sant'Agnese, as is proven by a date—1700—still conserved in that area below a relief with a Dominican symbol. A few years later—in 1724—Massari began the construction of the big new church and the rebuilding of the convent in the locality which, despite the property's change of hands, is still referred to as that of the Gesuati.

The scuola of the Carità also fluorished then, and it renovated its building, as is shown by the date 1679 carved next to the symbol of the scuola on the outside of the structure at the far end of the entrance courtyard (fig. LXXXVI), while on the inside of the same structure an inscription states that a restoration was completed there in 1769—that is, a bit after Massari had modernized the seat of the scuola and designed the new façade, which was later completed by Maccarucci (1766). Meanwhile, when the campanile of the poor canons' church collapsed (1744), they did not reconstruct it. Only a few of them remained; then, in 1768, the government decided to concentrate the small religious communities together, and the Lateran canons were forced to leave their great monastery.

The church was entrusted to the scuola of the Carità; the staffing was left to a chaplain, and, finally, on September 7, 1792, the suppression of the canons was completed and the effects of the church were given to the new church of the Maddalena, which had been costructed by Temanza.[2]

After the republic fell, the building hosted foreign troops during the comings and goings of the French and Austrians; finally, on March 9, 1807, the government made it the seat of the new Accademia di Belle Arti, including a school and a picture gallery, against the advice of the professors of the Academy. Those who took an interest in the matter preferred the Scuola di San Marco, but later the architect Giannantonio Selva, titular professor of the reformed Academy, gave in and accepted the complex of the Carità, despite the evident inconveniences that the professors, students, and works of art would have to sustain. He hoped to save whatever remained of the sixteenth-century convent, and every use suggested for it would have entailed destructive and irremediable alterations.

The task of adapting it to its new functions was first entrusted to Giovanni Antolini, who proposed a massive project, now lost, which accorded with the ideas of Selva and the academicians. But the duties of Antolini, who had been made the chief clerk of works for all of Lombardy-Veneto, were so extensive that the task of execution passed quickly to Selva, who was left free to ignore the proposals of the Lombard architect.

Palladio's works were scrupulously conserved, but the Gothic church was devastated, with full awareness; not even Palladio had respected it, as one can see not only in his additions to the apse's exterior mentioned above (fig. LXI) but also in the wall where the Corinthian atrium was supported, where the long Gothic windows were covered in a barbarous manner in the sixteenth century. The scuola was used without alterations, perhaps because after its modernization by Massari its sytle accorded gracefully with the sixteenth-century monastery, or perhaps because the great upper hall was useful for ceremonies and exhibitions. But it was difficult to unify the buildings, to work out a continuous circulation pattern, and to overcome the existing changes of levels between the various buildings.

After the initial modifications had been completed, the Palladian courtyard assumed the appearance shown in the above-mentioned print of 1828 (fig. CIII). It was urgent to have a storage area for the numerous paintings of the institutes and of the secularized churches, and so the Ionic loggia was walled up, with only the lunettes left open. As in the seventeenth century, the return arches on each side of the courtyard were again respected, and still visible under the arcade is a walkway that was later hidden from view when the pavement was raised; in the print one can see between the pilasters the new steps that were made necessary when the level of the ground floor was raised, in order to reduce the infiltration of damp from the subsoil into the area intended for studios. On the right in Moschini's print, in the area Palladio intended for the refectory, one can see the new picture gallery, which Selva designed and which was constructed after his death by his student, Francesco Wchowich-Lazzari in 1828 (plates 8, 22; fig. LXXXV).

Selva's original project is lost; all that remains of it is the brief description with which the neoclassical architect presented his designs to the president of the Academy, Leopoldo Cicognara.[4] This does reveal that the place destined for the new picture gallery contained a coal storage bin belonging to the Zecca and a small transport barracks. The barracks created difficulty for the adaptation of the institute, because the soldiers were constrained to use the services of the students and this introduced a deplorable promiscuity. To bring the basement for the new hall into line and to align the public street, Selva proposed the removal of some old construction from the two lower stories, using it as the residence of the academy's custodian; this suggests that beyond the calle del Dose, in the vineyard, the canons had storage rooms and a little house. With the projected construction, Selva suggested, one reunites "nuovamente ciò che formava in addietro un solo corpo di proprietà, giacché questo locale [the barracks] apparteneva al soppresso convento della Carità, dove si è fondato il presente stabilimento, ed era anzi quello su cui dovevasi continuare il disegno palladiano, come si vede nel suo 2° Libro dell'architettura p. 30."

Selva therefore had proposed here to enlarge the building, carrying it to the proportions projected by Palladio. In fact, if he had built the refectory, the monastery would have been 230 feet long (that is, 74.60 meters) along the rio di Sant'Agnese; now, with the eighteenth-century additions, which can be assessed and recognized in the roof, that side is 73 meters long (scale drawing *b*; fig. LXIV). Similarly, the other dimensions of the new picture gallery correspond to those projected in the sixteenth century and would have extended the building over nearly the entire asymmetrical zone foreseen toward the rio della Carità (fig. LXXXV). The exterior along the rio di Sant'Agnese scrupulously extended the sixteenth-century structure, with the motif of metopes and triglyphs, the Ionic frieze, and the rhythm of the openings (scale drawing *f*). The interior of the new picture gallery, however, corresponds only to its new function.

Installed on the façade overlooking the rio della Carità was the monumental portal of San Nicolò di Castello, a church that Selva destroyed when extending the public gardens. Inside, in the upper hall, four Greek marble columns from the Scuola of the Misericordia were set up.

The architect had the highest respect for the tablinum; he adapted it to a studio and preserved its original level. He substituted a portal for the window that then existed; traces of it remain on the outside wall, and inside there is a suture in the stucco frieze, which shows that earlier the window's arch broke into it (plates 38-39; fig. LXXIX). Such a hiatus certainly had an aesthetic significance, which we can succeed in grasping only with difficulty. Selva justified his making this transformation by noting that Palladio, in his design of the plan, had envisaged a door here. Beyond this new portal four steps make up the difference between the nineteenth-century and sixteenth-century levels. The altar was brought here and placed in the great niche on the right. The other portal that permitted access from the other niche into the church entrance and then into the church was also closed.

The pavement of the tablinum was also preserved, for the moment, only to be destroyed in 1827.[5] But the other brick pavements in the monastery were destroyed at this time. Among them the most notable must have been that in the Ionic loggia which must have had a special importance, because it was located in front of the guest rooms and the abbot's room. At the ends of the loggias two entrances to the new hall were opened. The top floor, which had been intended to serve as a dormitory and to accommodate the eleven cells, was not greatly altered; eight cells are still preserved here in their original dimensions. An elaborate solution was required to carve out a passage between the monastery, the church, and the former scuola; it also had to give access to the hall that was obtained by adding a median floor to the church. Selva had thought of lowering the level of the convent to that of the scuola in the lodgings hall, opening a portal, and connecting the two different levels with some steps. After Selva's death, the work was continued, in the midst of the usual economic difficulties, by Francesco Wchowich-Lazzari, who also succeeded Selva in his teaching position at the Accademia.

To mention something we have discussed elsewhere,[6] we maintain that the nineteenth-century work was intended to make the best use of the space and to provide a proper setting for the gallery and the Accademia; in so doing, criteria of the period were used, and these required, among other things, that symmetry be respected. Thus, Lazzari destroyed the two return arches that his master Selva had saved, because the older man still dreamed of completing the Palladian project and did not dare to lay a hand upon any of it that was extant. After the arches and pilasters were knocked down in 1829, the corner solution became visible and one could then discover what the Palladian proportions would have been in the completed work (fig. LXXIV). Selva, a cultivated and refined man, had rendered a good account of himself. Lazzari, a man destined to destroy, reduced the ends of the three orders by two bays and reproduced in the second and third order on the left the motif that Palladio had envisaged only for the right. Moreover, he reopened the arches in the second order, added balusters, and then closed them with glass (fig. LIX). Later, glass was also placed in the arches of the first order, thus sacrificing all the chiaroscuro effects that Palladio had studied so carefully. Lazzari left a detailed report of the destruction and reconstruction in a publication, which is important because it contains a great deal of information about the original condition of the building; it does not seem, however, that he believed himself to be opposing the prevailing culture and aesthetic. Indeed, he appeared to his students to be a vigorous defender of Palladio against the new criticism represented by Pietro Estense Selvatico, as the architect Camillo Boito testified.[7]

After the modifications of the courtyard were finished, the façade of the scuola was transformed (1830), the hospice was adapted to its new function (1831), and an exhibition hall was fitted out in the former guest rooms on the *piano nobile* (1829-30).

Finally, the construction of other rooms in the area of the hospice of the Scuola della Carità was approved. This was the origin of the so-called "newest" halls (1845), which one uses to go from the reception *salone* in the old scuola to the new picture gallery. The "sale nuovissime," the product of successive and elaborate projects of Lazzari, required tearing apart the small medieval cloister that was in the center of the hospice and all the interesting structure that surrounded it; both are still recognizable in views made by Lazzari and in the carefully made topographic plan of Combatti (1847; fig. VII). There is a reference to the little courtyard in some lines of Fapanni: "Esisteva un chiostretto quadrato, con pozzo nel mezzo, di stile del secolo XVI. Fu atterrato circa il 18 ... quando si eressero le fabbriche nuove. Piccio economo, e Zenoni cancelliere se lo ricordano."[8]

The exterior of the monastery was changed relative to how it had been envisioned by Palladio when the rio di Sant' Agnese was filled in (1863); it is visible in the Perissini plan of 1866. Selva, with the addition of the new halls, had extended the building to the proportions projected in the sixteenth century; the reflection of the rippling water played along the façade until the canal was covered. The majestic "cavana" was now useless, and so it was closed (plate 7; fig. LXV); with the raising of the street level, a great part of the basement in *pietra d'Istria* vanished. Lost now were the reflections and the changing play of light projected from the canal inside to the guest rooms, the cells, the tablinum, and the stairs. During the flood of November 4, 1966, the rio Terra' again filled with water and the event evoked the original appearance of the monastery (fig. VI).

The closing of the *cavana* brought about the demolition of the mezzanine level above, producing an area of full height, while the arch of the *cavana* and its great stones remains visible. The vaulted opening that gave access to the area of the guest rooms and a window in the mezzanine level that let in light from the Doric portico were closed, and near it a Palladian-type portal was opened (figs. LXXX-LXXXI; LXXXIV).

For a long time there were no further important modifications. In 1938 the president of the Accademia, the architect Guido Cirilli, in order to add space to the school and to the gallery, separated the two connecting courtyards, thus reestablishing the partition that in the sixteenth-century project had divided the atrium from the peristyle. Then, in 1948, under the sponsorship of Giuseppe De Logu, the tablinum was restored. The beautiful armadios formerly belonging to the monastery of the Gesuati and probably designed by Massari, which interfered with the appearance of the little niches and lateral doors, were removed. The pavement was also restored, following the scheme recorded in a polychrome watercolor discovered by the present writer. The dawing had perhaps been made when it became necessary to remove the original brick pavement, which had been ruined by wear and humidity (1828; color plate *d*). The person who directed the work of restoring the tablinum believed it opportune to cover the shafts of the pilasters that stood behind the two great columns with marble (plate 43); Palladio, however, had obviously wanted all parts of the walls to be plastered uniformly. That error was born from the desire to pay homage to the artist by enriching the harmonious area; therefore, we should not blame the restorer but should simply admire one of the most elaborate and genial spaces designed by the great master.

As has been said, when the Accademia was installed in the former monastery, it became necessary to raise the level of all the sixteenth-century construction in order to retard the infiltration of damp and the usual subsistance of the ground level. The original level was retained only in the tablinum. Some steps were constructed between the columns of the peristyle, and five steps of the oval stairs were covered up. In 1968, when restorations were executed under the direction of the Soprintendenza ai Monumenti, the steps and the original pavement in the stairwell were exposed, as was the full height of the door, now walled up, that opened into the tablinum (figs. XCIII-XCIV).

In 1970 the Soprintendenza alle Gallerie undertook the restoration of the top floor with the cells. That work is underway at the time of writing; documents published for the first time in this monograph are being used in the project. The long corridor where the dormitory was located is being restored to a single space by tearing out the median floor, which was constructed to make fuller use of the space (fig. LXXIII). At the end of the corridor, in the wall that originally faced the vineyard and the calle del Dose, traces of two balconies facing the south have been found; these are visible in a print by Coronelli (figs. LXXVI, IC), where they are shown in an imprecise way. The balconies would have been taken out had the refectory been constructed according to the original project, and therefore it is improbable that they were designed by Palladio; they disappeared when the *sale nuove* were set up.

The restoration has finally permitted the verification of the existence of the cane vaults in the corridor and cells (figs. LXXI, LXXII, LXXV). The imposts of the vaults, which would have turned the corner had the passage between the atrium and the peristyle been built, have come to light. This vault, of course, is above the one already mentioned in the ground floor, which was torn out by Lazzari when he destroyed the return arch of the peristyle (figs. LXXI, LXXIV). In the restoration it has been possible to reduce the weight of the plaster added during successive renovations. The mouldings of the original doors between the dormitory and the cells have been found; some of these have been recovered after having been walled in during the renovations of the nineteenth century.

Since the group of buildings that formed the complex of the Carità are now used intensively, a comprehensive restoration does not seem a likely possibility.

Just as it is only in our imagination that

we are able to see the interior of the church reconstructed in its entirety, so, too, only in this way are we able to imagine the space formerly occupied by the solemn atrium as emptied of its unfortunate additions, or the arcade and the loggia as closed off in a less primitive way (or, rather, as open in accordance with their original significance and function). Only in the mind can the *cavana* be better assessed, in order to give importance and value to the majestic stones that form it. And only in this way can the walls of all the sixteenth-century spaces be appreciated as they were four hundred or so years ago, when "mistro" Paleari, for a salary of "ducati sedese," gave them over to be "adorned" according to the rules of art.

NOTES TO CHAPTER V

[1] 1666, p. 338.
[2] Venice, Correr, Cod. Cic., 2008, *Chiesa di Santa Maria della Carità*.
[3] Venice, Archivio dell'Accademia, Anni 1807 ff.
[4] Venice, Archivio dell'Accademia, 26 March 1817.
[5] Moschini-Marconi, 1955, p. xx.
[6] 1934, passim; 1936, p. 78; 1941, p. 43.
[7] 1880, pp. 34 ff.
[8] Marciana, mss. Italiani, Cl. 7, n. 2283.

VI
VISUAL AND LITERARY RECORDS

The little book in which Temanza wrote, "Non va il Palladio...." is perhaps the first piece of writing inspired by the Corinthian atrium. Nevertheless, although there are no documents to prove that he referred to the atrium, one should begin an "excursus" on the literature concerning the monastery by turning to what Giorgio Vasari wrote of it in the life of Jacopo Sansovino, published in 1568. The author had been in Venice twice; his first visit was rather long, lasting from 1541 to 1542, which was before Palladio had built anything in Venice, while the second was very brief, lasting only from the 21st through the 27th of May, 1566. That he had perhaps personally visited the works in progress at the Carità is suggested by the way he describes the stairs and the materials of construction; Vasari judged the complex "meraviglioso e notabilissimo," the most beautiful work executed by the master in Venice (naturally meaning up to the year in which Vasari wrote). Only passages devoted to the stairs and to the materials differ from the description Palladio himself had given; in the rest of the description Vasari repeats what appeared in the *Quattro Libri*, which had not yet been published. He gives the measurements and speaks of the monastery as if it were finished, perhaps because when he wrote there was still hope that it would be completed. Having done so, he deceived many students, including the illustrious Temanza. It is possible to believe that Vasari, like other friends of Palladio, would have known the *Quattro Libri* before publication, and this would explain the identity of many phrases in the two works:

"... In Venezia ha principiato il medesimo molte fabbriche; ma una sopra tutte che è meravigliosa e notabilissima, a imitazione delle case che solevano far gli antichi, nel monasterio della Carità. L'atrio di questa è largo piedi quaranta e lungo cinquantaquattro, che tanto è a punto il diametro del quadrato, essendo le sue ali una delle tre parti e mezzo della larghezza. Le colonne, che sono corinte, sono grosse piedi tre e mezzo e alte trentacinque. Dall'atrio si va nel peristilio, cioè in un claustro (così chiamano i frati i loro cortili), il quale dalla parte di verso l'atrio è diviso in cinque parti e dai fianchi in sette, con tre ordini di colonne l'un sopra l'altro, che il dorico è di sotto, e sopra il ionico ed il corinto. Dirimpetto all'atrio è il refettorio, lungo due quadri e alto insino al piano del peristilio, con le sue officine intorno comodissime. Le scale sono a lumaca e in forma ovale, e non hanno né muro né colonne né parte di mezzo che le regga. Sono larghe piedi tredici e gli scalini nel posare si reggono l'un l'altro per essere fitti nel muro. Questo edificio è tutto fatto di pietre cotte, cioè mattoni, salvo le base delle colonne, i capitalli, l'imposte degli archi, le scale, le superficie delle cornici, e le finestre tutte e le porte."[1]

Henry Wooton, the English ambassador to the Republic, who resided in the capital of the duchy for various periods between 1591 and 1623, published a treatise on architecture in 1624. The Corinthian atrium served as his point of departure for stating his disagreement with those who thought that to build with columns and arches was proper only in countries rich in stone and marble. Thus, he explained, "I have often at *Venice* viewed with much pleasure, an *Atrium Graecum* (we may translate it an *Anti porch*, after the Greeke manner) raised by *Andrea Palladio*, upon eight *Columnes* of the *Compounded Order*; The *Bases* of Stone, without *Pedistals*, The *Shafts* or *Bodies*, of meere Brick; three foote and an halfe thicke in the *Diameter* below, and consequently thirty five foote high, as himselfe hath described them in his second Booke; Then which, mine Eye, hath never yet beheld any *Columnes*, more stately of Stone or Marble; For the Bricks, having first beene formed in a *Circular Mould*, and then cut before their burning into foure quarters or more, the sides outwards ioyne so closely, and the points concenter so exactly, that the *Pillars* appeare one *entire Peece*; which short description, I could not omit, that thereby may appeare, how in truth wee want rather *Art* then stuffe, to satisfie our greatest *Fancies*."[2]

Wotton dwelt on the technical; however, his lean prose pulsates with an unmeasured admiration for the architect who, using poor material, knew how to build magnificent works that one could contemplate "with much pleasure." The humility with which he stated that the English did not possess either the ingenuity or the sensibility identifies him as the first ambassador of Palladianism in England. Indeed, from Wotton dates that official rapport between Venetian and English art which eventually found an exponent in Consul Joseph Smith in the eighteenth century.

Inigo Jones, a contemporary of Wotton, also gave a strong impulse in that direction; he had been in Venice many times and had studied the Convento della Carità at length. In his copy of Palladio's treatise (1601 edition, now preserved in the library of Worcester College, Oxford) one reads, with some difficulty, his many comments, which were in part transcribed and published in 1741, but which had been known for a long time previously. The notes of the English architect are essentially technical; the extent of those devoted to the Venetian monastery shows that he had studied it with interest and care (fig. XXIII).[3] Vasari and the two Englishmen have left the only testimony derived from direct inspection of the grandeur and elegance of the Corinthian atrium; the remarks of the two foreign admirers and the bill of lading for the stone prove that a design that perished after the fire, along with all other records of its existence, was indeed executed.

Wotton and Jones almost certainly effected the removal of a great many of Palladio's autograph designs to England, which may account for the authenticity there of the Palladian cult, which elsewhere appeared cold and lacking in spontaneity, as tastes changed.

In the course of the seventeenth century only the English were given to Palladian studies; however, the *Quattro Libri* was not forgotten. In the eighteenth century, translations, commentaries and reprintings were issued. Then the *Quattro Libri* was published in London by Giacomo Leoni in English, Italian, and French (figs. XXV, XL); on the frontispiece it was announced that the notes and observations of Inigo Jones would be forthcoming. These did not appear in the first (1715), second (1721), or third (1726) editions, but only in the last edition of 1742. The successive reprints are sumptuous, and the engravings are quite beautiful and done with a line

LXI - *Convento della Carità and apses of the church: details*

LXII - *Convento della Carità: façades facing the former atrium and cloister in the interior of the monastery; the terrace next to the former dormitory is visible along the former atrium at center left*

LXIII - *Convento della Carità: the space of the former atrium at its junction with the church*

LXIV - *Convento della Carità: the flank along the rio terra' Sant'Agnese; on the left the nineteenth-century addition is discernible in the variation in the exposure of the eaves*

LXV - *Convento della Carità: arch of the cavana, closed in the nineteenth century: interior view*

LXVI - *Convento della Carità: details in brick from the terrace that encircled the "impluvium"*

LXVII - *Convento della Carità: stone slab with a medieval inscription, reused in oval stairs*

LXVIII - *Convento della Carità: stone slab with a medieval relief, reused in the oval stairs*

LXIX - *Convento della Carità, attic: in the foreground, the covering of the oval stairs; in the distance, the covering in wood and cane of one of the cells*

LXX - *Convento della Carità, ground floor: traces of a stair between the tablinum and the guests' rooms, indicated in the plan in the* Quattro Libri *and destroyed in the nineteenth century*

LXXI - *Convento della Carità: covering in cane of the corridor on the third floor, discovered during restorations (1970); traces are visible of the groin in the area where it turned the corner to the peristyle (destroyed in the nineteenth century)*

LXXII - *Convento della Carità: covering in cane of the cells uncovered during restorations (1970)*

LXXIII - *Convento della Carità: corridor on the third floor (formerly containing dormitories), during restorations (1970)*

LXXIV - *Convento della Carità, arcade: traces of the groin that turned the corner to the left-hand return arch, destroyed in the nineteenth century*

LXXV - *Convento della Carità: vault in one of the cells after the restorations of 1970-71*

LXXVI - *Convento della Carità: traces of a balcony formerly extant at the end of the corridor on the third floor; closed in the nineteenth-century modifications*

LXXVII - *Convento della Carità: arcade in the cloister*

LXXVIII - *Convento della Carità: ambulatory between the atrium and the medieval portion of the monastery after the reconstruction following the fire of 1630*

LXXIX - *Convento della Carità: traces of the window between the tablinum and the atrium, closed in the nineteenth century*

LXXX - *Convento della Carità: traces of the window between the atrium and the chapter hall*

LXXXI - *Convento della Carità: traces of the archway between the space of the "cavana" and the guests' rooms, closed in the nineteenth century*

LXXXII - *Convento della Carità: flank of the medieval buttressed structure*

LXXXIII - *Convento della Carità: guests' rooms on the ground floor; the cavity in the wall results from restorations (1958)*

LXXXIV - *Convento della Carità, ground floor: Doric portico; nineteenth-century doorway and traces of the window that opened into the "cavana" (the window is visible in the painting by Canaletto)*

LXXXV - *Flank of the Nuova Pinacoteca, constructed with a volume analogous to that of the refectory envisaged for the Convento della Carità*

LXXXVI - *Scuola and Convento della Carità: common courtyard with the well and the entrance to the hospice of the scuola*

LXXXVII - *The courtyard of the Carampane, Venice*

LXXXVIII - Vincenzo Scamozzi, *Scuola della Carità, courtyard: entrance portal to the scuola*

LXXXIX - *Scuola della Carità, courtyard: fifteenth-century loggia*

XC - INIGO JONES, *The Tulip Staircase in the Queen's House, Greenwich* (1616-29)

XCI - G. Sardi, B. Longhena, *Oval stair in the Ospedaletto, Venice* (1664-66)

XCII - *Convento della Carità, oval staircase: window and jamb toward the Grand Canal*

XCIII - *Convento della Carità: door between the* tablinum *and the stair hall under the oval stairs*

XCIV - *Convento della Carità: five steps of the oval stair case, covered in the nineteenth century, and now restored (1968)*

contrast that rather well evokes the original sixteenth-century woodcuts, but they are somewhat imprecise.

Giacomo Leoni had been born in Venice in 1686 and had left in about 1700, just when the city returned to an admiration for Palladio; the master was considered a symbol of that classicism to which Venetians thought they should return after the capriciousness of the seventeenth-century architects. The Convento della Carità had also found some new admirers such as Vincenzo Coronelli, who illustrated it in two prints executed around 1710 (figs. XCVIII-IC).

In the isometric plan of Venice (datable to 1693), he had already shown the monastery by simply copying the view of de'Barbari without accounting for the sixteenth-century reconstruction. Merlo had done the same in 1696 (fig. III). But in his later plan of the building, Coronelli was scrupulous in giving all the names of the separate areas and noting the "Calle del Dose" and the "Ponte del Dose di Pietra con una banda." That bridge is seen in the print, which has the inscription "Convento della Carità verso l'Rio, Architetto A. Palladio - Chiesa della Carità." The building's actual appearance was not reproduced with exact accuracy, but the document is interesting because it suggests the original proportions of the façade along the canal before the nineteenth-century additions.

The church has a single apse and the water seems to penetrate between the apse and the monastery. Knowing the location of the building, it is possible to imagine that the left apse is tucked within the acute angle formed by the meeting of the other apse and the monastery. With the ogive arch, one above the other, appear the two windows recorded in the bill of lading for the stone, the one "in la camera in testa al dormitorio sopra alla cappella," and the other "sopra alla cappella della chiesa." Still in place is the small projecting structure visible at the gound-floor level.

Ten rather than twelve windows are shown on each floor. But if Coronelli was imprecise, he was also observant; he recorded the door in the corner toward the bridge and the *cavana*, in which a gondola is moored.

The "Prospetto del chiostro maggiore della Carità d'Architettura del Palladio" persuades us that there were no memorable remains of the atrium. The prospect of the cloister appears isolated and complete in itself; on the other hand, it perhaps portends the way it would look were the ruins of the fire removed. Still, to the left of the major cloister, there remains on the inside the spiral stairs and the tablinum, and, above, the guest rooms and the cells. But by this time the construction has already lost its sense of unity, and one does not feel that the peristyle would have run around all four sides. On the ground floor the empiricist Coronelli added an arch to those existing; that arch was later executed by Lazzari, perhaps because he thought it to belong to the original scheme (fig. LIX). Visible on the right is the wall along the calle del Dose with the windows of the little study. With this we gain some sense of how mishandled that area was; we have no more precise record of it than this.

It is possible that Leoni knew this important monument by direct observation. Still, in his reproduction he took numerous liberties and, at times, even invented (fig. XL). In the plan the differences are not of great moment; some doors become windows and vice versa, some stairs are inserted around the persityle, and so on. But in the elevation he made a great pastiche (fig. XL); his six Doric arches do not have the same height as the Ionic ones, and the six windows above lack cornices. To make up for the bay he left out, he added two rooms of his own invention, demonstrating that he had studied the complex only superficially and that he did not understand the intention of Palladio. This plate (plate XXII) is anonymous; plate XV, which shows the stairs, was "gravé sous la conduite de B. Picart," one of Leoni's most accomplished collaborators. It is very elegant, and the interpretation of the architecture is quite judicious (fig. XXV). In this illustration Leoni has judged it opportune to add statues to the niches, which animates the spirals of the stairs; this change has given Palladio's design a Baroque flavor, as Wittkower has observed.[4]

Other English editions of the *Quattro Libri* followed; first among them was that of Hoppus Cole (1733-35), which reproduced Leoni's plates; then, in 1738, spurred by Burlington, Isaac Ware published an accurate edition of the treatise (figs. XLI, XLVII-XLVIII).

From about this same period date two paintings by Canaletto. In one, showing the Campo della Carità, only the highest parts of the monastery are visible but we are able to assess the scale of the complex, and we can still see the funnel chimneys that Coronelli had also illustrated (fig. IV). More significant for our purposes is the *Courtyard of the Convento della Carità* in the Royal Collection at Windsor (color plate a). As V. Moschini has said,[5] the painting was part of a series of overdoors with Palladian subjects executed for the little palace of Consul Smith at Santi Apostoli and can be assigned to about 1744. It is a poetic representation of what existed and an evocation of the original project. As Coronelli had done, Canaletto isolated the block of the main cloister from the rest of the construction. On the ground floor he extended the Doric portico and the terrace above it to the right and left, and he placed on each end the terminal bay with niches that the project suggested for only one end. The steep walls envisaged by Palladio along the sides are lacking; Canaletto has preferred an ample spread of the blue sky. Other variations are evident: the pilasters of the ground floor rest on steps; in the arches of the second order are the balusters envisaged in the project but executed only in the nineteenth century; within the Doric portico we see the window that gave light to the *cavana*, which was walled up in the nineteenth century (fig. LXXXIV). An Ionic arch and Corinthian window have been added in conformity with the terrace which was added on the left.

Various paintings by Canaletto had represented many Palladian buildings with fidelity; here, however, the painter presents a renovation perhaps drawn from the conversations with his friend Visentini and with Consul Smith, and it respects the aesthetics of architecture. In the nineteenth-century restorations Canaletto's suggestions were in part realized but not, unfortunately, with the evocation of the serene measure of the Palladian project that Canaletto was able to sense so felicitously even though he, like Coronelli, was ignorant of the execution of the atrium and of the fire.

With Muttoni one passes from the poetry of Canaletto to an elegant prose (figs. XLII-XLIII; IL-LII).[6] Often inexact in his drafting of monuments, in the case of the Carità Muttoni is accurate, perhaps because the illustration had been entrusted to Giorgio Fossati, who certainly was familiar with the entire building and had studied it well before engraving it with precision. In the comment he points out that the project in the *Quattro Libri* is a speculative vision and that many perplexities need clarification. Ignoring the execution of the atrium and the fire, he supposed that in the sixteenth century only the eastern part of the building had been constructed; Fossati did not come across any records concerning the condition of the building previous to the epoch he was recording.

Muttoni excused his having added the balusters for "ornament" in the second-story arcade; he boasted that he corrected "le ultime edizioni di Londra e dell'Aia," alluding to Leoni's edition that had erroneously shown half-columns instead of pilasters in the Corinthian order. Several details in the plates raise problems. For example, Muttoni shows a small stair behind the calle del Dose, whereas this had always existed, as was logical, contiguous to the *calle*. The function of the pier shown in the middle of the corridor next to the little stair is also curious. Muttoni also shows it in the large-scale plan (fig. IL), and it seems improbable that he would have invented such a pier. We may suppose that it was torn out in the nineteenth-century transformation; perhaps there was an exit to the calle del Dose here.

When he later reprinted the *Quattro Libri*, Muttoni[7] produced conjectural plans and elevations, coordinating them, however, with the original plates. For example, he put steps around the Doric portico in both the plan and the elevation; in the *editio princeps* they had been indicated only in the plan. Similarly, he removed the steps along the refectory, which had not appeared in the elevation of the sixteenth-century plate (fig. XLIII).

Of a very different character are Antonio Visentini's references to the monastery. These were formulated in the same cultural circle as that of Leoni. Leoni was only two years older than Visentini but like Muttoni, while condemning the Baroque taste, he later decorated his publications, as Leoni and Muttoni did, with the richest embellishments commissioned from painters stylistically related to Pellegrini, the most frivolous Venetian painter of the early eighteenth century. Indeed, Leoni associated with Sebastiano Ricci, and Muttoni entrusted the ornamentation of his volumes to Fontebasso and Francesco Zucchi; Visentini, long having professed a pictorial art learned directly from Pellegrini, provided his own illustrations with elaborate frames and extravagant borders.

Just as Palladio had believed that all the effects of Bramante's works belonged to classicism, so too did the neo-Palladians accept some elements of architecture that they intended to repudiate. This phenomenon is closely linked to the cultural circle of the Veneto; perhaps only at Venice would one believe that had Palladio known the architecture of Baalbek and of Palmyra, he would have considered it among the best Roman work and worthy of imitation, a point about which Visentini wrote.[8] The latter made a series of designs which today are in the RIBA; among them is a view of the Carità cloister with the legend, "Architettura del Palladio—Claustro della Carità, Venezia; Scala in piedi inglesi" (fig. C). The construction is rigorously symmetrical, identical to that which Lazzari left; the building is isolated on two sides, as it was in the views by Coronelli and Canaletto, and it is precise, but it shows only that one elevation, and the lateral niches of the upper orders are omitted.

Another view of the same project, which Zorzi published and discussed, is also in the RIBA (fig. CII).[9] It seems to have been taken from the plates of the *Quattro Libri*; in fact, it shows the returns in the corner arches of the second story that, as we know from the bill of lading for the stone, were never executed. This design, which is more elegant but less complete than the earlier one, refers to one of Muttoni's large designs; in each, for example, the frieze and every other decorative detail has been worked out in meticulous detail. In the Uffizi in Florence there is yet another version of the cloister (fig. CI) in which, without taking account either of the project or the remains, the structure is made to return along both sides with the most rigorous symmetry, ignoring the calle del Dose and the terrace that Palladio had thought of putting over it. There are six arches in each story, and the building appears isolated and finished. This is perhaps a student's exercise that could postdate Visentini, who taught at the Accademia from 1761 to 1778, by a few years, although he also had students before that period. The wide influence of his instruction, continued through the teaching of his student Selva, reaches to 1830; it is perhaps to Selva's period that we should date this design, which is perhaps a preparatory scheme for the tondo conserved in the Accademia, in which the courtyard is represented as complete on every side.

The "Trattato dele diligenti osservazioni fatte sopra le fabbriche d'Andrea Palladio visentino,"[10] should be dated before the *vita di Andrea Palladio* by Temanza (1762), in which a reference to the fire of 1630 appears. In fact, Visentini had supposed that the canons lacked the funds for completing the entire project. In the Trattato, which we have discussed elsewhere,[11] Visentini imagines himself taking leave in disgust of two gentlemen, one Roman, the other French, both lovers of modern and "corrupt" architecture, in order to show Palladian buildings to an English knight. After wandering around Venice and considering each work attentively, the Englishman and his guide express great praise for the insuperable master.

Visentini was not a polished writer, but it is possible to find some useful historical information in his works. He meticulously described the atrium, which had been refaced by Padre Gozzi, as if it were a remedy that had been worked out by Palladio himself; for a man who knew architecture well, that was quite a blunder.

Interesting is his remark about the sepulcher with the reliefs by Gambello, which was in the vestibule toward the sacristy, over the door that he called "a nichio" because it opened in one of the two exedrae. The spiral stairs led into the monastery; therefore the canons went from the first courtyard, which was held in common with the scuola, to the atrium and then to the oval stairs, having no entrance to the street other than through the portal on the campo della Carità.

Visentini made a great thing of the door in the Ionic loggia (plate 32), which narrowed as it rose like that of the Temple of Vesta at Tivoli reproduced in the *Quattro Libri* (IV, p. 94) with a woodcut taken from a design preserved in the museum in Vicenza (fig. XXVIII). Later Visentini stated that in the Ionic order the arches should have been closed with a balustrade, which we noted had been begun with the "mezze colonnelle che son poste al peduzo delle erte."

Concerning the exterior along the rio di Sant'Agnese, the record of the course of the "fascie che ripiega ... dalle cornici piglia sua figura vera" suggests that the metopes and triglyphs return along the calle del Dose, as they do along the other side toward the Grand Canal. This also seems to be what occurs in the print by Coronelli.

In Visentini's criticism there is considerable use of the term "bisaro" (that is, bizarre), which he perhaps uses to indicate originality. Although he considered the monastery to be one of the most exceptional designs of Palladio, the line of discourse dissipates in a fatuous panegyric vitiated by the chatter of the English knight, whom we may perhaps be able to recognize as Consul Smith.

We have often cited Temanza's studies, because with his record of the fire the history of the monastery begins to be clarified with greater verity, at the appearance of his biography in 1762. One must commend his interest in checking the measurements of what existed against what was recorded in Palladio's treatise and then composing a measured drawing of the surviving Palladian wing. He admired the tablinum in particular; he also appeared to be overwhelmed less by the beauty of the monastery than by the care with which the material was worked and by the unusual frieze.

Temanza's study was used by Bertotti Scamozzi, who in 1776 published his ponderous work, supplementing his plates with a notable commentary (figs. XLIV, LVIII).[12] The author reveals his preoccupation with bringing the precepts of Vitruvius concerning proportions into accord with the measurements indicated by Palladio and with the differing measurements of his executed works. He admired the concept of the complex, whose grandeur was appropriate for past times, but he was vexed because there was no possibility to build it in such a different period. Still, he praised the master who, having the capacity to conceive of a sumptuous work, knew how to adapt it to make that little bit which the times did permit. In his unconditional respect, he said nothing about the controversial frieze.

Bertotti took various things into consideration in his plates, but perhaps due to his imperfect knowledge of the topography of the site, he placed to the east—and therefore on top of the rio di Sant'Agnese—the assymetrical additions that the architect had placed on the west.

The second enclosed area, the one beyond the refectory, is shown as more extensive than it was in the *Quattro Libri*, and thus he had a more complete image of Palladio's concept, but there is no indication of the contiguous church which, in Palladio's plate, is useful for creating an impression of the area. Bertotti scrupulously coordinated sections and plan. The plate with the plan and the other one with the section are signed by Mugnon; plate XXV, which is of the greatest interest because it has the section of the atrium and of the two tablina (fig. LVIII), is instead anonymous. Here Bertotti, uniquely among the interpreters of Palladio, clearly represents the section of the "impluvium" between the church and the peristyle; we see the door of the cloister and the window behind the balustrade at the level of the third story. Records for such a window are found in the bill of lading for the stone. Bertotti wrote, concerning the "Casa degli Antichi," "... il pezzo che ancora esiste, e le Tavole disegnate dall' Autore mi bastarono per disegnarla bella ed intera." In fact, he gives here an intelligent and scrupulous graphic representation. To this, Mucci's republication of the *Quattro Libri*, illustrated with engravings by Silvestrini, can be compared (figs. XLV, LIII-LIV).[13]

Milizia also spoke at length of the monastery, finally giving a positive judgment.[14] His usual caustic criticism is directed not only toward the frieze but also toward the proportions of the Ionic order, which is not tall enough with respect to the lower order. Bertotti had observed this also, although he attributed the implicit accusation in his objection to a "delicacy of mind" and, with this, he indicated that he believed that Palladio belonged among the robust minds.

Milizia admired Palladio sufficiently to call him the "Raphael of architecture," but he did not analyze the monastery critically. It would have been useful if he had done so, given the influence that he had on the aesthetic consciousness of his time.

Instead, we can penetrate the taste of the times in the pages of Goethe; his remarks are especially lively in the first period of his travel journals (1768). In Vicenza he would have wanted to have taken a tour of the architecture with Bertotti Scamozzi; in Padua he acquired the *Quattro Libri*, and it then served him as a guide for uncovering the works of his favorite architect. On his visit to the Convento della Carità, which he had already admired in the pages of the *Quattro Libri*, he anticipated a strong impression, but he was disconcerted and surprised when he found the building incomplete. Upon his first visit on October 2, he wrote in his diary:

"Carità. I had found in Palladio's works that he had intended to build a building which imitated a private dwelling of a man of the highest standing in antiquity. I hurried there with the greatest anticipation but, ah, hardly the tenth part of it had been completed. But even this part is worthy of his heavenly genius. There is a completeness in the general layout and an accuracy in the execution which was formerly totally unknown to me. The materials there are for the most part brick (as I have seen before on occasion), but done with priceless precision. I made a few drawings from his work today, and I will gladly become more familiar with this work.... I cannot forget the Carità; he installed a set of stairs there which he praises himself and which truly are very beautiful." [15]

A few days later (October 5, after dinner) he again gave thought to the building:

"It seemed to me that when he was giving consideration to a piazza, a height and breadth, a church building which already existed, an old house, all of which he was going to put a façade upon, that he had thought: 'How are you going to bring this to the most noble form? You are going to have to break up this or that little detail, here or there an incongruity will remain, but that will allow the building as a whole to have a noble style and you will be working for your own pleasure.' And thus did he have in his soul a complete picture of what he wanted, and he brought it forth even though the site was ill-suited for it and he had to truncate and mutilate it. Still, for me, the wing of the Carità is so precious because even in it, his entire spirit soars. Were it finished, it would perhaps have been the finest piece of construction ever built in the world." [16]

Less than a week later he was back for his second visit (October 11, in the evening):

"I was once again in the Carità ... wandering around within the great concept of Palladio. A person could spend years in contemplation of such a work. I will return again early tomorrow morning. I think I have never before seen anything so noble. And I am certain I am not mistaken about that. But I also think that the exquisite artist who was born with an inner sense for the great, which he has then developed with greatest energy (no one has any idea how much he exhausted himself when he gave himself to works of the ancients), found the opportunity to execute a work of loving labor, the imitation of a house of the ancients, an opportunity for which his thoughts were perfectly suited. He was troubled by nothing, and he allowed nothing to trouble him. About the original concept and the design I say nothing; only a word about the execution. Only the capitals and the bases of columns and a few other parts that I observed are in stone. All the rest (I could hardly say of brick) are of burnt clay, for I know of no such bricks as these; you can imagine that the sharpness of the frieze with its ornamentation is also from burnt clay and the various parts of the cornice as well. He has also had all the forms made in such a way that they must have had just enough extra material in them that after the material was fired and it was then placed in the building, only a little mortar was used to hold them in place. The ornamentation of the arches is also fired. This technique is not entirely new to me, but as it is done here it is quite beyond my imagination. In Dessau they have also thrown things up in this way, and Palladio had probably taken it over from the ancients. But, still, the entire thing is a whole, and had it been stuccoed and given one color, it would have been fascinating. Oh Destiny, you who have patronized and immortalized so many stupidities, why did you not allow this work to be finished!

"About a small stairway (a spiral stair without a column in the center) which he himself praised in his work—which succeeds marvelously—I believe I have said nothing. You can believe that when Palladio said that it succeeds well, he was saying nothing. Indeed, it is nothing except a spiral stair, but one which a person never grows weary of going up and down. I have also seen the sacristy today, which lies right next to the stairs and was executed according to his drawings; tomorrow I will come back here. In that way I will be able to recall it correctly in my head and heart."[17]

Goethe had also made some drawings of the monastery, as he said, but as time passed dream and reality merged with one another, and when reorganizing and publishing the travel journals (1816-29), he returned to Palladio's treatise and, when he came to the Carità, he recorded "having entered an atrium of Corinthian columns which is an enchantment." The atrium, however, had not existed since 1630. Nevertheless, the monastery had hypnotized him, and he proved it by the extent of the writing he dedicated to it. Compare, for example, how concise and laconic he had been when judging the painting of the great Venetian masters. He defined the project as an ambitious one, which, had it been completed, would have required the destruction of many buildings; his caustic comments on the incompleteness of the work are always vehement.

From this interpretation of the late eighteenth century we may go on to the precise descriptions in the *Fabbriche di Venezia* published for the first time in 1815-20, edited by the Accademia di Belle Arti; a second edition appeared in 1838-40, and a third in 1858 (figs. XLVI, LV-LVII, LIX). Leopoldo Cicognara, president of the Accademia when it was reestablished by Napoleon, Giannantonio Selva, its professor of architecture, and the architect Antonio Diedo, secretary of the academy, directed the students from the academy housed in the former monastery to measure and make precise drawings of the buildings of Venice and to engrave plates. Selva compiled the ample notes on the Carità; the plates that reproduce the plans from the *Quattro Libri* were designed by his student Francesco Lazzari. The various parts that were projected and that still existed were indicated by different quality lines. It is clear that the description was compiled after the execution of the first part of the restorations (1807) and before settling the project for enlarging the new wing (1817). The author, repeating Temanza's error, believed that both tablina had been executed.[18]

Selva left the record of the little study constructed on the calle del Dose, the origin of so many disputes with the scuola, and gave measured drawings of it: "Eccetto che i due lati NO, OM del chiostro, tutto l'esposto fabbricato era completamente condotto a termine, allorché fu soggetto alle fiamme. Di ciò che il Palladio seguita a descrivere al di là della pubblica strada, non era stato costruito che il pezzo P.Q. tuttora esistente, eretto sopra un volto attraversante la strada stessa."

The architect had studied the building foot by foot when he adapted it to its new function; still, he said that he did not know if, in addition to the entrance from the campo della Carità, the canons had other entrances available to them. Evidently he did not know the complex very well before he became its restorer. For our part, we would be grateful to him if, after having come to understand the consistency of the building before putting a hand to it, he had left a detailed graphic record; he would have made one only if he had considered the monument to be one of a kind, which was extraordinary in the activity of Palladio. Instead he scrupulously analyzed the proportions of the orders, exhorting the students to continue in that depressing exercise in order to deduce what the measurements of the constructed work were and how they corresponded to the theories in the treatises. But Selva also noted and admired the simplicity of the relationships in the cloister's proportions, and he valued the ability of the artist to organize the building in a regular manner on an anomalous site, and to do it with grace. With Milizia, chief among the acerbic "modern philosophers" of architecture, he recognized Palladio's greatness.

In the last edition of the *Fabbriche* there is an addition to the passage by Selva written by Francesco Zanotto;[19] it reports about the works resulting from the government decree of January 29, 1829, which had been documented in near completeness in the pamphlet Lazzari wrote in 1835. A new plate illustrates the Palladian prospect in the courtyard after that work had been carried out (fig. LIX).

Cicognara, reading the "Elogio di Andrea Palladio" at the Accademia in 1810, mentioned the monastery, which already housed the school and gallery while the modifications were being executed. Meanwhile Quarenghi, who had taught painting for years and had decided to take up architecture after having come to know the *Quattro Libri*, wrote to his friend and fellow student Selva from St. Petersburg, where he had been for some time. In two letters that Lazzari refers to[20] Quarenghi affirms his unchanging admiration for the Vicentine architect, taking in part as his point of departure the fact that the monastery was to be put to this new use. In the first, dated October 7, 1807, one reads: "la scelta del convento della Carità a mio giudizio è molto opportuna per tale oggetto [for the Accademia], e quantunque sfigurato per la dimora delle truppe, nelle sue mani son sicuro ripiglierà la primiera forma, e suprattutto la sagrestia, che per me era un oggetto di stupore e di meraviglia tanto per la proporzione in generale, come in tutti i suoi dettagli d'un gusto il più puro, e il più semplice che immaginare si possa." In the second, from April 23, 1812: "Vorrei pure prima di morire veder ancora una volta la Sagrestia della Carità, e il Redentore, che sempre ho presenti, e non ho ancor veduto nulla onde paragonarli; tanto sono sublimi e maestosi che nulla più."

The friendship and mutual admiration between Quarenghi and Selva had been born in the common Palladian cult that provided the basis of the works of the two men, the one in great Russia and the other in the little Veneto. Neither the Venetian nor Quarenghi was hesitant on occasion to break the rules of classicism. For example, in the shops near the Anichow bridge (annexed to a room of the imperial palace in St. Petersburg) Quarenghi attached a building with Ionic columns to the palace with its decorations in the Corinthian order, and he surmounted the Ionic order with a Doric frieze. He boasted of that adulteration in a long letter to Canova, and it was also reported by his son Giulio.[21] He defended the artist's liberty of invention, although he failed to discuss the topic by referring to the frieze in the Venetian monastery, as is proven by a postscript in which Giacomo Quarenghi added: "Après avoir achevé la lettre, je viens d'apprendre qu'il-y-a eû quelqu'un qui a pris mon parté, en avançant que Palladio a fait à Rome un batiment du même, genre que le mien.... Ayant visté moi même, tous les batiments de ce Sublime Architecte, je peux rassurer qu'il n'y en a aucun de cette espèce."

In addition he mentioned that in Rome an altar in the Ospedale di Santo Spirito, where no unorthodox decoration exists, is attributed to Palladio. He also noted that at the Palazzo Nani in Venice (fifty meters from the Palladian monastery), he had designed a relief in which Doric and Ionic were coupled, a motif he had copied from the antique. At the Carità, however, he held the tablinum in high regard, but not the frieze, which had provoked so much confusion in the theories of his contemporaries.

Two tondi [22] in which the peristyle and the tablinum are represented may be attributed to Giuseppe Borsato (1770-1849), holder of the *cattedra di ornamenti* in the Accademia in Napoleon's organization (figs. CIV-CV). There are many important similarities between these works and the documented works of the artist, such as *The Austrian Emperor visiting the Canova Hall in the Treves de Bonfili Palace*, and *The Tribute Paid to Canova in the Hall of the Gallery in Venice*, now in the Palazzo Treves and the Museo Correr in Venice, respectively. The tablinum is scrupulously taken from the plan in the *Quattro Libri*; it indicates the door in the center of the wall toward the atrium and the numerous niches that were not, in fact, built. In adding decoration to the tablinum, the artist took his inspiration from the plate in the *Quattro Libri* that shows the Corinthian rooms;[23] he filled the niches with statues and placed long reliefs in the style of Canova along the walls.

In the tondo with the peristyle we see a free interpretation of the project; the terrace along the refectory has been done away with, and the cloister has become decisively Roman and Bramantesque. Borsato had collaborated with Selva in the work of adapting the complex, and the tondi seem to convey the dreams of what, when working in the new seat of the Academy, they hoped they might still see completed in the majestic building. Instead, the new use of the complex accelerated the wear and tear no less than if it had been destroyed.

Perhaps that aspiration had also been determined by the depressing actual appearance of the building, which we see in the small print published in G. Moschini's guide to Venice (1828; fig. CIII). He was the first among the guidebook authors to recall attention to the architect of the former monastery, noting that the completed work had been admirable and that the fire had had its effect. The guides of the seventeenth and eighteenth centuries had mentioned the few paintings to be found in the monastery, but they had ignored Palladio. In the print by Moschini the tufts of weeds growing among the old stones do not evoke a Piranesian fantasy so much as the negligence derived from the misery that, for decades, gripped Venice after the fall of the Republic. Some figures seem to exit cautiously from the shadow; this was the form of the courtyard after its modification by Selva. Then, with the renovations of 1828-30, the loggias assumed the appearance illustrated in the pamphlet by Francesco Lazzari (this is the same illustration as the one that appeared in the *Fabbriche di Venezia*; see fig. LIX). These loggias, considered necessary in such a restoration, were neither justified nor satisfactory; they simply point up the difficulties that were overcome in camouflaging the new part. It succeeded in its intention such that, if we did not know the history of the monument, we should perhaps not have seen the extent of the transformations carried out in the nineteenth century. Lazzari's text is especially interesting for the information it gives about the technicalities of Palladio's construction;[24] it is there that one learns about the polychrome pavement in the sacristy and about the technique worked out for sealing it from the damp by putting a functional matrix of bricks underneath.[25]

As was the case with other neoclassical architects, Magrini also venerated Palladio and, in uncovering the history of his various buildings, for the first time he consulted documents of great interest in the archives that permitted him to attest to the correctness of the date read by Lazzari on the building. But Magrini did not know what part of the Palladian project had been constructed.[26]

Very different is the tone we find some years later in the pages of Pietro Selvatico Estense, who for years had lived in the former monastery, both as a student and a teacher. Concerning Palladio, he wrote: "Di questa sua invenzione sembra ch'egli medesimo si compiacesse, giacché ne dà accurata descrizione nel capo VI del libro II dell'opera da lui scritta; ed usa modi e parole che rivelano l'uomo contento del proprio lavoro. Ed aveva ragione, perché in fatto anche nel solo pezzo che ancora ci rimane si può veramente ammirare il bell'ingegno di lui, e la elegante correzione della sua sesta. Io non disputerò se questo convento sia disposto in modo da ricordare le prescrizioni di Vitruvio intorno alle abitazioni romane o piuttosto le case degli antichi, come ce le porge la dissepolta Pompei. Forse ci sarebbe su tal proposito molto da eccezionare. Ciò per altro importa poco, giacché nulla giova che la pianta sia o non sia conforme all'antiche norme. Anzi tanto più ne verrebbe onore al genio del vicentino, quanto più si potesse provare che la casa degli antichi non ha a che fare nulla colla invenzione di cui imprendo a ragionare.

"L'atrio corintio, che or più non sussiste, perché incendiatosi sin dal 1630, insieme a gran parte dello edifizio, presentava bellissime proporzioni. Quelle sue quattro colonne per lato ad intercolonnio eustilo doveano dare apparenza magnifica ed agile ad un tempo: ...Severamente elegante era pure ciò che il Palladio chiama l' 'Inclaustro,' e che i grecisti direbbero peristilio. Di questo rimane intatto ancora un lato che ben lascia conoscere quanto nelle proporzioni ioniche e doriche, studiate sugli edifizii romani, fosse addentro Palladio, e come, allorché il voleva, fosse anche indipendente da grette imitazioni. Codesto peristilio è a tre ordini dorico, jonico e corintio: i due inferiori ad arcate formanti gallerie, il terzo chiuso a finestre, per dir vero, né ben profilate né grandiose."

After having recapitulated what had been said about the frieze, he concluded that "il Palladio era uomo di troppe cognizioni e di troppo senno, per non sapere che gli antichi non si teneano obbligati di mettere sempre i triglifi nel dorico." Selvatico then added some criticism about the tablinum, "la parte che in questa fabbrica più si guadagnò l'encomio degli illustratori e dei biografi del Palladio." His judgement was: "L'iconografia è, a dir vero, pregevole per linee correttamente mosse. A codesti pregi peraltro non mi pare rispondano quelli dell'alzato, perché in esso si conterranno sì tutte le possibili regole architettoniche, ma quella a me pare manchevole, che solo l'occhio richiede, una certa cioè, snellezza e grazia di proporzioni, ed una decorazione la quale concordi col ben ideato concetto. Quelle colonne doriche che lasciano correre fra esse uno spazio di quasi dieci diametri intozziscono tutto il vaso; e più lo intozzisce la volta scema che vi si slancia sopra. Le spaziose pareti appariscono d'una cappuccinesca povertà: le nicchie stanno a disagio in quelli angoli che offrono spalle disuguali: le finestre sono troppo nude e male distribuite nel vano." [27]

Selvatico, who was not scandalized by the Ionic frieze, discussed the tablinum, whose plan he liked but whose elevation seemed to him to be squat and impoverished, the way he presented it to his readers in a pleasing lithograph (fig. CVI).

The critic was justified; the tablinum, inserted with such facility in the plan, became in execution a commodious sacristy for a spacious church but it did not have the finesse of other analogous spaces, such as the entrance to the Villa Pisani in Montagnana.

To those who are accustomed to the sharp and reasoned explanations of the professor, the expressions used in discussing the monastery do not make a great impression: he affirmed that Palladio, knowing Vitruvius but also knowing the practice of architecture, took his point of departure from the house of the ancients without producing a pedantic imitation, drawing suggestions from "Trissino, poeta antiquario," as Selvatico wrote later. "E così riesce a dare mirabile armonia di rapporti fra i pieni e i vuoti," conserving the "catenamento delle forme organiche fra di loro." Therefore, he is "uno dei primi architetti i quali segnano una separazione fra la scultura e l'architettura." [28]

In the pages of Selvatico are lively references to the punctilious Selva and to Lazzari, whom he praises for his system of restoration. Such encomiums imply a condemnation for the restorations that were then being carried out in Venice by Federico Berchet—the refacing of the Fondaco dei Turchi, in fact, is not many years later than the writings of Selvatico.

Quatremère de Quincy also took up the monastery, which he called San Giovanni Laterano della Carità. He described the initial project and gave an account of its construction.[29] Similarly, Burckhardt, who recorded the justified enthusiasm of Goethe, affirmed that Palladio preferred to build with bricks, "knowing that, later, there would have been no interest in plundering them as there would be with cut stone." He did not seem to comprehend the aesthetic criteria of the architect.[30]

The passage from neoclassical theories to those of the idealists is vividly conveyed by Camillo Boito in a ceremony honoring Palladio, held on the occasion of the third centenary of his death. He revealed a different temperament from that of the old Francesco Lazzari and the young Pietro Selvatico, both of whom were his masters within the walls of the former monastery. For two years the tablinum had been his studio; he mentions having worked, lived, and dreamed there. Boito, in his pathetic expatiations, shows that he had looked closely at the architecture. He noted that Palladio, in superimposing the orders, had from time to time done things not done in the middle ages, in the Renaissance, and by Sanmichele and Sansovino. He accepted the latest aesthetic and wrote that beautiful architecture must be looked at as a work of art if one is going to be able to understand anything about it. That had been Temanza's failure when he had described the anomalies of the frieze.[31]

For decades after the centenary nothing of importance was written about the monastery. Then Adolfo Venturi, in his *Storia dell'arte italiana*, brought the attention of students back to that forgotten work. The information he gives there is schematic; he did not confront the problems belonging to the complex history of its construction: "What remains ... is the design of Palladio, which presents itself here as an entity—the eurhythmic series of arches, in a double order, divided with the Doric columns below and the Ionic ones above, is graduated according to the finest musical sense of the Vicentine architect, in a crescendo of slenderness and grace, with superimposed series of doors, little niches, and light encasements. It leaves an impression of Olympian peace. All is accounted for in the careful, perfect work: the placement of the frames, the mellowness of the frieze of bucrania, shields, and flags, the turning of the balusters, which along the arcade of the second order are bathed in the sun as if to temper with a note of youthful freshness the grave silence of the Doric portico and its classical frieze."[32] Despite the late date, Venturi made an accurate inspection of the site and recorded his interest in the information that he was able to give; unfortunately, in editing his study, his collaborators inserted among the illustrations the nineteenth-century portal that had been opened by Selva, attributing it to Palladio.

In the same years Pée, studying Palladio's buildings with scientific rigor, calculated the degree of dependence of Palladio on classicism. For Pée, this was the basis of any respect he might have for the architect, but he stopped short of subordinating to it the logical exigencies of clients. A comparison between the house of the Romans in Barbaro and the project for the monastery showed, according to the author, that the artist had obtained an extraordinary augmentation of perspective effects, determined by the placement of the tablinum, by the widening of the atrium, and by the insertion of Composite columns in the atrium he had called Corinthian. He also noted that at the Carità the artist was much freer than he had been when designing the rigid scheme for the Palazzo Thiene.[33]

We have previously noted concerning the restoration of the tablinum that "every revival of classicism is a pretext Palladio uses for cleverly inventing totally personal works. Such is the case here in the tablinum where *in nuce* appears part of the plan of San Giorgio Maggiore. The forcep transept of the church grows out of its rigid perimeter with an effect analogous to that of the two parts that at the Carità are constrained by the two columns. But here the limited area allows the embrace of the complete play of line and the musical alternation of the flat and curved planes, a motif taken up again in later periods and developed in an unexpected manner. Analogous to this idea of Palladio's for the Venetian churches is the sober coloristic effect; the white of the plaster is enlivened by the gray of the stone, where the architectonic movements are underlined more nervously. The two serene columns add a third color, a rosy gray, which in the architect's initial concept probably had the function of tying together as if by a subtle brush stroke the white and the gray of the upper part to the reddish tones of the original pavement.

"Thus with the lines and masses gracefully echoing classical concepts and with the juxtaposition of sober tints, a complex rich in effects has been composed. According to one's point of view, the lines create different effects, and when one moves in the space it appears that the architecture itself moves. In short, the element of surprise of which Bernini and Longhena were so fond already appears here."[34]

In the sessions on architectural history held at the Centro Internazionale in Vicenza many profound theories have been presented, which are useful in explaining problems in all the works of Palladio. From time to time the monastery becomes the subject. Thus, Fausto Franco affirms: "Palladio's 'grand' town planning derives from a procedure analogous to that described for the 'small' town planning. The constructions of forums and of their surrounding buildings, which Palladio broaches in the *Quattro Libri*, demonstrate that he had always taken account of the relationship between masses and interior spaces in his palaces with courtyards. If, in these, we think not in the usual terms of 'façades' but of 'organisms,' we must stress the fact that the artist thought less of courtyards than of actual piazzas surrounded by public buildings. The vast spaciousness of the Convento della Carità in Venice ... would demonstrate this were it not one of the unfinished works." [35]

In the course of this study we have considered how in this project Palladio concentrated his attention on the interior of the building and its great spaces and remained unoccupied with the exterior; this demonstrates the correctness of Franco's observation.

Pane, analyzing the complex, judged the large cloister to be closer to a Bramantesque courtyard than to a peristyle. The rectangular structure of the building is rather simple. The walls of the main chapter hall and of the sacristy are in line along one side of the atrium with the pilasters of the cloisters, and, similarly, so are the pair of columns with the continuous wall that corresponds to the interior wall of the cells. However, the successive spaces are neatly separated, differing from those which are connected by perspective in many palaces and villas. [36]

The same scholar in 1947 had devoted an ample monograph to the architect, extending the argument in a later, more complete study: "The Sacristy, between the floor and the ceiling, is an invention that recalls the T-shaped atria of some villas and the columned halls with intersecting groin vaults; the remarkable perimeter inserts itself in a very organic manner between stairs and room of different size, so as to form with these a rectangular block on each side of the atrium: here fantasy and reason together compose a recurrence of niches, apses, columns, and pilasters, while in elevation groin vaults and lunettes are juxtaposed. The result is not an expression of tension but of an agreeable rhythm, which renders perfectly acceptable the unique disposition of the structure.

"In the cloister, the superimposition of three orders, the first two with half-columns set against piers, the third with pilasters and rectangular windows, presents a scheme that from the point of view of the overall structure offers no novelty, while it suggests the precedent of other sixteenth-century compositions that were similarly inspired by the Colosseum and by the Theater of Marcellus. But it is still clearly original in that it presents a perfect execution of the scheme in bricks and terra-cotta, with the use of stone limited, as usual, to the sills, the capitals, and the bases, while the architrave is divided in each intercolumniation by a corbel formed by an upside-down wedge whose side faces furnish a support for the moulded bricks. The subtle layer of mortar and the tight, impeccable execution of the joints and mouldings also helps to confer an entirely new sense to the traditional articulation, giving the impression, as Goethe put it so well, that the walls were made in a single casting." [37]

With these pages Pane became the first to approach the analysis of the complex monument with a direct sensibility.

Wittkower's remarks are also interesting: "Palladio planned and partly executed his most elaborate reconstruction of the Roman house.... His programme was never misinterpreted.... Here, at last, he had an opportunity of building a real atrium with an open ceiling.... From the atrium one proceeds into the chiostro which, being too large for one giant order, was given a system in three tiers derived from that of the Colosseum."[38]

Bruno Zevi mentioned the monastery in passing, but he makes observations on Palladio's sensibility that can justly be applied to this work: "Although in general Palladio adopted the elements of the classical Roman canons, he undermined their accepted applications and combinations, thereby altering their significance, not for some Baroque ideal of movement and spatial interplay but in order to translate into stone a poetry, an ardor of spirit, that was sustained by architectural traditions but proceeded from tendencies essentially pictorial. Bases, capitals, pilasters, and columns—all taken from the classical orders—became the means for an expression that is equally removed from the classical structures of antiquity and from the perspective systems characteristic of the Renaissance."[39]

Another of his remarks seems written especially for the monastery: "Prosperity without security may lead to a sense of alienation, and the megalomaniacal plans of Palladio's unexecuted or incomplete buildings are perhaps one sign of this."[40] Palladio did not resist the temptation to extend a grandiose project for the Carità, although he was practical and not just a dreamer, knowing very well that he would never have been able to bring it to its full completion.

The worthy Zorzi has had many opportunities to occupy himself with the monastery, and in the volume devoted to Palladio's public works he speaks very broadly, repeating what he had said earlier: "Although Palladio had affirmed that in the open atrium of the monastery of the Carità he had wanted to approach the Vitruvian scheme, still in this part of the building he did not abandon his usual practical approach to construction. In fact, as it is reproduced in the *Quattro Libri*, it is not at all the Corinthian atrium described by Vitruvius but is unfortunately one of the usual porticoed atria derived from those with the giant columns designed by the master for some of his Vicentine palaces (for example, for the courtyard of the palace of Giuseppe Porto in Vicenza and, later, for the first courtyard of the projected palace of Giacomo Angaran near S. Faustino in the same city). Nevertheless, the great columns, rising in all their grace to support the rich trabeation and the open terrace above, already suggest the final development of Palladio's style, inspired by Michelangelo's eloquent art."[41]

As happens from time to time with Zorzi, a formidable collector of documents, he did not take account of some significant details; thus, he admired the bricks that lend a particularly strong color to the extremities of the façade of the cloister,[42] not noticing that it was a neoclassical restoration, different in age and in the quality of material.

Turning to consider the publications of the *Bollettino del Centro Andrea Palladio*, we find a sound article by André Chastel,[43] which clarifies the source and the impact of the oval staircase in the Carità. Guglielmo De Angelis d'Ossat, confronting the problem of "I Sangallo e Palladio," makes a thoughtful and profound comparison with Antonio da Sangallo the Younger in regard to the monastery. "Decidedly stressed are the analogies, or, rather, the essential harmonies, as found in an actual Palladian building—the courtyard of the monastery of the Carità in Venice. The incomplete but beautiful work, in fact, in its solid proportions and in its broad, impressive cadences, recalls the modules of mid-sixteenth-century Roman attitudes, and more precisely, those of the Sangalli, an influence that I judge to be more valid and pertinent than the imitation of Bramante or, even less to the point, of the Colosseum, which has usually heretofore been referred to. Indeed, the proportions of the arcade of the projected courtyard at the Palazzo Farnese appear to be equal to those in the Carità. For our specific ends, this comparison presents itself as highly indicative and valuable. In Palladio's works it is very rare to encounter either the simple motif of arcades framed by an order of half-columns or piers, or the broad proportions of the plan. Concerning this second point, we cannot cite a better example than the arcuated 'barchesse' in the Villa Muzani alla Pisa (Malo), no longer extant, whose relationship, it seems, was chosen to contrast with the extremely narrow arcade of the central block. Documents pertinent to the construction of the villa indicate a date of 1559, exactly when Palladio would have been engaged in the project for the Venetian monastery.

" The fragmentary monument of the Carità therefore constitutes a conscious exception, a generous act of admiration, almost a moment of abandon toward the whole Roman world that had its proper exponent in Sangallo. It may be considered an evocation, indeed, even an isolated posthumous homage." [44]

A cultural relationship certainly existed between the two architects; however, even if when designing the Venetian cloister Palladio had remembered the courtyard of the Palazzo Farnese (fig. XXVII), it slipped his mind by the time he got around to working out the very different chromatic character of the Venetian building. And it is plausible that the peristyle of the Carità, had it been completed, would have appeared very different from the austere Roman courtyard, both because of the pleasant warmth of the bricks and because of the dramatic module, because Palladio not only produced a variation on the theme but renewed the motifs that he certainly shared here with his immediate predecessors.

It has also been noted by Lionello Puppi, who accepted Pane's observations that the monastery derives from the house of the ancients "only in the analogy offered by the cloistered character of the interior spaces." This he confirmed by writing about "the persistence in Palladio's actual stylistic articulation of an absolute freedom with respect to the model, which is deprived of any institutional character and made instrumental to the imaginative execution. Contemporary practices (next to that of Bramante, it seems that Palladio also benefited from Michelangelo at the Palazzo Farnese—but here one sees the entirely pictorial use of exposed bricks) are put into use where necessary, but always with a clear knowledge of the expressive function." [45]

For James Ackerman, only the color of the bricks distinguishes this work from those by Bramante. After having stated that the monastery is the last of the archaeological works designed by Palladio, he adds: "The Venetian character of the San Giorgio cloister is far removed from Palladio's other cloister design, for the monastery of the Carità in Venice, of which only one wing is preserved in the court of the Accademia delle Belle Arti. There, Palladio explained, the attempt was not only to be Roman, but actually to recreate a grandiose Roman house which in the *Quattro Libri* he used to illustrate the Corinthian atrium.... Palladio knew the Roman house from Vitruvius's description rather than from ancient remains, so that his reconstruction is guesswork; in fact, he made no effort to present the cloister as a *peristylium*, but used motives from the Theatre of Marcellus and the Colosseum in a context that is much closer to Bramante—except that it has a warm brick colour—than to antiquity.... The design is anachronistically classical in the unclassical mid-Cinquecento; probably it seemed provincial and out-of-date to the Venetians, who were not as avid antiquarians as the Vicentines, and for the rest of his career in Veince, Palladio avoided the archaeological mode."[46]

Ackerman's observations are acute; in fact, after this "casa dei Romani" Palladio no longer took up erudite exercises. He became a constructor who accompanied his usual learned proportions with a completely modern character. But even within the monastery, had it been completed, the images of the Colosseum, of the Theater of Marcellus, and of the Arena in Pola would have blended with many other levels that existed in the architect's conception (fig. XCV): the learned integration is revealed in his black and white designs, but not in his finished works. If we force ourselves to see the atrium with the eight great columns of brick, the bases and capitals of white stone with the coffers and terrace above, the archaeological evocations and the qualities drawn from the works of other masters of the sixteenth century vanish, and instead the Loggia del Capitaniato, the atrium of the Palazzo Chiericati, and the courtyards of so many Palladian palaces and villas, easily come to mind.

This has been affirmed also by Nicola Ivanoff, who, when writing of this monument, said that Palladio "made it with the considerable archaeological open-mindedness ... of the palazzo di Iseppo da Porta."[47] He added that "the fabulous little city that Palladio built as the Convento della Carità was, in the past, hidden by the Gothic construction of the church and the scuola. The only visible part was the flank along the canal. In Venice, therefore, Palladio was faced with the same problem that he had faced at the beginning of his career with the encasement of the Basilica in Vicenza—that of making the old and the new, the traditional Gothic and the Renaissance, coexist. But the solution he now gave was exactly the reverse of the earlier one."

One must here recall that the monastery never excited universal interest; only the erudite have from time to time examined it, for the most part considering it as a notable piece of research into classicism. It is quite possible that the enthusiasm of Goethe would have been more tenuous if Palladio had not evoked the phantom of the house of the ancients when he himself spoke of the work. In the following decades, as in our own epoch, this work appears expressive to only a few; the innumerable visitors to the Gallerie are not stimulated by a vision of the cloister. After Canaletto and Borsati, no artist has attempted to interpret Palladio's ideas in a work worth mentioning even though, since the beginning of the nineteenth century, many painters, sculptors, and architects have been both teachers and students within the walls of the former monastery.

An architecture that is "without a façade," with an "unimportant" exterior, produced at a moment in the development of an architect who had only slowly reached maturity, which concentrates on the poetic episodes of the interior—stairs, tablinum, cloister (to enumerate only the most outstanding)—is not able to draw as many admirers as the villas, churches, and palaces that offer visions completely lacking in mystery. Francesco Sansovino, illustrating the Church of the Carità, recorded the "chiostro con belle, grosse e spesse colonne composto da Andrea Palladio nobile architetto."[48] Later only the scholars, one might say, have visited the exemplary monument with interest and reverence.

XCV - Daniele Barbaro, *Elevation of the theater*. From *I Dieci Libri dell'Architettura di M. V. Vitruvio tradutti ...*, 1556, V, p. 152

XCVI - Antonio Visentini, *The Chiesa della Carità (etching after Canaletto)*

XCVII - Luca Carlevarijs, *The Chiesa and the Scuola della Carità: between the two, the entrance to the monastery and the scuola (etching after Canaletto)*

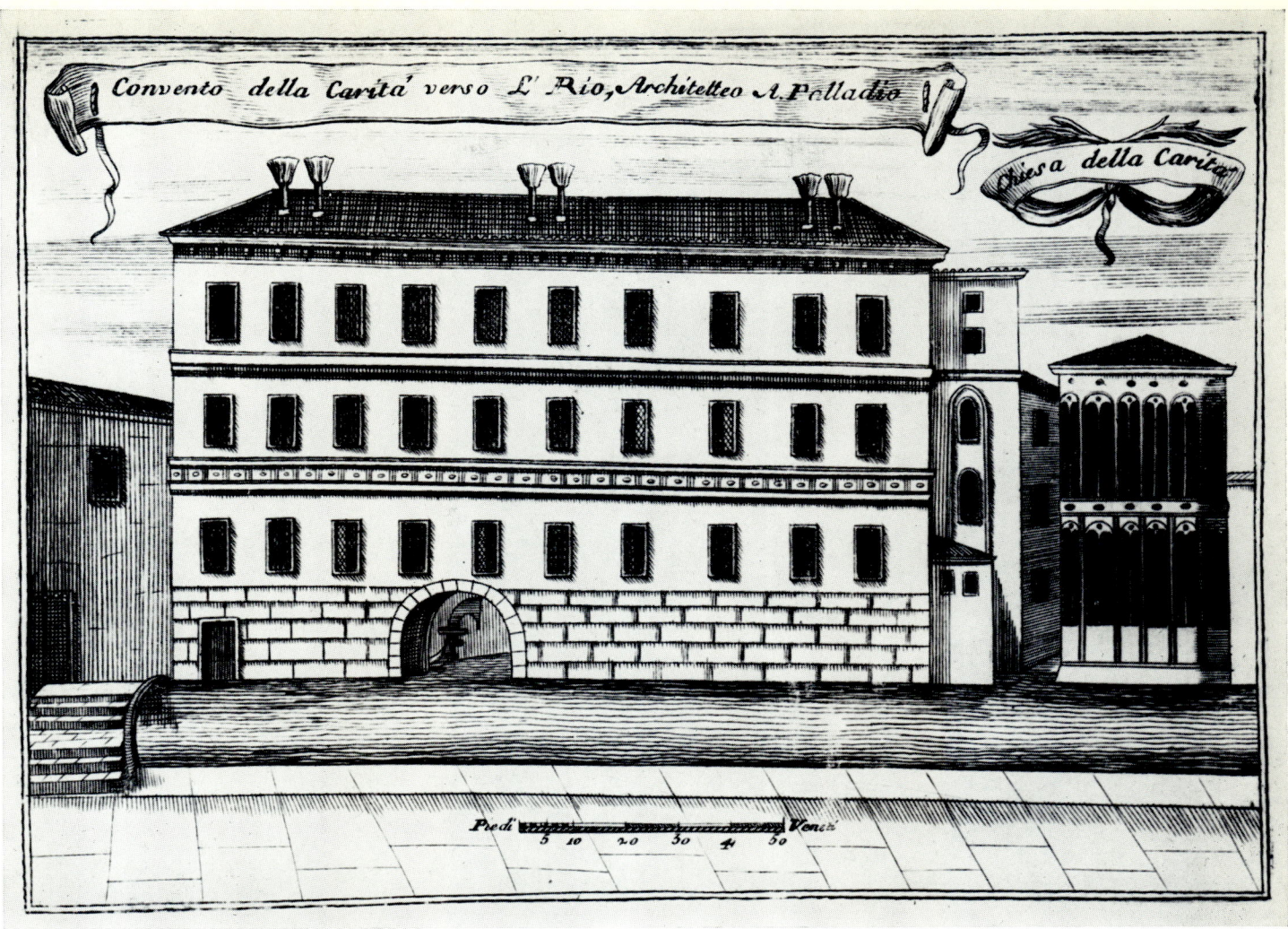

XCVIII - Vincenzo Coronelli, *The Convento della Carità toward the rio di Sant'Agnese.* Venice, Museo Correr

IC - Vincenzo Coronelli, *View of the cloister of the Carità.* Venice, Museo Correr

C - Antonio Visentini (?), *Façade of the cloister of the Carità.* London, RIBA

CI - Antonio Visentini (?), *Elevation and section of the cloister of the Carità.*
Florence, Soprintendenza alle Gallerie, 3510 A

CII - Antonio Visentini (?), *Elevation and section of the cloister of the Carità.* London, RIBA, XIII, 2

CIII - Giannantonio Moschini, *Atrium and cloister of the Convento della Carità in 1828.*
From *Nuova Guida di Venezia,* 1847

CIV - GIUSEPPE BORSATO (?), *The cloister of the Convento della Carità (imaginary reconstruction)*. Venice, Accademia di Belle Arti

CV - Giuseppe Borsato (?), *The tablinum of the Convento della Carità (imaginary reconstruction)*.
Venice, Accademia di Belle Arti

CVI - PIETRO SELVATICO, *The tablinum of the Convento della Carità.*
From *Sulla Architettura e sulla scultura in Venezia dal Medioevo fino ai nostri giorni*, 1847, p. 329

NOTES TO CHAPTER VI

[1] 1943, III, pp. 618-619.

[2] 1624, pp. 43-44.

[3] 1741, p. 71:

"Plate XX.   A. The Breadth of this Atrium is 1/3 of the Length.

C. The Tablino is 2/3 Parts of the Breadth of The Atrium, and Square besides the two Half-circles. Columns.

G. The Courts are 1/3 longer than they are large.

Plate XXI.   D. The uncovered Gallery or outside Passage, which leads to the Stairs and brings you up into the Rooms at right and left.

Plate XXII.   A. Logia. B. Refectorio. C. Calizola Scoperta. D. Vault Sotto Sesta a Fascia. E. Most of these walls are 2 Bricks and 1/2 thick.

F. So far as this finished; the rest is not finished, by reason of the great Expences one of the fathers told me, that each Arch of the Peristylo would cost a thousand 'Venetian Ducati,' meaning throughout finished with Inrichments. The Atrio is finish'd, the Columns are of Bricks, with red Stucco, the Base and Capitals are of Stone, the Roof of the Gallery above the Entablature is of Timber, and was paved with Bricks; but by reason of the Rains passing thro' they have been obliged to make another Roof to the top of the Building, and supported by Pilasters, and covered with Tyles; so that about the Opening of the Atrio above is a covered Terrace to walk on.

All this Building is of Brick, and the Ornaments of Stone; on the side of the Peristylos is done clean, and the Coings; the oval Stairs are excellent; and The Rail of the Stairs is up to the top. The open oval Stairs with a Rail and Banister of Stone upon the Steps is extreamly well executed.

Plate XXIV.   A. B. Shews the Dripping of the Pavement of the Terrace.

B. Shews likewise, that this Plinth is raised over the hinder part of the Cartooch, as you will find or see in the Profile of the Cornice.

C. The sfondati to the Ovolo are all in one without the Corona, and the Cartooches are turned into a Corona, with a Cimasia and a Wave. The Bases and Capitals of the Columns are of Stone and the Columns of Bricks, and the Freze of Wood."

The transcription is not exact, but the sense is not altered. The transcription, however, is useful even when reading tre original, because certain lines clear then have since been rubbed.

Page 30, concerning the plan: "Logia. Refectorio. Calizola scoperta. Sotto sesto a fascia Most of this walls ar 2 bricks and 1/2 thick." In the margins of the page, near the sketch of the three steps in the oval stairs, are some illegible words. Near the unbuilt tablinum the following line runs across the area: "this porticus is continued along ad the strock and Atrium."

Page 31, next to the statue of the atrium: "This statues are in right 1/6 of collonna and architraw"; near the top of the steps: "This rail and baluster is ... "; near the coffers: "The sfondato to the ovolo are al onw; the t. Corrona ... out and the cartouche are tourned in to a Corona and on that a cimasium and a wave"; near the profile of the cornice: "This is a plinth rising out this hinder part of a cartouch, under the rail and ballauster"; near the pavement of the terrace: "is the pound on of the terrace"; on the base and shaft of the column, and on the frieze, respectively: "stone, brick, wood."

Page 29, in the margins and under the description of the building: "This building is not finished by reason of the great charge for one of the fathers tould me that every Arch of the Perristillio wold cost 1000 duc. I mean thought on the in ... the Attrio is finished the Pillars are of Brick finished rodd and the base and Capitals ar of stone the roof of Timber wo rond Paved with Bricks but by reason that the water paised throu they have mand an other roof born up by Pilasters and covered with so that about the opening of the Atrio along ther is a terrace covered to walk about al this Building is of Brick and the ornements of stone. Ther is in side of the Peristillio is done clean the Coyns the Ovall staircase is excellent and thor good an apogio of Iron up to the top."

[4] 1954, p. 310.

[5] 1954, p. 36.

[6] "Le osservazioni...", 1740, I, p. 1.

[7] IV, 1743, p. 15.

[8] Venice, Correr, "Contro Rusconi," Cod. Cic. 3656.

This is not the place to take up the details of the contacts between this curious polygraph, engraver, and architect with Canaletto and Consul Smith. It is known that for Smith he designed a small palace on the Grand Canal at Santi Apostoli, and a villa at Mogliano in the terra firma, now unfortunately destroyed. Visentini engraved many paintings by Canaletto for English patrons, and he made drawings of Venetian buildings, both churches and palaces, collected in the *Admiranda Urbis Venetae* in the British Museum.

[9] 1964, p. 241.

[10] Venice, Correr, Cod. Cic. 3658; see document XX.

[11] 1962, p. 368.

[12] 1776, p. 40.

[13] 1791, p. 55.

[14] 1785, p. 36.

[15] 1887, pp. 254-55.

[16] 1887, p. 268.

[17] 1887, pp. 292-94.

[18] 1858, II, p. 105.

[19] 1858, II, p. 109.

[20] 1835, p. 20.

[21] 1843, I, p. 39. The French original is in the Museo Civico in Bassano, II-158-1679.

[22] Venice, Accademia di Belle Arti, oil, 12 cm. in diameter.

[23] 1570, L. II, Cap. LX.

[24] "Data mano allo scavo trovai che sotto a ciascun piedritto degli archi, compresa la sporgente semicolonna, vi corrisponde un solidissimo masso formato di regolare muratura, avente un primo

strato composto a pezzi irregolari di pietra tenera, e che allargandosi gradatamente verso la sua base termina sui fianchi col congiungersi al masso vicino. Questa muratura che in profondità corrisponde a circa 1/6 dell'intiero edificio, s'appoggia sopra grossi tavoloni di larice sotto a' quali sembra che siasi apparecchiata una platea di soli frantumi di fabbrica. Avendo in seguito dilatato alcun poco lo scavo rinvenni, a non molta distanza dalle ridette fondazioni, dei pali incerti piantati paralleli a quelli; dal che mi parve di poter dedurre che forse al momento di costruirle abbiasi dovuto usare il chiuso o cassero all'oggetto importantissimo di tener in asciutto lo scavo durante il lavoro di quelle. Incontrai inoltre entro a questo spazio dei grossi pezzi informi di pietra, che probabilmente s'impiegarono a maggior presidio delle stesse fondamenta, sotto le quali non mi fu dato rinvenire la palafitta, solito solo mezzo usato a rinforzo di certi terreni, e tanto comune a Venezia. Se ad onta di avere il nostro architetto ommesse le palafitte, la fabbrica si mantenne inalterabile, ove se eccettuare si voglia un parziale avvallamento, forse accidentale, accaduto nell'angolo a destra ove si univa l'arco ora demolito, è a dedursi che ciò sia derivato dall'aver rinvenuto alla stabilita profondità un terreno carantoso misto a sabbia, come mi è parso anche di riconoscere, nel quale l'uso del pilotajo anziché utile poteva tornare pregiudizievole, giacché in aggiunta alla somma difficoltà che incontrai a conficcare i pali, non servono questi che a squarciare il terreno a scapito della naturale sua tenacità, che ne costituisce la maggior resistenza " (1835, p. 11).

[25] " Tale appariva la precisione e la somma esattezza del lavoro da doversi a ragione presumere che tutt'i pezzi usati per comporre il detto pavimento, dopo usciti dalla fornace, siensi ridotti nella stessa maniera che dallo scalpellino si lavorerebbe un pavimento di marmo. Ed a proposito di questo pavimento non voglio lasciar di esporre la giudiciosa precauzione usata dall'autore affine di preservarlo dalla umidità, che non a torto temeva vi potesse comunicare il terreno. Apparecchiato dapprima il fondo con frantumi di fabbrica bene spianati, vi stese sopra uno strato di grossi mattoni in pieno che servivano di base ad altri posti in coltello, i quali tenuti fra lor discosti formavano tanti canali paralleli. Si appoggiava su questi un altro strato di eguali mattoni pur in pieno, e finalmente il pavimento or menzionato " (1835, p. 13).

[26] 1845, p. 48.
[27] 1847, p. 329.
[28] 1856, II, p. 818.
[29] 1872, II, p. 193.
[30] 1855, p. 267.
[31] 1880, p. 35.
[32] 1940, II, pt. III, p. 359.
[33] 1941, p. 93.
[34] 1947, p. 142.
[35] 1959, p. 19.
[36] 1960, p. 65.
[37] 1961, p. 293.
[38] 1962, pp. 80-81.
[39] 1966, col. 64.
[40] 1966, col. 79.
[41] 1964, p. 243.
[42] 1964, p. 245.
[43] 1965, p. 11.
[44] 1966, p. 43.
[45] 1966, p. 33.
[46] 1966, p. 106 and p. 153.
[47] 1967, p. 62.
[48] 1581, p. 96 verso.

VII
CONCLUSION

For the student who has followed the history of the Carità there remain some choice problems to resolve. In the interval between Palladio's original conception and its execution and what survives to the present time, there exists a consistent paucity of information, and it is difficult to unravel the threads that tie together the original intentions and the present state of the building.

Goethe wrote of the monastery that, had it been completed, there would perhaps be no other building in all the world that would have been more perfect; let us see whether his unconditioned enthusiasm is still justified.

The plan of the monastery is strung out in a manner similar to that of other buildings designed in the decade 1550-60, buildings that were constructed, or remained projects, or were only partially executed (figs. XI, XXXIX). But in the Palladian projects designed to be the setting for a family, the spaces often penetrate one another and always permit an airy perspective view, which unifies the complex and allows one to comprehend its consistency and articulation. At the monastery Palladio preferred instead to use a simple idea that was rhythmic and episodic.

Surrounding the open area, the tablina, the stairs, the guests' quarters, and the refectory are independent units; this is one of the characteristics translated from studies for the *casa degli antichi*, in which the architect had always imagined spaces that were successive and self-sufficient. He believed, therefore, that it was an apt plan for a conventual family as well. The religious were able to isolate themselves or to congregate together; they could circulate without interfering with one another on the ample terraces above the atrium and flanking the refectory or within the porticoes around the "impluvium" and within the Doric and Ionic loggias. The cells with their harmonious proportions have the dignity appropriate to the ease of the congregation.

Such a plan could be adapted to any kind of city, but it was worked out to fit the dimensions of the site constrained by the rio di Sant'Agnese and the rio della Carità (fig. VII; plates 1-3; scale drawing *a*). However, it did not respect the property of the Scuola Grande, perhaps because of the desires of the euphoric patrons. The flank of the church determined the way the monastery would be developed, and the asymmetrical area was designed for the particular space available. But since it is not explicit, it has come down to us as a riddle open to many solutions (figs. XI, XXXIX).

In Venice something like seventy or so religious houses flourished. In those of the thirteenth and fourteenth centuries, the cells and the other areas were strung around cloisters in which isolated small columns of stone supported brick walls.

This is the form of those of Sant'Apollonia, of the Madonna dell'Orto, and of San Michele. In the fifteenth century the spans of the arcades widened and the columns became less slender, as in the old cloister at San Giorgio Maggiore. In the early sixteenth century trabeated colonnades were used from time to time, as at Spirito Santo and at Santo Stefano. Then followed reconstructions that coincided with the activity of Sansovino, who was constrained to give substantial advice concerning San Salvatore and San Zaccaria, monasteries whose sumptuous and elegant tone suggested the presuppositions found in Palladio's work. It is not known in what chronological sequence the monasteries were reconstructed, but it is possible that they fall within the decades 1530-50, which means that they preceded the Carità.

Palladio got little from these precedents; he adapted the disposition of the spaces according to local tradition, perhaps, among other reasons, because he was not permitted to depart far from an established rule. But in the elevations he disassociated himself from every example and conceived a peristyle that was Roman in proportion and in rhythm but not in materials (plates 8-9). He invented an atrium and a stair and a sacristy-chapter hall-tablinum totally without precedent (plates 48-54, 33-38). In Venice superimposed loggias were used from time to time in major projects—in the Fondaco dei Tedeschi, in the Sansovinian buildings for the Zecca, for the Dolfin, and for the Corner—but in monasteries, even in the most important ones, only a single portico supported the upper floors. On the terra firma, on the other hand, one could already see cloisters with many loggias, and Bramante had left examples that Palladio had certainly seen. At the Carità, however, he was original in his use of rounded bricks in the columns and in the pilasters, as well as in leaving visible and enhancing the chromatic contrast between the bricks and the white stone of the bases, the capitals, and the dripstones (plate 21).

Thus, in a city in which for decades contractors had been importing ton after ton of *pietra d'Ossero* and *pietra di Rovigno* (and Sanmichele and Sansovino were the most important architects to make use of it), Palladio was able to look to the terra firma for Ferrarese bricks "ben condizionati," like those employed in the construction of Venetian buildings during the thirteenth and fourteenth centuries, used together with the famous "altinelle" like the connective tissue and the skeleton.

It has been said time and again that his use of this material attests to Palladio's desire to adapt his building to the predominant color of the city ("Venise la rouge"), but that theory is open to dispute. Bricks pleased Palladio as a material, and he wrote about them many times. At the monastery he wanted the rosy tone of his bricks to approach that of the still-new and brown ones in the church, which had been finished a few decades earlier.

The architect wanted warm bricks for the eight big columns in the atrium, the most "antique" area and the only one that he was able to bring to full completion. "Né ci dovemo meravigliare se le colonne vengono così alte, perciocché la magnificenza di quelle case così ricercava, et è proprio loro l'altezza et larghezza," Barbaro had written in book six of his treatise, when discussing the *casa degli antichi*. The only work in which the architect put robust, high columns was the atrium of the Carità; not even in the courtyard of the Palazzo Angarano, had it been built, would the engaged pilasters have presented the majestic appearance of the Venetian columns, isolated as they are and strictly confined within the space encompassed by the limited proportions and bathed by the sober light that entered from the "impluvium." At the base of that area the wall was lightly stuccoed in white and had the voids of the windows opening on the two floors. The pavement presumably would have been brick laid in a herringbone pattern and would have lent another rosy tone.

From the columns one's gaze was directed to the white capitals, to the elegant coffers, and to the empty infinity of the sky. Nothing similar was to be seen elsewhere in Venice; never had Palladio had the opportunity of experimenting with a similar chiaroscuro relationship, concluded at its summit by well-moulded balusters and limited by an open terrace. The lofty statues would have represented, as seems to be indicated in the design, an inventory of the heroes then in vogue—Hercules, Athena, Persephone. This would have been the single concession made to the novelties imported to Venice by Sansovino (figs. XII-XIII).

Everything else was all Palladio's invention, and only he would have been able to compose such *poesia*. In a city given over to the strictures of Sanmichele and Sansovino, he proposed an alternative that permitted one to dream of the antique through the magic filter of fantasy.

We might try to imagine the impressions of one who followed the itinerary proposed by the architect in this project: church, atrium, peristyle, refectory, peristyle. From the atrium, wrapped in light and dynamic in form, a few steps lead to the arcade where the exit into the cloister would have provoked a different kind of amazement (plates 8-9) by the rhythmic superimposition of the orders, the repeated accents of the stone, and the contrast of light and shade produced by the deep arcades sunk back beyond the bright walls. Here one would find himself before a palimpsest in which, following the suggestions of the latest Roman architecture, he could recall the courtyard of the Palazzo Ducale in Urbino, and elements from the Arena in Pola and the Colosseum. But the primary material was brick (even Vasari had written that the convent was made all of "pietre cotte"), which climbed to the level of the ample terrace and to the great block of the refectory and took life from the innumerable shadings in the undisciplined frieze that ran around the four sides of the great peristyle. This would have been kept as a garden, as we learn both from the custom of the time and from the term "horto" that is written in that space in the project in the archives. In the elegant garden, the rare light snowfall would have formed a sort of matrix like a woodcut, whitening the projecting frames and leaving black the bucrania and covering over the wide walkways of the two first stories and the gutters above.

Attempting to reconstruct the dignified façade of the *casa degli antichi* the architect would have been able to suggest a hypothetical design such as those illustrating Barbaro's Vitruvius. Instead, the exterior of a monastery could only be allowed the luxury of a very large stone basement and of a "cavana," the arch of which is made of rugged and majestic pieces of stone (plates 4-7).

To the artist the antiquities of Rome appeared ruined and disheveled. He could therefore be relieved of attempting to design suitable antique decorations for the interior of the monastic *casa degli antichi.* We know very little about how he intended to finish the interior, which he did not illustrate in his treatise. In substance, the only parts to retain their original proportions unaltered are the stairs, the tablinum, and some cells. In these areas a bright tone prevails on the walls; in the tablinum was a polychromatic pavement; the Doric frieze and the two rich columns were rose-colored, as were the stairs and stair landings (plates 33-38). It is probable that the architect had thought of completing the ornamentation of the sacristy with festoons and marble or stucco statues; a tablinum, by its very function, demands images in its niches, and the theoretical tablina shown in the *Quattro Libri* were endowed in this way. Similarly, a sacristy constructed in Venice in the middle of the sixteenth century would not have been allowed to retain such plain walls and ceilings. The rich pavement and serene columns and the altar with the altarpiece by Benedetto Caliari (fig. V) presume a completion similar to that of the church at Maser; the niches in the stairs, according to the custom of the time as well as to what we can see in the designs in the treatise, would also have hosted figures in the round. Perhaps in the ceilings of the guest rooms one could likewise imagine stucco and painted decoration; in imagining this we might recall certain Palladian settings and villas around Vicenza and the rooms of the Palazzo Ducale, which were decorated by the artist or by his students.

Some fact of which we are ignorant interrupted the relationship between the architect and the canons, and for this reason not only was some of the essential structure not built but also part of the decoration was left incomplete.

Atrium, peristyle, sacristy, stairs—some of each of this remains incomplete, but still these parts constitute unique events in Palladio's activity. Thus, while we can find the plan of the building referred to in others of his projects and in the monastic tradition, in the elevations we find singular solutions that are coherent with other aspects of his activity but that are without an exact analogy to others of his buildings, either built or projected. The plan does not appear to be a spontaneous creation but the result of long study; in the elevations, on the other hand, the resolution of spaces interrupted by heavy vertical structures and the elaborate tablinum, in which empty space seems to be moulded, still allow one to sense the architect's extemporaneous creation, as he resolved problems while actually on the building site.

Observing the project as it is presented in the *Quattro Libri* and what remains of it today, we understand that the author had hoped to achieve a memorable and grandiose work to demonstrate to the Venetian lords that, in addition to Sansovino and Sanmichele, there was also Andrea Palladio, architect, prepared to propose new ideas and original inventions, elaborating them from the antique while remaining completely outside traditional solutions. These were the years in which he longed to become established in the capital, as his request to be made "Proto al Sal" shows. But his goals were too high, and the project he presented to the Lateranensi canons was too ambitious; as he later learned, to install himself in Venice as "princeps" he had to take a different route. In the monastic buildings of successive decades in Venice the idea broached at the Carità was not taken up. The oval stair appeared again in the seventeenth-century hospital of Santa Maria dei Dereletti (Ospedaletto; fig. XCI); and, in the eighteenth century, Giorgio Massari drew some inspiration from the great Palladian spaces when projecting the reconstruction of the Dominican monastery called the Gesuati alle Zattere (plate 2). Here, too, a small oval stair appears on the plan, an homage to the great architect. The monastery was only partly constructed.

The heart of the Palladian project, the Corinthian atrium, was burned and immediately forgotten. But we can once again assess the organic conception in which, as always, the builder subordinated the allocation of light and elements that he would have entrusted to painters and sculptors who were friends to an emphasis on structural dynamism.

We can, with Goethe, heap reproaches on fate for not allowing the complex to be completed. The poet believed that, perhaps, this would have been the most perfect piece of architecture in the world. But here we cannot follow him because, for us, the concept of perfection does not correspond to anything that is concrete. We know that Palladio did not aspire to raise the perfect work but proposed to build something functional and adapted to a use that he discussed during its designing with his scholarly, critical, and artistic friends. His works always provoke unequalled aesthetic responses, sometimes intense and always harmonious, like those derived from the creations of nature: this occurs also at the Carità, from its solemn, serene proportions and its refined colorism (color plates *b-c*).

The subsequent history of the monument provokes some thought. Vasari in Florence in 1568 and, later, Jones and Wotton in England stated that at the Carità Palladio had given a clear demonstration of his genius. But in Venice, among the architect's own contemporaries, only Francesco Sansovino, son of Giacomo and a native of Tuscany, in 1581, mentioned it meaningfully. His words, "le colonne belle, grosse e spesse," show that he had looked closely and well at the new architecture. Immediately after that the monastery was forgotten in Venice; only the English theorists preserved a lively image of it and dreamed of seeing the notable building completed. In the eighteenth century Coronelli hesitantly reconstructed it in his prints, as did Canaletto in his paintings, reconstructing the ruins and the interrupted work with grace; Visentini spoke of it at length at the behest of, and in response to, the "Cavaliere Inglese." The admiration of these artists perhaps derives from an ideological outlook put into circulation by the English colony in Venice. Everyone knew the *Quattro Libri*, but no one suspected that the proposed atrium had been a reality for more than sixty years, alongside the incompleted peristyle. Later, Temanza discovered the record of the fire, and he especially admired the monument for its structural technique. Selva, his student, integrated a veneration for Palladio into his neoclassical culture, but when adapting the former monastery to the uses of the academy, he did not think of leaving measured drawings of the condition of the Palladian building before his work in it. Moreover, in the *Fabbriche di Venezia*, he published plans and elevations derived from the *Quattro Libri* rather than from the extant remains of the monument.

No Italian, and no Venetian, paid the warm tribute to the Convento della Carità that was given it by the scholarly English and by Goethe, perhaps because the rational, learned, and unimprovised character of the Palladian concept here renders it more comprehensible to the northern than to the Latin temperament.

The architect had evoked a contrivance foreign to his time and an abstract philosophy that remains an anomaly for Venice, and for this reason the work has been respected but not loved for these many decades.

In the sixteenth century the local culture was not disposed to pay attention to such a new idea: the all-pervasive presence of Sansovino did not permit any attention to be given in Venice to an architect who wanted to construct in the city an elegant and solid work, the product of a long cultural search, and still a work endowed with a poetic mystery.

d - Nineteenth-century watercolor with the design of the sacristy pavement in the Convento della Carità.

QUESTO BENEDETTO TEATRO

On February 23, 1565, Palladio wrote to Vincenzo Arnaldi in Vicenza: " Ho fornito di fare questo benedetto Theatro, nel quale ho fatto la penitentia de quanti peccati ho fatto e sono per fare. Marti prossimo si reciterà la Tragedia, quando V. S. potesse vederla, io la esorterei a venir, perché si spiera che debbia essere cosa rara."[1]

The presentation of *Antigono* followed on February 27, 1565. We know the date with precision from the letter cited above. Temanza said that the play was presented on February 29, but Palladio had given a precise indication of the date. In addition, 1565 was not a leap year.

Vasari gave a diffuse description of the theater: " Ora Federico [Zuccheri] se bene era sollecitato a tornarsene da Venezia, non poté non compiacere e non starsi quel carnovale in quella città in compagnia d'Andrea Palladio architetto: il quale avendo fatto alli signori della compagnia della Calza un mezzo teatro di legname ad uso di Colosseo, nel quale si aveva da recitare una tragedia, fece fare nell'apparato a Federigo dodici storie grandi, di sette piedi e mezzo l'una per ogni verso, con altre infinite cose de' fatti d'Ircano re di Jerusalem, secondo il soggetto della tragedia; nella quale opera acquistò Federigo onore assai, per la bontà di quella e prestezza con la quale la condusse."

These are the only firsthand accounts of the theater, but neither Palladio nor Vasari said where it was installed. The arrangements for its presentation had been made by a part of the Compagnia della Calza called " degli Accesi."[2] It was composed of fourteen members, among whom the prior in office for the three-year term was a Contarini, while three more members of the same family were members. There are notices of ties between some Contarini and Palladio. The Compagnie della Calza, composed of patricians, assumed the task of organizing sumptuous public and private festivals on the occasion of the arrival of some illustrious personage, for marriages, or when they accepted a member of importance among themselves.

The lay company was encouraged in its activities by the senate; we have no information that it organized celebrations on recurring religious occasions or for institutions dependent upon persons in the Church. The celebrations were presented as private festivals and as public ones offered to the citizens; for the most part they consisted of the presentation of theatrical works within a palace. One might suppose that in their pomp they might rival the grand religious exhibitions; recitations in palaces could create a parallel to the religious events that were held in the cloisters of monasteries and that often were daring. It is recorded that *La Mandragola* was presented for the first time in the Convento dei Crociferi.

The Compagnia degli Accesi was founded in 1562, the last among its sisters. It had a brief but intense life which ended, for all one knows, in 1565, when it presented for a single time the *Antigono*, a tragedy by the Vicentine Antonio Pigatti, Conte de Monte. No more was ever heard of the work, but accounts of the theater continue.

If we put accounts of the presentations organized by the Accesi in chronological order, we find first a record by Francesco Sansovino, according to whom, in 1562, in the Palazzo Dolfin at the Rialto, " s'appresentò una Tragedia così fattamente, che in questa parte non si hebbe ad haver punto d'invidia à gli antichi. Percioché il Teatro fu capacissimo di molte migliaia di persone. All'incontro del quale era posta la ricchissima scena, rassomigliante una città con tanto bell'ordine di colonne e di altre prospettive, che fu mirabil cosa a vedere."[3]

Francesco's father Giacomo had worked at the reconstruction of the Palazzo Dolfin from 1536 to about 1550. The son, in *Venezia nobilissima*, mentioned the courtyard " circondato di logge all'usanza romana," which survived until the last decade of the eighteenth century when Selva modernized the building, respecting only the façade. The neoclassical architect would personally have preferred to obliterate that, too, judging the palace to be one of the least notable works by Sansovino,[4] but he encountered opposition among the conservative elements of the city.

Before its restoration, the courtyard had a Doric portico, which had two loggias above it, one Ionic and one Corinthian; above the loggia there was a story with little rooms that had a series of windows forming a nearly continuous series of openings. With the rhythm of solids and voids and with the effect of the loggias, the courtyard was much more airy than that of the Palazzo Corner dalla Ca' Grande, another building by Sansovino.

From notices in the archives we know that later, on January 23, 1563, the Provveditori all'Arsenale ceded to the Accesi eight light galley sails;[5] then, on March 3, 1564, for the induction of Francesco Maria della Rovere into the company, a festival was held for which the architect G. A. Rusconi, noted for his work at the Palazzo Ducale, constructed a theatrical machine called "La cappa," erected on a barge that was moved along the Grand Canal.[6] Next is a document concerning the presentation of *Antigono*, which brings us to February 27, 1565. After that date, we have no further records of either the Accesi or the Compagnie della Calza.

In 1762 Temanza took up the question of the Palladian theater of the Accesi, locating it in the Carità and explaining it in this way: " Io ho un ragionevole sospetto che codesto Teatro sia stato rizzato nel grande atrio corinzio del Monistero della Carità, poco prima ordinato dal Palladio. Veramente toltone i luoghi pubblici, mon v'era forse a piana terra, in Venezia, Sala maggiore né più sfogata di quest'atrio." Then Temanza referred to an inscription " dipinta in un ampio tavolaccio sopra la porta del coro, posto nel secolo scorso da P. Abbate Gozzi, il quale su le rovine dell'Incendio rizzò le fabbriche, che ora si veggono." He read it in this way: " Ubi ligneum extabat Theatrum Opus eximium Palladii - Ab igne vorante consumptum - Palladis Amica Columba - haec Atria lapidea - Virgini, quae pacem peperit Mundo Pacifera erexit - Cui pectus incenderat Caritas - Ne foret incomodus - Diutius ad Templum accessus."[7] It is not clear why Temanza, with such evidence as this right at hand, expressed himself hesitantly about the location of the theater, which he nonetheless judged to be the cause of the fire of 1630, which occurred, according to the author, by spontaneous combustion.

The " reasonable suspicion " of Temanza became a certainty for later authors. The present writer has also had occasion to vouch for the supposition. But now the more profound study of the building and of its history has caused certain doubts to arise about Temanza's statement; we have already found him to be in error when he asserted that the second tablinum had been constructed, as well as on some other points.

Among those who have written about the theater, the references of Gradenigo are interesting. He wrote: " 1565 del mese di febbraio in Canareggio fu fatto un teatro di legno all'antico per opera di Andrea Palladio nel quale un giorno di martedì fu celebrata una Tragedia cioè Ircano Re di Gerusalemme scritta da Antonio Da Monte Vicentino e professore di medicina nello studio di Padova." But the same author, concerning " gli stabilimenti per la musica" in Venice, noted, " merita ... d'essere qui ricordato che nell'anno 1565 la celebre Compagnia della Calza ordinò al sommo Palladio la erezione di un Teatro nel grande Atrio corinzio del Monastero della Carità dentro il quale venne fabbricato di legno sulla forma degli antichi (e forse stimato più di quello di Vicenza)...."[8]

This chronicler is often imprecise and poorly informed. The entries he gives are not dated, but one might suppose that the first was compiled before the edition of the *Vita di Andrea Palladio* by Temanza, and the second after its publication. However, Gradenigo confuses two notices; that which refers to the presentation of the *Talanta* of Aretino, organized by the Compagnia dei Sempiterni in 1541 and fitted out by Vasari in a Cannaregio palace that is also recorded in the *Venezia nobilissima*, and another that concerns the presentation of the Accesi in the theater of Palladio.

We have no information about Padre Gozzi, and every trace of the " tavolaccio " has also disappeared. Temanza said that is was installed above the door in the choir; but would it have been on the ground-floor level over the door used to enter the church from the ante-sacristy, or on the second floor, above the portal by which one entered the " barco " from the corridor that opened into the guest rooms, the abbot's room, and the snail-plan stairs (a portal recorded also in the bill of lading for the stone)? This second supposition seems closer to the truth; Temanza's statement, " affinché non fosse incomodo l'accedere per un percorso più lungo al tempio," makes one think so.

To be sure, many people from Tassini to Zorzi have supposed that the theater was in the part of the peristyle already constructed, a hypothesis which seems more certain from the point of view of logic than Temanza's is. In fact, the atrium, judging from the plans of Palladio, Muttoni, and Selva, had an area of about 18.23 by 8.34 meters (within the columns); that would not have been enough to have housed a theater for which, as Vasari wrote, Zuccheri had prepared twelve square panels of 2.60 meters on each side. In the peristyle, however, the available area amounted to about 27.12 by 21.90 meters. In addition, the installation could have been set up even during the course of construction, as occurred at other times in other locations in Venice.

But if the theater was in the peristyle, why did Gozzi place the inscription so far from it, above the door in the choir, boasting of having built on its site the " Atria lapidea"?

It is certainly not possible that the wooden construction was preserved until 1630, causing the disastrous fire of that year. According to the custom of the time such apparatus, which was made for special occasions, was dismantled immediately; and in a building site full of activity, whether in the atrium or in the peristyle, the theater would have been a noticeable encumbrance.

Moreover, Sansovino, writing in his *Venezia nobilissima* where he recorded the activity of Palladio at the Carità,[9] would have mentioned it. He gave notice of the theater of the Sempiterni built in a Cannaregio palace and that of the Accesi in the Palazzo Dolfin. He also recorded the latter's destruction, which occurred according to custom. Why did he not record a theater still visible in the cloister when he mentioned the " belle, grosse e spesse colonne "?

Nor did Henry Wotton mention it when he wrote at length, and with such admiration, about the Palladian atrium. And Inigo Jones, annotating his copy of the *Quattro Libri* with various observations about the monastery, did not speak of it. He had discussed theaters with Scamozzi, and in his own country he was occupied with architectural theaters inspired by Palladio's works; if there had been a theater by his favorite master visible at the Carità, he certainly would have noted it.

We are able, therefore, to affirm that the theater was not preserved until 1630; such an assertion implies that it was not the cause of the fire.

The fire broke out, as we know for certain, on November 16; in that season of the year, the Venetian fogs hardly make spontaneous combustion a likely possibility in a wooden construction exposed to the elements for sixty-five years and therefore, presumably, rotten. The fire spared the oval stairs, the sacristy, and the entire east wing; it perhaps had its origin in the west wing, where the kitchen and the " camera del foco " were located. Nothing had been built here in the sixteenth century, and the great medieval walls still visible there bear faint traces of what could have been a fire. Jones, in his marginal notes, noted that the upper part of the atrium was for the most part wood of quite solid thickness, as can be seen in the designs (fig. XII). In Venetian construction such material was always used with extravagance; many fires are recorded that were caused by braziers and by other, similar heating systems. At the Carità, a furnace would probably have been in the covered gallery (an element we know through the citation by Jones and from the design already cited) where, probably, there was an abundance of wood (fig. XVI).

Thus, in the long inscription, Padre Gozzi boasts of having substituted the " Atria lapidea," which would not have been a simple thing to burn, for Palladio's "Atrium ligneum." We know that with poetic license it is permitted to use the plural " atria " and the singular " atrium " to mean the same thing. In the inscription given by Temanza one should read in the first line, not " ubi ligneum extabat theatrum," but " ubi ligneum extabat atrium." An inscription installed above a doorway, perhaps in the shadows and written on a " tavolaccio," could have been difficult to read, especially in its highest and most distant lines. At times, Temanza suffered from a " flussione d'occhi " which made it difficult for him to read well.

If the inscription was placed at the second story where one reached the upper choir, it would have alluded instead to the creation of a simpler access to the church, created by building at that level a corridor placed between the perimeter walls of the atrium and the area where the four facing composite columns rose. Before the fire, to enter the choir of the church one followed a long and inconvenient path.

One might, instead, suppose that the theater had been installed in the courtyard of the Palazzo Dolfin, which was about sixteen meters on each side and was surrounded by loggias, as has been mentioned above. In that case, we would be dealing with the same theater described in that palace in the *Venezia nobilissima*; Francesco Sansovino could have dated the presentation of the *Antigono* in 1562 rather than as in 1565, by committing an understandable error; when he wrote, several years had passed since the event.

We have brought out here some possible hypotheses, in the hope that they might be useful to specialists; but " questo benedetto Theatro " has been associated by scholars with the Convento della Carità perhaps only through a string of errors.

NOTES

[1] Vicenza, Biblioteca Comunale, 1565.
[2] L. Venturi, 1909, p. 117.
[3] 1581, p. 406.
[4] Venice, Correr, P.D. 529, *Epistolario Canova-Selva*.
[5] *La Civiltà veneziane del Rinascimento*, 1958, p. 232.
[6] L. Venturi, 1909, p. 112.
[7] 1778, p. 312.
[8] Venice, Correr, Cod. Cic. 3276.
[9] 1581, p. 96 verso.

COMPARATIVE MEASUREMENTS OF THE PROJECTS AND THE EXECUTED BUILDING

LEGEND: A = Project preserved in the Archivio di Stato
B = Project from the *Quattro Libri*
C = Executed parts as they exist

The metric measurements have been calculated on the basis of Palladio's having used a Venetian foot equal to 0.3477 meters.

		A	B	C			A	B	C
EXTERIOR	Length along the rio Sant' Agnese	73	74.60	73	SACRISTY	Length	9.56	9.04	9.60
						Breadth	7.65	9.04	9.60
	Length along the rio Sant' Agnese; part constructed in 16th c.			55.90		Height	5.21	6.26	7.35
	Length, along the calle del Dose	57.03	41.60	57.40	LARGE CHAPTER HALL	Length	14.44	9.04	
	Asymmetrical area		30			Breadth	7.48	9.04	
	Length, along the church	38.25	41.40	38.60		Height	8.69	6.26	
ATRIUM	Breadth	17.38	19.47	20.70	SMALL CHAPTER HALL	Length	9.56		
	Length	15.99	18.23	20		Breadth	7.65		
	Bays	3.47	3.13			Height	5.21		
	Portico	3.47	2.78	3.30					
CLOISTER	Breadth	23.12	21.90	32.00	STAIRWELL	Length	8.51	10.50	10.50
	Length	28.51	27.12	34.00		Breadth	2.45	4.52	4.10
	Bays	3.47	4.52	4.55	CLOISTER GROUND FLOOR	Ceiling height	5.21		6.30
	Portico	3.30	3.30	3.30		Column height		6.26	6.00
REFECTORY	Breadth	8.52	10.43		CLOISTER SECOND FLOOR	Ceiling height	5.21		6.25
	Length	21.73	21.90			Column height		5.56	5.40
	Height	10.43	15.65						
GUESTS' ROOMS	Lengths	6.80			CLOISTER THIRD FLOOR	Ceiling height			5.60
	Breadths	7.65	6.30	6.30		Pilaster height		4.87	4.75
	Heights	5.21							

CHRONOLOGICAL TABLE

1538, 18 February. "Alvise quondam ser Zuanne de pasotti" provides 30,000 bricks for the monastery at a price of L. 5½ per thousand (doc. I).

1541, 26 April. "Messer Hieronimo et messer Piero Corner fo del magnifico messer Philippo" pay 31 ducats to the monastery, and "Antonio Dandolo fo de messer Hieronimo" 60 ducats "in conto della fabbrica del detto monasterio over da essere investidi per conto della detta fabbrica, et non se possino alienar, vender né obligar per alcun altro" (doc. I).

1547, 12 May. By a public grant all the goods, fields, and rights that belonged to the monastery of the Portuensis congregation are turned over to the monastery in Ravenna (Cappelletti, 1885, IV, p. 332).

1548 (before). Some arches located in the first cloister of the monastery have been removed for building (Paoletti, 1893, III, p. 271).

1555, 30 January. Agostino Pasoto, and his nephews Agnolino and Iseppe, undertake to make 20,000 *piere ben conditionate* for the monastery (doc. I).

1561, 1 June. Palladio begins to supervise the construction of the monastery (doc. V).

1561, 1 June. "Accordo et mercato" between the monastery and master mason Antonio da Marcò concerning the reconstruction work (doc. VII).

1561, 24 June. Agreement for carrying away debris and for bringing good earth (doc. I).

1561. The date carved in the frieze of the peristyle.

1562, 1 April. "Bastian fornasiero" (brickmaker) will provide 100,000 *piere ferrarese* at L. 9, s. 15 per thousand for the fabric of the monastery (doc. I).

1562, 14 May. Palladio is paid for the *modello* of the fabric and for having directed the works for the year ending on the first of June next (doc. V).

1563, 20 January. Some work is done with the old stone (doc. VIII).

1564, 13 April. The monastery has bought a load of lead for the works (doc. VIII).

1568. In the "Vita del Sansovino" Vasari publishes remarks about the monastery, speaking of it as if it were completed (Rome, 1953, p. 618).

1568, 3 June. The foundations of the building are measured to evaluate the work of the chief mason (doc. I).

1568, 22 June. In the presence of Antonio da Marcò and the abbot the stone used in the work along the rio di Sant'Agnese is measured to estimate the value of the material used by the stonecutters; the results show that 2,872 feet of stone had been put into place (doc. I).

1568, 29 June. The measurements of the foundations of the fabric taken for the mason's account are again reported (doc. I).

1569, 22 March. To discover if the wages requested by Antonio da Marcò for his services rendered in construction are just, four masons are selected, two by the monastery and two by the master mason (doc. VI).

1569, 15 April. Because the two parties of the compromise referred to above are in disagreement, a fifth mason is nominated to arbitrate; he judges that the agreement will be valid until the end of May (doc. VI).

1569, 3 August. Palladio is charged by the canons to rebuild six coffers in the atrium that were defective (doc. I).

1569, 18 October. The five masons elected to judge the work of Antonio da Marcò decide that he should be paid 2,949 ducats and 5 grossi, subtracting from that figure 16 ducats for the walls which had not yet been whitened (doc. VI).

1569, 30 November. The arbitration cited above is deposited with a notary (doc. VII).

1570, 5 June. Antonio da Marcò declares to the notary that he would be satisfied with 757 gold ducats, subtracting from the stipulated sum that which he had earlier received in anticipation of expenses (doc. VII).

1570, 13 June. An accord between Palladio and the canons for remaking, at the architect's expense, the six coffers (doc. I).

1570, 24 July. The Guardiano Grande of the Scuola della Carità protests that the works has passed beyond the wall that formed the boundary between the monastery and the scuola (doc. I).

1570. Palladio publishes his treatise; the author speaks of the monastery as an already completed work.

1573, March. The stonecutters Antonio da Bissone and Gerolamo Testagrossa present a bill for L. 17,712, soldi 4 for all the stone used in the fabric (doc. VIII).

1574, 11 October. Antonio da Marcò and his brother Giambattista contract to build the new refectory for 260 ducats (doc. I).

1580, 19 August. Death of Andrea Palladio.

1581. In the *Venezia nobilissima*, Francesco Sansovino mentions the " chiostro con belle, grosse e spesse colonne composto da Andrea Palladio nobile architetto " (p. 96 verso).

1595, 14 November. The Scuola della Carità protests because the canons have built above the calle del Dose (doc. XIII).

1595, 17 November. The judges of the Proprio enjoin the canons to destroy what they have illegally constructed (doc. XIV).

1596, 11 January. The canons obtain from the judges of the Proprio the declaration that they have constructed nothing *ex novo* (doc. XV).

1597 (circa). Jones sees the terrace constructed above the atrium of the monastery.

1610, 9 October. The Sindaci del Piovego make measurements of certain buildings along the rio di Sant'Agnese where the prior of the monastery wants to begin new construction (doc. XVII).

1630, 30 November. Fire in the monastery (doc. XIX).

1772. 3 September. The government decides to abolish the Augustinian monasteries, and therefore that of the Carità.

1792, September. The community of the Lateran canons of the Carità, which by that time had been associated with others, is supressed (doc. XXI).

1807, 9 March. The Viceroy of Italy, Eugène Beauharnais, designates the former monastery, scuola, and church of the Carità, where at that time troops were quartered, as the Gallerie ed Accademia di Belle Arti (Archivio dell'Accademia, 1807).

1807, 11 April. The Viceroy approves a project, prepared by the Milanese architect Antolini for modifying the old buildings (loc. cit.).

1807, 3 September. The task of preparing another project is given to the architect Selva (loc. cit.).

1811, 10 April. The first part of the work of modifying the monastery and the church is settled upon (loc. cit.).

1812. Selva has prepared a project for expanding the building into the area that Palladio had designated for the refectory (loc. cit.).

1817, 10 August. The second part of the work, for modifying the building is terminated; this phase pertains especially to the former scuola (loc. cit.).

1819, 22 January. Death of the architect Giannantonio Selva. The continuation of the work is entrusted to his pupil, Francesco Wchowich-Lazzari.

1821, 30 April. Laying of the first stone for the building that will rise on the site formerly designated for the refectory (*Gazzetta veneta*, ad datum).

1829, 29 January. The decree to " repair " the Palladian wing of the peristyle is issued. In consequence of this Lazzari destroys the two return arches on either side of the peristyle and lengthens the arcade to the left and right. He reopened the arches of the Ionic order which had been walled up in 1811, installed the balusters projected by Palladio but never executed, and closed the arches with glass (F. Lazzari, 1835).

1863. The rio di Sant'Agnese is filled in.

1864. The " cavana " on the rio terra' Sant'Agnese is closed.

1938. With the project of the architect G. Cirilli, president of the Academy, the space of the peristyle is divided from the area where the atrium had been in order to obtain some usable space here.

1948. Restoration of the tablinum, removing the great armadios that interfered with seeing the side doors and wall niches. The pavement is reconstructed according to the original scheme. The pilasters on the walls behind the columns are faced with slabs of marble.

1967. The steps in the oval staircase covered in the course of the restorations of 1807-11 are restored; in this way, the original level of the pavement of the stair well is recovered. The work was executed under the direction of the Soprintendenza ai Monumenti.

1970. Restoration of the story with the cells, under the direction of the Soprintendenza alle Gallerie.

DOCUMENTS

The transcription is as faithful as possible to the original, but to facilitate the use of the documents, abbreviations and conventional symbols have been rendered in full. Photographs and transcriptions of some documents which are only referred to here are on deposit at the Centro Internazionale di Studi di Architettura " Andrea Palladio " in Vicenza.

I

Venice. Archivio di Stato, " Inventario del Monastero di Santa Maria della Carità, Sommario delle Scritture ... compilato da Giacomo Cagna e da Girolamo ed Andrea Pisoni," for the years 1578-79, Canonica della Carità, (lacking a signature number). The "Sommario" is cited by Magrini; it contains important information (1845, p. xiv) and has been called irreplaceable by students who have been occupied with problems related to the monastery since Magrini's studies. The present writer had the good fortune of finding it and of transcribing all the information relating to the history of the monument. The "Sommario" is an ordered catalogue of documents, the arguments of which it succinctly reports; that we have been able to add very few documents to the ones it mentions attests to its importance.

... 1411, 4 Novembrio. Baratto fatto tra li Reverendi Canonici de Santa maria della Charità, da una, et il guardian et compagni della scuola de essa charità, per lo qual detti canonici li danno due casette in capo della corte dove è il pozzo, et un altra casetta la quale è in capo del ponte per la qual si và a San Gervaso, con patto che non possino far chiesa ne far altro, ne far celebrar senon per necessità, et ella con licentia del priore, et all'incontro esso Guardian et compagni li dà ducati 2000 d'imprestidi della camera di imprestidi con condicione che non si possino alienare così in Collo. In copia senza sottoscritione con n°. 779.

1411 5 novembrio. Baratto fatto per li ditti canonici da una, et la Scola Carità da l'altra delle due case et horto dove ora è l'hospitale della scuola per 2000 ducati d'imprestidi

. . . . .

1497 (*From the chronology of the documents that precede and follow this one, one can conclude that it was written in December.*) Supplica fatta per li Reverendi Canonici di Santa Maria della Charità di Venetia alli loro convicini di far un pontesello sopra la chale che va à Sant'Agnese di legno per servirsi d'alcune loro case. In copia con le contente fatte per messer Antonio Vituri fo domino messer Andrea et il guardian grando della sua Scuola della charità con n.° 1685.

. . . . .

1498.28.marzo. Parte presa nel maggior consiglio per la quale vien data licentia alli Reverendi canonici petenti di poter fare il ponte del qual nella loro supplicatione per andar dal monasterio loro ad alcune loro case, et stabili, con patto che mai essi Reverendi canonici non possino fabricar ovvero far muro appresso la casa delli nobili de chasa Memo nella Vigna di essi Reverendi canonici per quanto tiene la casa preditta da chasa Memo salvo che per spatio de piedi cinque remoto da detta casa in copia nodaro messere Enea Caspenio nodaro della Corte mazore con n.° 1705.

. . . . .

1498.2.Aprile. licentia data per li magnifici signori alli pioveghi alli Reverendi canonici di santa Maria della charità di Venetia di poter far un volto sopra una calle pubblica che discorre da san Trovaso à sant'Agnese. item che li Reverendi canonici di ditto monasterio possano andar suso (non legitur) da ditto loro monasterio alle sue case che sonno per opposito di quelli. In copia sottoscritta per essi Reverendi di mano propria. con n.° 1706.

. . . . .

1503.4.Aprile. Supplica delli Reverendi Canonici de Madonna Santa Maria dalla Carità de Venetia al Serenissimo Prencipe per poter serrar una Cale qual discorre tra esso Monasterio, et una casa che fù da cha bonza per essi Reverendi Canonici aquistata per potersi allargar con ditto suo Monasterio con la Commission fatta alli signori officiali alle cose pubbliche, che debbano rispondere insieme con la loro resposta, et d'altri in copia sottoscritta da diversi respondenti à favor d'essi Reverendi Canonici, con n.° 1780.

. . . . .

1503.7.Aprile. Supplica delli Reverendi Canonici regulari de santa Maria dalla Charità de Venetia porta a sua serenità nella quale supplicano per potersi allargare il monasterio si degni di concederli, che serrar possino una strada, che discorre dal Canal de san Trovaso piccolo al Rio de santa gniese ch'è tra ditto Monasterio, et la casa de cha bozza che fù del quondam Nicolo aquistata da esso per loro con il respondeat delli signori giudici del piovego che il si può fare, in copia non appar de man de chi sia con n.° 1781.

. . . . .

1538.18.Febraro. Accordo fatto tra il Monasterio de santa Maria dalla Charità de Venetia da una, et ser Alvise quondam ser Zuanne de pasotti per nome suo, et de altri delli pasotti in materia di dar al monasterio della charità miara 30. de piere cotte à pretio de lire 5. e meza il mier, et de ditto pretio si habia à scontar soldi 20. per mier per li debiti à essi pasoti con ditto Monasterio in copia Nodaro messer Bonifacio sulian quondam Mathio da Venetia con n.° 2196.

. . . . .

1541.26.Aprile. Partide de cecca per le qual vien scritto per il magnifico messer Hieronimo et messer Piero Corner fo del magnifico messer Philippo, al Monasterio de santa Maria della Charità de Venetia per portadi in conto della fabrica del detto monasterio over da essere investidi per conto della detta fabbrica, et non se possino alienar, vender nè obligar per alcun altro L. 31 de grossi et un'altra per messer Antonio Dandolo fo de messer Hieronimo al detto Monasterio de ducati 60 del suo cavedal delli 8 per cento condicionadi come in quelle, in copia Nodaro messer Hieronimo di Reni con il recever del ditto Corner delli prediti danari, con n.° 2245.

. . . . .

1555.30.zenaro. Instrumento per il qual ser Agustin Pasoto della contrà de san Nicolò sotto pieve de Sacco facendo per nome suo, et Agnolino, et Jseppo suoi nepoti per li quali promette de ratho si obliga far al Reverendo Procurator del Monasterio de santa Maria dalla Charità de Venetia miara 20 de piere ben conditionate come in quello in copia Nodaro messer Stephano di Astori quondam Zuane da pieve de sacco. con n.° 2472.

. . . . .

1561.24.zugno.
Acordo fatto tra il Reverendo Don Paulo de Venetia per nome del convento de Santa Maria dalla Charità da una et ser Stephano ditto Caster, et Gasparo Zavatin da ovado burchieri dall'altra, in materia de portar via il ruinazzo della fabbrica de santa Maria predetta, et condur terra per bisogno d'essa fabbrica, in copia sottoscritto da esse parti, con n.° 2738.

. . . . .

1562.primo Aprile.
Scritto per il quale ser Bastian fornasiero promette dar al Monasterio de santa Maria dalla Charità de Venetia miara 100 de piere ferrarese à L. 9 s. 15 il mier per la fabbrica di esso Monasterio, in copia de man Zanantonio murer co n.° 2764.

. . . . .

1568.3.Zugno.
Nota delle mesure, et fondamenta della fabbrica per conto del muraro maturade e di ditto insieme con messer Hieronimo Marcolini da Treviso, et maestro Antonio de Zuane muraro in copia non ne è sottoscrittion, con n.° 2974.

. . . . .

1568.22.zugno.
Nota delle mesure della fabbrica del convento de santa Maria della Charità per conto del tagliapietra per li scalini della fondamenta sopra il Rio et canal quali fondamenta sono state mesurade presente il Reverendo Abbate, et il Reverendo Domino Hieronimo da Treviso, et maestro Antonio murer de Marco, quali sono in tutto de netto piedi 2872, come in quella in copia non vi è sottoscrittion. con n.° 2976.

. . . . .

1568.29.zugno.
Mesure delle fondamenta della fabbrica del monasterio, et convento de Madonna Santa Maria dalla Charità de Venetia, per conto del muraro mesurade con la presenza de ser Antonio de Zuane muraro, et messer Hierolimo Marcolini da Treviso, in copia non appar de man de chi sia fatta con n.° 2977.

. . . . .

1569.30.Agosto.
Accordo fatto tra messer Andrea Paladio architetto Vicentino da una, et li Reverendi Canonici del Monasterio de santa Maria dalla Charità de Venetia dall'altra, in materia de riffar sei quadri dell'atrio che sono nel monasterio della charità de Venetia li quali sono stati disfatti, et sono quelli che vanno appresso i capitelli, che confinano con il foro di mezzo, in copia sottoscritto da ditto messer Andrea palladio, con n.° 3011.

. . . . .

1570.13.zugno.
Accordo fatto tra messer Andrea Paladio architetto et cittadino de Vicenza da una, et li Reverendi Canonici de Santa Maria dalla charità de Venetia dall'altra, in materia de disfar a tutte sue spese, et danni li sei quadri del coperto della corte i quali sono de fuori dalle colonne in copia sottoscritto da esso messer Andrea con n.° 3024.

. . . . .

1570.24.Luglio.
Chiamor fatto per il guardian della scola de santa Maria dalla Charità sopra tutti li lavori fatti nel muro del ditto Hospedal per li R.di Canonici della Charità, item sopra tutti i lavori che passa oltra il muro preditto, in copia n.° 3027.

. . . . .

1573. marzo.
Polizza delle pietre vive, che sono nella fabbrica del Monasterio de Santa Maria dalla charità de Venetia date per maestro Antonio Tagliapietra de bissone a san Vidal e maestro Hieronimo testagrossa, in copia senza sottoscrittione con n.° 3116.

. . . . .

1573.primo marzo.
Nota delle pietre vive che sono nella fabrica del monasterio delli Reverendi Canonici de santa Maria della Charità date per maestro Antonio Tagliapietra da bissone a San Vidal, et maestro Hieronimo testagrossa stimate per maestro Antonio de gasparo tagliapietra da S. Apostoli,

et maestro Stephano de Zuane de gazaniga per nome delli sopradetti tagliapietra, et per nome delli Reverendi Canonici preditti per maestro Pasqualin del Zago, et bortholo de domenego tagliapiera eletti per le sopra ditte parti per stimar tutte le ditte piere del sopraditto monasterio date per li sopradetti tagliapietra come in quella copia non vi è sottoscrition. con n.° 3117.

.....

1574.11.Ottobrio.
Scritto per il quale mistro Antonio Murer insieme con mistro Batta suo fratello si obbligano de far alli Reverendi Canonici del Monasterio de santa Maria della charità de Venetia il Refrettorio novo per pretio de ducati 260 come in quello, in copia senza sottoscrittion con n.° 3134.

II

Ibidem, Inventario del Monastero di Santa Maria della Carità, Scuola di Santa Maria della Carità, Busta 43. "Copia tratta dal Capitolare Bergameno della Scuola di Santa Maria della Carità di Battuti di Venetia a carte 25 recto." (The copy refers to the request made by the canons to build the "pontesello" over the calle del Dose; it is more explicit than the source concerning this that we find in the previous document, dated 1497.)

III

Idem, ibidem, busta 43. "Copia tratta dal Notatorio secondo della Scola di Santa Maria della Carità à carta 173 verso." (This reveals that the canons had undertaken construction in their "proprietà e casa;" on August 24, 1543, they promised their neighbor, Anzolo Memmo, who had complained to them about certain corbels that projected into his little courtyard, that when the work was finished, everything would be in its original condition.)

IV

Idem, ibidem, busta 2, loose sheets, "Documenti relativi a lavori." (In this box are the designs for the doorway (fig. XXIV), for the covering in the atrium (fig. XVI), and for the ground floor of the monastery (fig. XVII). The plan of the second floor (*primo piano*; fig. XIX) is in busta 17 ("Documenti relativi a lavori"), and the only comments on it indicate the uses of the various spaces shown there. However, on the parchment that contains the study of the ground floor there is a long statement in the hand of the architect, which is transcribed here, that explains various things. On the back of that sheet is writing that is almost completely rubbed off and that appears to be in Palladio's hand: "Disegno per il Monastero dela Carità." Also written there, in a more recent hand, is this: "N. 1. Disegno del Monastero della Carità.")
The transcription of the caption is as follows:
" Descriptione delli edificij in terra tutti sono manifesti unito presente dissegno coi suoi numeri de piedi in longo et largo. Resta descrivere gli mezadi. quali vanno in questo primo ordine. Sopra la cantina se compartiscono tre mezadi. Una camera per il portinaro larga piedi 8 1/2. seguita la factoria larga piedi 12. Dopo una dispensa da piedi 12. Item sopra la cavana. Uno mezado che sia camera dal farmiliar. Item magazino da grandezza come la camera. El secondo solaro sara nel secondo claustro. Cosci saranno per ordine. contiguo alla giesia sopra la sacristia una camera per il sacrista da piedi 15 Larga. Seguita la libraria da piedi 25 larga. Dopo una camera da piedi 15. Poi seguita anditi et scala si come da sotto. A l'altra banda sopra il lignaro sara il granaro il qual se podara allongare più del legnaro, a piacimento. La longhezza e larghezza sì come il legnaro. Seguita sopra il forno et lavatoio et cirg (*non legitur*) dalla corte Lozza. Seguita il claustro dietro all'ospitale. Et l'altro claustro sopra la cusina se (*non legitur*). Immediate seguita la camera dal foco, qual se intenderà sopra la cusina et dispensa, longa piedi 34 sopra il loco del refrectorio se fara scala per andare su la lozza et in dormitorio. Sopra gli mezadi da la camera fino al muro della giesia sara il Reverendo capitolo. Tutti gli edificij de questo secondo ordine saranno de altezza si come et gli bassi ossia piedi 15. Excepto il capitulo il qual se intenderà alla altezza del dormitorio et lozza. El terzo solaro sarà il dormitorio, el pavimento del qual sara alto da terra 30 piedi. Et a questa altezza item vanno il Refrectorio.
El pavimento in terra "

V

Idem, Sala diplomatica Regina Margherita, n.° 13-LXXIV, raccolta autografi.
(A receipt in Palladio's hand for having made the model of the monastery and for having directed the construction for a year.)

Recto, left side:
" 1561 adì 7 marzo

Messer Andrea Paladio Architetto die dar per scudi 10 forestieri dati per il modello val.	L. 67.
29 luglio per contadi a buon conto per il suo salario de esser soprastante alla fabbrica scudi 6 forestieri	L. 40.4
5 agosto per contadi per stampi di piere	L. 9.
14 per contadi a buon conto del salario scudi 3 forestieri	L. 20.2
6 settembre per contadi scudi 3 venetiani	L. 20.8
3 ottubrio per contadi scudi 3 forestieri meno soldi 6	L. 19.
27 per contadi scudi 6 venetiani	L. 40.16
21 decembrio per contadi scudi 3 venetiani	L. 20.8
11 zener per contadi scudi 4 forestieri	L. 26.16
11 febraro per contadi L. 15 soldi 16	L. 15.16
ultimo per contadi L. 11.2	L. 11.2
1562 adì 11 marzo scudi 2 venetiani	L. 13.12 "

Recto, right side:
" 1561 adj primo zugno
Messer Andrea contrascrito die haver
per il modello della fabbrica scudi 10 fo-
restieri   L. 67.
per stampi di piere L. 9.   L. 9.
per esser soprastante alla fabrica a scudi
40 forestieri al anno incominciando il
sopraditto giorno fino adj primo zugno
1562   L. 268.
adj 14 Mazo del 62
Ricevo io Andrea Palladio dal padre don
Francesco da la carita per compito paga-
mento del mio salario de questo anno
che finisce adj primo zugno che venira et
del modelo de la fabrica et per li stampi
lire trenta nove et soldi diece vale   L. 39 s. 10 "

Verso, left side:
Ricevuta del Palladio
(Note: *Palladio's own handwriting is limited to the actual receipt where the following appears*: " Ricevo io Andrea Palladio... ").

VI

Idem, Notaio Benedetto Soliano, protocolli 1569-70. Zorzi (1964, p. 245) discusses this arbitration almost in its entirety. On March 22, 1569, the abbot Illuminato of Padova and the mason Antonio da Marcò, " murer de San Zorzi," enlisted four masons who were to examine the request for wages made by Antonio da Marcò for the work executed up to that date at the monastery. Antonio had selected Maestro Antonio del Grande, *proto* of the Ufficio del Proprio, and Maestro Giacomo Mazzocco; the abbot chose the masons Battista de Elia and Zannantonio de Cristin. They began on April 15 and dragged their deliberations out through all of May. It was then decided to begin again at the beginning, but because the parties had come to no agreement, a fifth judge, the mason Innocenzo di Francesco Lombardo, was named to the panel.

VII

Idem, Inventario del Monastero della Carità, parte I, busta 27.
The most important parts of this report on the arbitration concerning the construction at the monastery, dating from November 30, 1569, are also given by Zorzi (1964, p. 246). The five judges, taking into consideration the agreement entered into by the fathers and the mason Antonio da Marcò on the first of June, 1561, visited the monastery to inspect the work done there. In a detailed document signed by all five and dated October 18, 1569, they stated:
" che tutti i lavori fatti per ditto mistro Antonio, ... così quelli compresi nel ditto suo accordo de di primo zugno 1561 come quelli fatti oltre suo accordo, montano ducati duemilia, novecento, quarantanove grossi cinque delli quali ducati 2949 grossi 5 li batemo ducati sedese, da L. 6 g. 4 per ducato, per li muri che mancano à smaltar, et così li ditti ducati 2949 g. 5 se intendono da L. 6 g. 4 per ducato, et più delli sopradetti ducati sedese sia abbattudo tutto quello, che ditto mistro Antonio havesse recevudo dalli ditti padri à bon conto delli sopraditti d. 2949 g. 5 che montano i suoi lavori et restante veramente sia pagato per li Reverendi Padri al ditto mistro Antonio subito senza alcuna contraddition, con dechiaratione che la scrittura del suo accordo de di primo zugno 1561 resti firma, et valida per una parte et per l'altra et anchora disemo, che tutta la spesa, che si farà per causa de ditta stima, sia pagata la metà per parte." From the same document it turns out that Paleari was paid up, deducting from the sum what he had received in advance: " Anno nativitatis Domini JC 1570, Ind. XIII, die vero lune, quinto mensis Junij supradictus ser Antonius Paliari de Morcho murator confessus fuit se habuisse, ac sibi bonificatus fuisse a Reverendo in Cristo patre Domino Francisco de Venetijs ad praesens Abbate suprascriptis monasterij Sanctae Mariae Charitatis ducati septingentos quinquaginta septem aurj currentes ad rationem L 6 grossi 4 parvorum pro singulo ducato et grossos quatordecim ad aurum... ".

VIII

Idem, ibidem, busta 6.
The document transcribed here is fundamental for the history of the construction. Although cited by some scholars, no one has ever given careful attention to it. The stonecutters Antonio da Bissone and Girolamo Testagrossa presented an accurate " polizza delle pietre vive " incorporated into the building. Four stonecutters, two representing each of the two parties to the contract, estimated the value of the accepted stone. We thus know what point the construction had reached at the date of the bill of lading (March, 1573); furthermore, from the " Sommario delle Scritture " and from the notes of Inigo Jones we know that construction had been interrupted after the works indicated in the document had been finished; therefore, we are also able to deduce what parts of the building were destroyed in the fire of 1630.

" Adi Marzo 1573:
Polizza delle pietre vive che sono nella fabbrica del Monastero delli Reverendi Canonici di Santa Maria della Carità, date per mastro Antonio tagliapietra de bisson a S. Vidal, et maestro Gierolimo testa grossa, et stimate per magistro Antonio de Gasparo taglia pietra, in contrada di S. Apostolo; Et maestro Stefano de Zuane da gazanega per nome delli sopra detti taglia pietre; Et dall'altra parte per nome delli Reverendi Padri maestro Pasqualino del Zago, et fratello di Domenego taglia pietra eletti per le sopradette parte per stimar tutte le sudette Pietre, nel sopradetto monasterio datte per li sopra detti taglia pietre.

Tutti li scalini della fondamenta sopra il rio, et dentro atorno alla cavana sono piedi 2872 a soldi 24 il piede monta   L. 3446 s. 8

Per il volto della cavana qual sono pezzi n.° 15 computando li doi pezzi delle jmposte qual sono redutti tutti in piedi 34 a s. 2. 4 il piede monta   L. 40 s. 16

Per il Crescimento della porta appresso il ponte cioè delle fondamenta, insuso sono pezzi n.° 5 computando el sogier di sopra sono p. 13 a s. 24 qual monta   L. 15 12

Per il crescimento qual sono alla porta della Cavana dalla fondamenta in suso pezzi n.° 2 qual fanno le erte di detta porta, sono p. 8 a s. 24 il piede monta   L. 9 s. 12

Per pezzi n.° 8 su la Cantonada del ponte quali fanno Cadena alla rustica sono tutti p. 22 1/2 a s. 24 monta   L. 27 s.

Per li scalini apresso alla scala approdo n.° 53 sono tutti p. 212 a s. 27 il pe, monta   L. 286 s. 4

Per il zocholo ch'è sotto alla base delle colonne doriche in terra piana qual camina da uno capo all'altro della fazada del Claustro et volta sotto le due colonne che sono per testa sono tutto p. 88 1/2 a s. 30 il pe monta   L. 132 s. 15

Per le Cimaze delle imposte, delli volti delli Pilastri n.° 9 delle loggie da basso dell'ordine dorico sono in tutto p. 113.08 a s. 70 el pe monta   L. 397 s. 17.

Per li socholi soto li detti 9 Pilastri sono in tutto p. 103 1/2 a s. 45 il pe monta   L. 243 s. 4

Per li Architravi pezzi n. 8 quali fanno cadena sopra alli volti del primo ordine longhi pie 3 l'uno sono tutti p. 24 a s. 36 1/2 el pie monta   L. 67 s. 16

   L. 4667 s. 4

(pagina seconda)

Per le base delle colonne dorice del primo ordine n.° 7 in terra piana a L. 31 l'una monta   L. 217 s.

Per li capitelli n.° 7 sopra dette colonne dorice, à L. 19 s. 2 l'uno montano   L. 238 s. 14.

Per doi basi delli cantonali che compagna le dette colonne a L. 25 l'una s. 10 monta   L. 31 s. —

Per li doi capitelli sopra detti cantonali à L. 15 s. 10 l'uno monta   L. 31 s. —

Per due porte in le stancie da basso e pe piano di una pietra e mezza alta p. 6 large pe. 3 in luse sono tutte due p. 40 a s. 33 il pè, monta   L. 66 s.

Per una porta da necessario da basso de una pietra sono p. 17 a s. 14 il pe monta   L. 11. s. 18

Per porte n.° 3 soazade delle stanze da basso à pe piano in nel Claustro alte de luse p. 7 large p. 3 1/4 à precio de L. 83 s. 14 l'una monta   L. 251. s. 2

Per un armario in una stanza da basso à muro d'una pietra alto p. 4 largo p. 2 1/2 sono pezzi 15 à s. 14 monta   L. 10. s. 10

Per la porta della foresteria sopra la Cavana de una pietra alta in luse, p. 6, larga p. 3 sono tutta p. 20 a s. 16 il pe. monta   L. 10. s. —

Per una porta che va in chiesa soazada all'incontro de quella della sagrestia, alta p. 8. 1/4 larga p. 4 con scalini n.° 3 apprestata detta porta fornita con le sue erte, friso, cornice, et scalini con quanto fornimento se contiene di pietre vive in detta porta, monta L. 189. s. 10: val.   L. 189. s. 10

Per la porta che va in sagrestia all'incontro della su detta alta p. 8. larga p. 4 s. 50 il pe., sono pe. 26 monta   L. 65. s. —

Per due porte soazade in sacrestia, alte p. 6 large p. 3 a L. 105. s. 8. l'una   L. 210. s. 16

Per due colone mandolate in sacrestia con base et capitelli   L. 955. s. —

Per due base, et doi capitelli sopra alli pilastri all'incontro delle dette colonne monta   L. 37. s. —

Per le cornise sopra le dette colonne con architrave sono p. 15 l'una a L. 5.s. 21.— el pe misurade à torno monta   L. 155. s. —

Per una finestra che guarda sotto all'Atrio in sagrestia, alta p. 7. 1/2 larga p. 5 sono pe 21 a s 33 il pe, monta   L. 34. s. 13

   L. 2790 s. 3

(pagina terza)

Per una finestra tra il Claustro grande, et l'Atrio, sopra alla porta della tramesera alta p. 6. larga p. 3. di una pietra, sono pie 20 a s. 16. il pie, monta   L. 16. s —

Per una finestra nel cantone dell'atrio nel muro della Sagrestia con la ferriata alta p. 6 larga p. 3. sono p. 20. d'una pietra e mezza à s. 33 il piè monta   L. 33. s. —

Per una finestra picciola in sagrestia sotto alla scala co' ferri, larga p. 2. alta p.2 1/2 de una pietra sono tutta pie 11 a s. 16. il piè, monta   L. 8. s. 16

Per una porta terrena nel canton sotto l'atrio, sotto la finestra alta p. 6. 1/2 larga p. 3. d'una pietra e meza sono tutta p. 21 a s. 33 al pie, monta   L. 34 s. 16

Per finestre n.° 2 che guardano sopra al Canal grande nella scala a buovolo, una alta p. 6. larga p. 3. sono. p. 20. l'altra alta. p. 5. 1/2 larga. p. 3. tutte due à muro de una pietra e meza, sono. p. 19. sono tutte due. p. 39. a s. 33. il pie, monta — L. 64. s. 16

Per una finestra sopra alle dette alta. p. 5. 1/2. larga p. 3. di una pietra e meza, sono. p. 19. a s. 33 il pe, monta — L. 31. s. 16

Per la porta soazada sopra il. primo solar, nella scala à buovolo, soazada con friso, et cornise alta p. 7 1/2 larga p. 4. senza soier da basso, monta — L. 148. s. 16

Per la porta che va sul Coridor alta. p. 7. 1/2 larga. p. 3 a muro da due pietre senza soier da basso, sono. p. 19. a s. 24 il pie, monta — L. 50 s. —

Per doi scalini sotto detta porta longi tutti dui. p. 7 a s. 24 il pie, monta — L. 8. s. 8

Per le piane del Coridor che vanno in Choro longe tutte. p. 34. large. p. 32. à 1.5; s. 5. il pie, monta — L. 179. s. 17

Per modioni n.° 8 sotto dette piane soazadi, a L. 14 s. 10. l'uno, monta tutti — L. 116. s. —

Per la porta alla Camera. del Reverendo padre Abbate alta pie. 6. 1/4. larga. p. 3. soazada, monta — L. 83. s. 14.

Per due porte in detta Camera schiette, d'una pietra e meza, alte. p. 5. 1/2; senza soier da basso sono tutte due. p. 29. a s. 33 il pie monta/ — L. 47. s. 17.

———

D. 822 g. 15

Per finestre n.° 4. che guardano sotto l'attrio nell'Andito della Camera del Reverendo padre Abbate d'una pietra e meza alte. p. 6.

(pagina quarta)

large p. 3. l'una, sono in tutte. p. 80. a s. 33 il pie monta — L. 132. s. —

Per il Zocholo che è sopra la coperta della cornice dorica tramezo gli archi delle colonne joniche, et sotto le base di dette colonne sono. p. 116. a s. 29. il pe monta — L. 168. s. 4

Per la coperta della cornice dorica. P. 81. à s. 90 il pe: — L. 364. s. 10

Per pezzi n.° 4. di detta coperta quali sono fuori d'opera sono p. 8. 1/2. a s. 90. il pe, monta — L. 38. s. 5

Per la sotto base over Zocholi sotto li Pilastri del ordine jonico che tuol suso l'imposto delli su la prima loggia sono tutti 8 pilastri. p. 100 once 9. a s. 40. il pie, monta — L. 201. s. 10

Per le cimase sotto l'imposte delli volti, de detti pilastri. 8. sono. p. 120. 1/2 a s. 66 il pie, monta — L. 397. s. 13

Per base n.° 7 delle colonne joniche su la prima loggia a L. 26 s. 11. l'una monta — L. 186. s. —

Per capitelli n. 7. di dette colonne joniche a L. 31. s. — l'uno, monta — L. 217. s. —

Per due base, et dui capitelli delli cantonali che compagnano dette colonne, joniche, monta — L. 87. s. 11.

Per pezzi n.° 7. che fanno chiave dell'Architravo della cornice jonica longi. p. 3. l'uno, sono. p. 21. tutti, a s. il pe, monta — L. 89. s. 6

Per porte n.° 4. soazade su la. prima loggia con cornisi, friso, alte. p. 6. once. 2. large pie 3. once 2. a L. 83. s. 14. l'una, montano tutte dette — L. 334. s. 16

Per due porte in le foresterie d'una pietra è meza schiette, alte, p. 6. large. p. 2. 3/4 sono tutte pie. 39. a s. 35 il pie, monta — L. 64. s. 7

Per una portella da necessario in una di dette forestarie alta. p. 5. larga pie 2. 1/4 d'una pietra picciola, sono tutta pie. 16. e 1/2 a s. 14. il pie monta — L. 11. s. 11

Per una porta in la foresteria appresso alla scaletta à muro d'una pietra, alta, p. 5. 1/2 larga p. 2. once 4 sono pie. 17. 1/2. a s. 16. il pe, monta — L. 14. s. —

Per la coperta della cornise jonica la qual è longa. p. 96. a s. 80. el pe, monta — L. 384. s. —

Per base. 9. delli Pilastri Corinti a L. 7. s — l'una monta — L. 63. s. —

Per Capitelli. 9. sopra a detti pilastri a. L. 21. l'uno monta — L. 189. s. —

———

L. 2882. s. 13

(pagina quinta)

Per porte n.° 12. delle celle schiette d'una pietra e mezza, alte p. 5. 3/4 large p. 2. 1/2 sono pie 18 1/2 l'una, sono tutte dette. p. 222. a s. 33 il pie monta — L. 366. s. 6

Per finestre n.° 7 soazade nel dormitorio che guardano sopra al Claustro grande, con friso et cornise disopra, alte, p. 6. large p. 3. a L. l'una computando le cornise sotto alle piane monta — L. 500. s. 6

Per finestre n.° 4 che guardano su l'Atrio computando quella che fa da porta, alte. p. 6. large. p. 3. sono pie. 20. l'una, a muro d'una pietra e mezza, sono tutte pie 80 a. s. 33 il. p. monta — L. 132. s. —

Per una porta in cima alla scala a buovolo alta p. 7. 3/4 larga pie. 4. senza soier da basso, a muro de due pietre, sono tutte pie. 20. 1/2 a s. 50. il pie la qualè in capo del dormitorio, monta — L. 51. s. 5

Per una finestra in la camera in testa al dormitorio sopra alla capella, alta. p. 5.

larga. p. 3. d'una pietra e mezza, sono tutte. p. 18. a s. 33. il pie, monta L. 29. s. 14

Per la gorna sopra al muro della chiesa, guarda su l'Atrio, sono. p. 62. 1/2. a s. 30. il pie, monta L. 92. s. 15

Per li scalini della scala à buovolo, n.° 96. a L. 12. s. 10 l'uno monta L. 1200. s. —

Per patti n. 8 in deta scala a L. 21. l'uno, monta L. 168. s. —

Per una porta che va sopra alla capella della chiesa, d'una pietra e meza alta. p. 6. larga p. 3. sono tutta pie 20 a s. 33 il pe, monta L. 33. s. —

Per una finestra in detta camera alta pie 4. 1/2 larga. p. 3. sono tutte. p. 17. d'una pietra e mezza. a s. 33 il. p. monta L. 27. s. 4

Per una finestra in la scala à buovolo, guarda sopra alla porta della sagrestia, d'una pietra, alta. p. 6. larga. p. 3 sono tutta. p. 20. a s. 16. il pie monta L. 16. s. —

Per un portale che va sopra alla loggia, delle foresterie alto. p. 10. 1/2 largo. p. 4. once 8. soazado con friso, et cornise co due cartelle, monta L. 242. s. 9.

Per finestre n. 12. su la fazada del rio, delle stanze da basso, d'una pietra è mezza, alte. p. 7. large p. 3. sono pie. 22 l'una, sono tutte. p. 264. a. s. 33. il pie monta tutte L. 435. s. 12

(pagina sesta)

Per finestre n.° 12. delle camere del secondo ordine delle foresterie alte. n. 6 large. p. 3. d'una pietra e meza, sono pie. 20. l'una, sono tutte. p. 240. à s. 33. il piè, monta L. 396. s. —

Per il crescimento di 11 piane delle dette finestre, butando fuori quella della scala a buovolo, sono: p. 20. a s. 33. il pie. L. 33. s. —

Per finestre n.° 12. delle celle, computando quella della scala a buovolo, alte. p. 5. large. p. 3. sono piè. 18 l'una, a muro d'una pietra e mezza; sono tutte. p. 216. a s. 33 il pie, monta L. 356. s. 8

Per la gorna sopra al claustro. p. 100. a s. 62. il p. monta L. 310. s.

Per la gorna sopra all'Atrio sono. p. 57. 1/2 à s. 62 il. p. monta L. 177. s. 15

Per la gorna sopra alla fazada del rio, sono. p. 182. 1/2. con li voltari delle teste à s. 62. il pie, monta L. 565. s. 15

Per doi pezzi di pietra grezzi, per far doi modioni sotto le gorne su li cantoni della fazada sopra il rio, li quali modioni fece maestro Agostino, quali pezzi era de. p. 2. p. quadro, et grossi once 6. sono tutti doi miara. 1. a L. 5. il Miaro L. 5. s. —

Per la piera grossa di doi base grande delle colone dell'Atrio sono miara. 16. a. L. 5. il miar, monta L. 80. s. —

Per la fattura delle due dette base à duc: 15 l'una monta tutte due L. 186. s. —

Per due tavole di pietra grezza soto due delle dette base dell'Atrio, sono miara, 6. 1/2 a. L. 5 s. il miar, monta L. 32. s. 10

Per un altra tavola delle dette base grezza, sono miara 3. 1/2 a L. 5. s. — il miar, monta L. 16. s. 5

Per la pietra grezza d'un'altra base del detto attrio sono miara 8 à L. 5 il miaro L. 40. s. 1

Per un pezzo grezzo per coprir una delle dette base che era fatta delle pietre del Monasterio longo. p. 3. 1/2 largo. p. 1. e 1/4 grosso, p. 1. monta L. 4. s. 4.

Per li. 8. Abachi delli capitelli delle colone dell'Atrio, montano tutti L. 236. s. —

Per una nappa rossa nella camera sopra la cavana monta L. 93. s. —

Per una napa bianca nella terza camera nelle foresterie di sopra monta L. 50. s. —

Per quattro pietre da fuogo nelle. 3. foresterie et una nella camera del Reverendo padre Abbate de. p. 5. l'una sono tutte. p. 20. a L. 2. il. p. monta L. 40. s. —

L. 2621 s. 17

(pagina settima)

Per fattura di dette pietre, monta tutte a s. 50. l'una L. 10. s. —

Per un' altra nappa rossa nella camera del Reverendo padre Abbate monta L. 93. s. —

Per la fattura delle. 3. base delle colonne grande dell'Atrio a ducati 15 l'una monta L. 279. s. —

Per una pila in barbaria da lavar la testa L. 12. s. 8.

Per una nappa schietta nel camerino della foresteria di mezzo L. 6. s. 4.

Per la manifattura del portal rustico davanti la sacristia L. 9. s. —

Per una pila della cisterna senza rodolo: L. 6. s. 4.

Per la fattura della finesterella del reloio L. 1. s. 4

Per dui pezzi de scalini con il baston, tondati, per testa fuori d'opera L. 6. s. 12

item dovemo haver per la fattura de alcuni lavori de pietre vecchie, delle quale non è stato fatto debitor al libro, fu a di 20. genaro 1563 L. 35. s. 5.

item fu adi. 13. aprile. 1564. per la partida del piombo posta al detto libro in suo debito L. 11. s. 8

L. 490. s. 1

per una napa mandolata alla francese nella camera de mezo nelle foresterie monta   L. 93. s. —

per una napa francese in la terza camera nelle foresterie di sopra monta   L. 50 s. —

L. 633 s. 1
L. 2621 s. 17
L. 3994 s. 11
L. 2882. s. 13
L. 822. s. 15
L. 2790. s. 3
L. 4667. s. 4

L. 17712. s. 4

IX

Idem, Inventario del Monastero di S. Maria della Carità, Scuola di S. Maria della Carità, busta 43.

This box contains various manuscript and printed documents that permit one to follow the decades-long litigation between the monastery and the scuola. On March 26, 1586, the public official Andrea de Guaschi was sent by the government to discover in what parts of the building the symbol of the scuola (two concentric circles intersected by a cross) was visible. His inspection was very careful; because his information is especially detailed for the courtyard that the monastery and the scuola both used, one can draw the conclusion that the canons intended to continue construction in order to complete the Palladian project and that this would have led them to encroach upon the courtyard.

X

Idem, ibidem.

In a document that on the basis of other documents may be dated to 1590, the canons protest because a dormer window (" luminale ") had been constructed above the roof of the hospice of the Carità; from it one could see into the interior conventual spaces. Up to that time their independence had been respected.

XI

Idem, ibidem.

Andrea de Guaschi, who in 1586 had made the report about the symbols of the scuola visible in the courtyard, measured the distance between the new dormer window, another that already existed, and the conventual property. The document is not dated.

XII

Idem, ibidem.

In an undated document the canons affirm that they have no desire to impede the scuola from " alzar esse sue case dell'hospedal," but they demand that all the windows of the hospice be high above the ground and equipped with iron bars and glass in a manner that " non si possi da esse finestre veder nel Monasterio medesimo, né da esse uscire, et venir in esso Manasterio."

XIII

Idem, ibidem.

" Chiamor sopra il volto del ponte ": the scuola protested because the monastery had constructed over the calle del Dose and had occupied it, contrary to the pact signed on June 25, 1497. The judges of the Proprio ordered an inspection to be made; it revealed that there was indeed new construction in that area. This probably pertains to the so-called little study (*studietto*) that on one side abutted one side of the monastery, and on the other, some other buildings of the canons that were beyond the calle. The inspection was made on November 14, 1595; the entire affair leads one to suppose that the scuola feared that the new works were preparations for the construction beyond the calle of the refectory that would have disrupted the site of their hospice.

XIV

Idem, ibidem.

On November 17, 1595, the judges of the Proprio enjoined the canons to destroy what they had illicitly constructed.

XV

Idem, ibidem.

" In causa clamoris."

In the following January (11 " zenero " 1595 in the Venetian calender) the canons obtained from the judges of the Proprio the declaration that they had not constructed anything new; the document of the *proto* Cesare Zoreto, the representative who had been along for the new inspection, was accompanied by a sketch that is now not to be found.

XVI

Idem, ibidem.

" Mesure tolte per me Ottavio Peruzzi."

On September 25, 1610, at the request of the monastery and on commission of the government, the measurements of the courtyard between the monastery and the scuola were once again checked.

XVII

Idem; ibidem, busta 17, documents concerning the work.

" Mesure de confini tolte de mandato de Magnifici Signori Sindici de Piovego." The measurements, which were taken on October 9, 1610, were requested because Padre don Agostino, prior of the monastery, " intende a refabricare da novo una sua proprietà " along the rio di Sant'Agnese. This could still be related to the area that was intended for the refectory.

XVIII

Idem, ibidem, busta 43.

In a printed "strida" dated July 18, 1628, the canons boast in a haughty tone of having always won their suits against the scuola, but they add that if the affirmations of the "Guardian grando" of the scuola that now the scuola members desire to "vivere in pace" with the monastery is true, the canons are satisfied "che sia levata la pena di Ducati mille d'oro concordata tra noi in occasione di trasgressione." It is not clear what all this alludes to; however, among the suits pressed by the scuola there is a record of one that concerned the construction of the studietto: "... pretendeste, che l'aria della Calle fosse vostra, con levarci l'autorità di fabricar il volto del Monasterio sopra il ponte, e il studietto della Casa nostra pur sopra la Calle, e pur la perdeste."

XIX

Idem, Miscellanea codice di storia veneta, Sansovino, "Cronica veneta," busta 68-70.

"... 1630 16 novembre si attaccò il foco nel convento della Carità et restò in buona parte incendiato."
This chronicle records many events of war and peace that are more or less notable; in the year 1630 the macabre events surrounding the plague then raging are cited with much emphasis. The note reported here, referred to by Temanza as well, records the fire that put an end to the expansion of the monastery.

XX

Venezia, Museo Correr, Cod. Cic. 1976, Coll. Mss. VI 799, "Trattato dele diligenti osservazioni fatte sopra le fabbriche d'Andrea Palladio visentino le qualli si mirano nella Inclita Città di Venezia, espresse in versi da Antonio Visentini veneto..."

Transcribed here is what Visentini said concerning the monastery. Some of the information is interesting, and certain considerations show how facts about the history of the monastery had been lost.

"Del Convento della Carità, e prima del Atrio"

L'Architetto

> Questo Convento con quanto gli hò descritto
> Il Palladio lo fece, e più credea
> Di compirlo intieramente, che dovea
> Li Canonici stessi ben politto
>
> Ridurlo a perfezion bensì compitto
> Goderebbe un Convento assai sontuoso
> Mà il tempo ogni cosa ha traditto
> E rimasto gli fù inoperoso
>
> Voglio dir così tronco è derelitto
> Idea grande gli mostra in poco sito,
> Potea perfecionarsi, mà i contanti
> Li mancò ai Canonici incostanti
>
> Non ostante però lei vederà
> Ciò ch'il Palladio disposto, e ben volesse
> Una fabbrica insigne, e convenisce
> All'Abbazia pomposa come và.
>
> Ecovi quì l'Atrio posto in prima
> Il Palladio lo dispose con dotrina
> D'Ordine Composito volea che fosse fatto
> Sì come gli se lo havea pensatto
>
> Di Colonnatti rotondi intieramente
> Isolati bensì tutti ugualmente,
> Di sopra un terazzato con renghiera
> Cosa legera sì, e di buona maniera
>
> Nel suo Libro lui pose li disegni
> Di quanto intendea che fosse fatto
> Mà al certo, qui nel Atrio non è statto
> Eseguito il pensier de suoi ingegni
>
> Le osservazioni dunque sieno talli
> Quanto saria il suo libro per modelli
> Il present'è diverso ben assai
> Più non si riconosce l'Atrio mai
>
> Non ostante però che sia diverso
> Ciò fece il Palladio per converso
> Pensò ben sì che tal cosa fosse
> Natta d'opinion per molte cosse
>
> Si potria dir che la spesa andasse
> Ad'una suma importante, e non bastasse
> Quantità di denari per compire
> Et risolvesse cossì, fè eseguire
>
> Al Palladio come che si vede
> Di un Ordin Dorico ben legato
> Con Arcatte e Pilastri appoggiatto
> Sopra di un sol gradino, che non cede
>
> Le Arcatte son quattro in ogni latto
> Alzano la Seraglia, e pogian su l'Imposte
> La Cornice che portan ben disposte
> Li Modiglioni suoi col riquadratto
>
> Questa cornice ha molto del variatto
> Circa l'Ordine suo qual'è Toscano
> Ma il Palladio che volse un bel inganno
> Formò la Cornice Ionica sol quanto
>
> Questa è legera, è con Modiglioni
> Fà bella vista, e core ne cantoni
> Tutta seguente, e licia in buona vista
> E sopra le mezarie, finestre aditta
>
> Da sole fascie queste vien legatte
> E di sopra in distanza ben seratte
> D'altra Cornice che sostien la gorna
> Con Modiglioni, e questi in buona forma
>
> L'Atrio s'è osservato quanto basta
> Entriamo adesso dov'è la Sagrestia
> E questa sì, ch'ella fu adempia
> Giusto il disegno, e come và la stampa

Qui v'è l'Ingresso quadratto e bello
Una porta per facciata riempe quelo
La prima è nell'Atrio e la seconda
Alla Sagrestia vi porta, ben adorna

Sopra di questa un Sepolcro vi è
Di Briamonte Capitano illustre,
Due bassi rilevi di Bronzo l'adorna ed è
Opera di Vitorio Gambello che riluce

L'altra alla Scalla a lumaca vi conduce
E la quarta nella Chiesa introduce
Entriamo pur per hora in Sagrestia
Per mirar la sua forma, e come sia

L'Ingresso a Nichio, e corisponde questo
Al compagno di fronte che ha Altare
Due Colonne Doriche quì stare
Isolate con Pilastri di buon sesto

Quatro Nichi son che adornan insieme
Con due porte di fronte, e tre finestre
Sopra delle Colonne le Cornici Sestte
Architravatte, e con goccie che stà bene

Il Sofito stà a voltto con Lunette
Graciose sì, e liscie ben politte
Di bel'aria in tutto compartitte
Così alla Sagrestia non manca niente

Altro da dir non vi è, se non andare
Ad'osservar la Scalla, che in buon fare
Comoda assai, e aperta stà nel mezzo
Fita nella muraglia ogni suo pezzo

La sua forma è a Lumaca giusta, e bella
Introduce in convento ben per quela
Questa è la prencipal, e stà arrichitta
Di Nichi con finestre assai politta

Nel primo Coridor che si assende
V'è la porta famosa che fà pompa
Il Palladio la fece giusta à posta
Simile à quella, che a Tivoli lui vide

Streta al di sopra, e larga più di soto
Questa maniera si dice Vitruviana
Essendo che Vitruvio ci dà tutto
Al Cap. 6°: nel suo Libro 4°, è acompagna

L'opinion sua il Palladio per bisara
Solo vi agiunse le rechie o sia cartelle
Per distinguersi un poco più da quele
E cossì abbelj il Coridor con pompa rara.

Andiamo hora nel Inclaustro e si osservi
La bisaria, il pensier per tutt'i versi
Che in questo il Palladio praticò
Per far conoscere il suo saper, e quanto oprò.

Di sei Archi è composto con Colonne
D'Ordine Dorico il primo qual compone
Le sue Pilastratte forte e più dispone
La sua Pianta sopra d'un zocolino con ragione

Le Arcatte che in questo son disposte
Libere senza seraglia è state poste
Sono ben sì appogiatte alle sue Imposte
Con ottima ragion ben composte

La sua Cornice Dorica che chiama
Le Metope, e Triglifi ch'acompagna
Qui si osserva variata e da mirarsi
Che in vece de Triglifi le Boine teste starsi

Le Metopi che honora tal Cornice
Altro non sono se non Scudi rotondi
Con binda al di soto, che alli Cornii
Delle Testte Boine ben si unisce

Di questa novità che se ne dice
Al certo il Palladio quì pensò
Di poter far cosa nova, e inventò
La legatura cossì far acciò compisce

L'Ordine ben compostto e se dicesce
Che l'ingegno sol basta per far bene
Unindo le cose sempre che conviene
Disponendole in forma ch'apparisce

Di perfetto saper, e comparisce
l'Ordine giusto e in buona semetrja
E chi pensar di più mai potrja
Per far cosa agiustatta, e che dovesse

Arichir ben cossì il nobil Fregio
Con la Cornice sopra e bel ripiego
Vi ha posti li dentelli assai gentilli
Che legiadra, e compitta, serva à queli

Questa Cornice al certo ell'è vistosa
E diversa da ciò vien praticatto
Ma il Palladio pur cossì ha pensatto
Variarla ne suoi membri, e sia pomposa

E parimente così anche l'Architrave
con due fascie ha posto, e Tenia in cima
Con caveto, e tendin che fà gran mina
Acciò la Cornice tuta sia eguale

Di sopra à questo vi è l'Ordine Ionico giusto
Con Colonnatti, e sue Arcatte parimente,
Pianta sopra zocolo conveniente
E nelle Arcatte poi, por il Balaustro

E si conosce questo ben a punto
Dalle mezze Colonnelle che son poste
Al peduzo delle Erte assai composte
Per terminarlo poi giusto il suo conto

O' quanto comparisce l'Ordine legero
Osservando il gentile Capitello
Con le Volutte sì ben lavoratte
Adorne de suoi ricci, giust'ed esatte

La Cornice che porta ell'è ben giusta
Al Ordine suo tutta compita
Con Modiglioni a cartelle e più politta
Comparisce col Fregii gonfio, e cossì aditta

Esser nel suo dover assai perfetta,
L'Architrave hà tre fascie con goletta
E così se ne stà tutta contenta
Nella sua proporzion come s'aspetta

Sopra di questo v'è l'Ordine Corinthio
Sono Pilastri semplici, e assai grevi
La Base sua è Toscana senza honori
Pogia questa, sopra fascia ben al drito

Qui non vi è Arcatte, mà tutto sta ripieno
Porta Finestre nel mezzo con ingegno
Pogian queste sopra un Pidestillo
Con Cimacia, e con Base, giust'a pieno

E da l'una e dall'altra passa in fascia
Così la legatura mostra grazia
Le Finestre ancor esse son'adorne
Di Cornici con Fregio gonfio in buone forme.

La Cornice degli Pilastri Corinthii
Questa tien del Compositto al quanto
Fregio drito essa porta con bel fasto
E Modiglioni fasciati, ben compitti

Nella gola di sopra sta la gorna
La qual versa l'aqua del Coperto
Sopra d'ogni Pilastro, Testa certo
Di Mascheron che dalla boca dona

L'aqua ch'egli riceve in buona soma
Di sopra pure si osserva alquanto drito
Ove son posti li copi, che politto
Conduce l'aqua alle gorne, e cosa buona

Il tutto s'è osservatto atentamente,
Quì altro non vi resta da vedere
Di tutto ciò che il Palladio con dovere
Sta ordinato in tal Fabbrica prudente

Anche il di fuori acorda unitamente
Con il corso delle fascie che ripiega
Dalle Cornici piglia sua figura vera
E così stringe a dover graciosamente

Hora la visita è fata, ne vi resta
Se non di dir come si manifesta
Queste fabbriche per una cosa rarra
Che se fosse compita saria vaga

Vaga per il pensier e per la molle
Del Inclaustro grandioso, e più di lode
Acquistarebbe il Palladio intieramente
Se il tutto fosse compito con tal mente

Convien ben dir che il Palladio intendesse
Assai ben giusta la vera Architettura
Ed in pocesso d'ogni sua misura
Fosse, accomodandola come lui volesse

E quante lui ne fece, sempr'è statte
Di bel aspetto e su l'antica forma
Conoscente ben lui, che si diforma
Scavalcando le regole pregiatte

Di bella proporzion sempre stimatte
Ne mai si vide del Palladio cosa
Che non fosse eccelente, e più pomposa
Come questa, e le altre osservate

Dunque si dica e dirà assai bene
Che il Palladio fù grande Architetto costante
Per il saper ch'avea di sienze tante
Distinguendosi come che conviene.

Io crederei che quanto s'è osservatto
Servir ben possi per esser pregiatto
Il suo Nome che tanto ha acquistatto
Di lode, e stima, ed da esser imitatto.

Il Cavalier risponde

Anche di questa son rimasto contento
E di quanto ho veduto architettatto
Del Palladio valente che ha operatto
Confesso il vero che tutt'è portento

Per veder cose tali ogni momento
Che si perdi gl'è tormento
Tanto son pago, e sodisfato insieme
Acquistando saper quanto conviene

Mai partirei da tali viste al certo
Dal contento che provo in veder questo
Ed ogni altro che il Palladio fece
Essendo tutto giusto, e ben si dice

Che le Fabbriche sue son distinte
Per la sua Architetura sì coretta
E ciò importa più semplice, e schietta
Giusto il metodo suo che si distingue

Da tutti gl'altri Architetti unicamente
Per particolar e giustamente
Avendosi fatta maniera propria sua
E nella proporzion che à lui parea

Ben cosa giusta, e assai regolata
Da tanti esempi che vide, e ch'amirò
Come lui stesso dice, ed aprovò
Per vera Antichità sola pregiata

Il studio che lui fece, e la racolta
Nel suo Libro stampò più d'una volta
E questo acciò ch'ogn'uno si valesse
De suoi studi in profito, ed imparasse

In soma se altro lei sà che quì vi fosse
Sarrà ben speso il tempo, là portarsi
Per veder tutto, e niente mai scordarsi
Ma intieramente osservar le belle cose."

XXI

Idem; ibidem, Cod. Cic. 2008, " Chiesa di Santa Maria della Carità."

" ...1792 settembre fu completa la soppressione de Canonici di Santa Maria della Carità, decretata dal Principe e alcuni effetti mobili di quella chiesa furono donati a quella di Santa Maria Maddalena."

XXII

Idem, ibidem, Cod. Cic. 3276, fasc. 13, extracts from the Codici Gradenigo concerning Venetian festivals, here an entry about " Teatri."

Palladio's Venetian theater is mentioned, stating that it was " in Cannareggio."

Idem., entry about " Memorie storiche sugli stabilimenti per la Musica eretti in Venezia." Here the same information is repeated, but with the statements that the theater was in the " Atrio corinzio " and that it was the cause of the fire in 1610 [sic]. Beside it is a note by Cicogna mentioning that the author of the report was Giuseppe Zoppa, writing in the " Memorie storiche della sua vita," Venice, 1840.

XXIII

Venezia, Biblioteca Nazionale Marciana, Mss. It. Cl. 7, n. 2283, Coll. 9121, F. Fapanni, "Chiese claustrali e monasteri di Venezia."

It is recorded here that before the construction of the new hall designed by F. Lazzari, there still existed some conspicuous remnants of the hospice of the Carità.

XXIV

Venice, Archivio dell'Accademia di Belle Arti, buste del 1807, 1808, 1809, 1810, and 1817, documents concerning construction.

Documents concerning the monies invested by the government in the work of converting the monastery into the Accademia di Belle Arti e Gallerie have been preserved, but there is no information there concerning the extent or the sequence of the work. One does learn from the notices that, initially, the restoration had been entrusted to the architect Antolini and then to Selva.

XXV

Venezia, Archivio di Stato, Prefettura dell'Adriatico, busta 60 (1807), 95 (1808), 319 (1810).

Here one finds information analogous to that in the archives of the Academy concerning the organization of the office entrusted with the work of adapting the building for the academy.

MANUSCRIPT SOURCES

ARCHIVIO DI STATO IN VENICE

— Sala diplomatica Regina Margherita, serie 74, a numero 13, raccolta autografi, Ricevuta del Palladio in conto lavori del 1561.
— Inventario del Monastero di Santa Maria della Carità, Sommario delle scritture compilato da Giacomo Cagna e da Girolamo ed Andrea Pisoni, a. 1578-79, canonica della Carità (senza marca).
— Notaio Benedetto Soliano, Protocolli 1569-70, pp. 70 sgg. Compromesso fra l'Abate del Monastero della Carità ed il muratore Antonio da Marcò.
— Inventario del Monastero di Santa Maria della Carità, Busta 2, Pergamene sciolte, documenti relativi a lavori.
— Ibidem, Busta 6, Serie III, Polizze di lavori, dal num. 2133 al 3116.
— Ibidem, Busta 17, Documenti relativi a lavori, 1574-1555.
— Ibidem, Parte I, Busta 27, Pergamene, Lodo fra il Monastero ed il muratore Antonio da Marcò.
— Ibidem, Canonici Lateranensi, Busta 43, Processi Scuola, 1411-1738.
— Prefettura dell'Adriatico, Busta 95 (del 1808); 60 (del 1807); 319 (del 1810), per i restauri ed adattamento a Scuola e Gallerie.

ARCHIVIO DEL CIVICO MUSEO CORRER IN VENICE

— Trattato delle diligenti osservazioni fate sopra le fabbriche d'Andrea Palladio visentino Le quali si mirano nel Inclita Città di Venezia, espresse in versi da Antonio Visentini veneto, Cod. Cic. N. 1967, Coll. Mss. VI, N. 799.
— Chiesa di Santa Maria della Carità, Cod. Cic. 2008.
— Estratti da' Codici Gradenigo intorno alle Feste veneziane. Memorie storiche sugli stabilimenti per la Musica eretti in Venezia, Cod. Cic. 3267, fasc. 13.

BIBLIOTECA NAZIONALE MARCIANA

— Chiese claustrali e monasteri di Venezia, Memorie raccolte da Francesco Fapanni, Mss. Italiani, Cl. 7, N. 2283, Coll. 9121.

ARCHIVIO DELL'ACCADEMIA DI BELLE ARTI IN VENICE

— Buste dal 1808 al 1825 (passim). Documenti relativi ai lavori di adattamento del Monastero ad Accademia e Galleria.

NOTE. In the library of the Accademia di Belle Arti di Venice is preserved a typescript, supplemented by a number of interesting measured drawings, that concerns "La Scuola e il Convento della Carità a Venezia." It was a project executed in the course on restoration in 1964-65 in the Istituto Universitario di Architettura, directed by the architect Angelo Scattolin and undertaken by the students Marcello Aquilina, Ennio Cervi, Fulvio Degrassi, Alessandro Lenarda, and Gilberto Nardi.

BIBLIOGRAPHY

1537 S. SERLIO, *Tutte l'opere d'architettura et prospettiva*, Book IV, *Delle maniere de' cinque ordini*, Venice, 1618 (Ist ed. 1537).

1544 S. SERLIO, *Regole Generali di Architettura*, Venice, p. xx.

1554 A. PALLADIO, *L'Antichità di Roma raccolta brevemente da gli Auttori Antichi et Moderni Novamente posta in Luce*, Rome.

1555 A. F. DONI, *Seconda Libraria*, Venice, p. 155.

1556 VITRUVIUS, *I Dieci Libri dell'Architettura tradutti et commentati da Monsignor Barbaro eletto patriarca d'Aquileggia*, Venice.

1568 G. VASARI, *Le vite de' più eccellenti Pittori, Scultori, e Architettori*, Florence.

1570 A. PALLADIO, *I Quattro Libri dell'Architettura*, Venice, p. 29.

1581 F. SANSOVINO, *Venetia città nobilissima et singolare descritta in XIII libri*, Venice, p. 96 verso.

1624 G. PENNOTTO, *Generalis totius sacri ordinis Clericorum Canonicorum historia tripartita*, Rome, p. 587.

1624 H. WOTTON, *The Elements of Architecture*, London (facsimile ed., introd. and notes by F. Hard, Charlottesville, 1968).

1666 N. DOGLIONI, *Le Cose notabili e meravigliose della città di Venezia*, Venice, p. 338.

1696 P. MERLO, *Vero e Real disegno della Inclita Cita di Venetia*, Venice.

1705 D. MARTINELLI, *Il Ritratto di Venezia*, Venice, p. 343.

1721 G. LEONI, *The architecture of A. Palladio in four books ... Translated from the Italian Original*, London.

1729 L. UGHI, *Pianta della città di Venezia*, Venice.

1736 *Cronica veneta sacra e profana*, Venice, p. 431.

1738 ISAAC WARE, *The Four Books of Andrea Palladio's Architecture*, London, II, pls, XX ff.

1740 [F. MUTTONI], *Architettura di Andrea Palladio Vicentino di nuovo ristampata... con le osservazioni dell'architetto N. N.*, Venice, I, pt. I, p. 1.

1741 I. JONES, *Notes and remarks upon the Plates of the second book of Palladio's Architecture*, Oxford.

1743 [F. MUTTONI], *Architettura di Andrea Palladio Vicentino di nuovo ristampata ... con le osservazioni dell'architetto N. N.*, Venice, IV, p. 13.

1744 [F. MUTTONI], *Architettura di Andrea Palladio Vicentino di nuovo ristampata ... con le osservazioni dell'architetto N. N.*, Venice, V.

1749 F. CORNER, *Ecclesiae venetae antiquis monumentis, Decas septima et octava*, Venice, p. 171.

1762 T. TEMANZA, *Vita di Andrea Palladio vicentino*, Venice.

1776-1783 O. BERTOTTI SCAMOZZI, *Le Fabbriche e i Disegni di Andrea Palladio*, IV, Vicenza, p. 38.

1778 T. TEMANZA, *Vite dei più celebri architetti, e scultori veneziani*, Venice, p. 312.

1781 F. MILIZIA, *Memorie degli architetti antichi e moderni*, Parma, III, pp. 38-40.

1791 A. MUCCI, *I Quattro Libri dell'Architettura di Andrea Palladio*, Siena, II, p. 55.

1795 G. B. GALLICCIOLLI, *Memorie venete antiche*, Venice, II, p. 239.

1796 O. BERTOTTI SCAMOZZI, *Le Fabbriche e i Disegni di Andrea Palladio*, Vicenza, IV, p. 40.

1798 T. VIERO, *Nuova Pianta Iconografica dell'Inclita città di Venezia*, Venice.

1810 L. CICOGNARA, *Elogio di Andrea Palladio*, Venice.

1815-1820 L. CICOGNARA - A. DIEDO - G. SELVA, *Le Fabbriche più cospicue di Venezia misurate illustrate ed intagliate dai membri della Veneta Reale Accademia di Belle Arti*, Venice, vol. 2 (sheets not numbered).

1828 G. MOSCHINI, *Itinéraire de la ville de Venise*, Venice (plate not numbered).

1832 A. C. QUATREMÈRE DE QUINCY, *Dictionnaire historique d'architecture*, Paris, II, p. 193.

1835 F. LAZZARI, *Dell'edificio palladiano nel monastero della Carità*, Venice.

1838-40 L. CICOGNARA - A. DIEDO - G. SELVA, *Le Fabbriche e i monumenti cospicui di Venezia*, Venice, II.

1841 M. PERISSINI, *Pianta della R. Città di Venezia*, Venice.

1843 G. QUARENGHI, *Fabbriche e disegni di Giacomo Quarenghi*, Mantua, I, p. 39.

1845 A. MAGRINI, *Memorie intorno la vita e le opere di Andrea Palladio*, Padua, p. 48.

1846 L. COMBATTI, *Nuova Planimetria della R. Città di Venezia*, Venice.

1847 G. MOSCHINI, *Nuova Guida di Venezia*, Venice (2nd ed.).

1847 P. SELVATICO, *Sulla architettura e sulla scultura in Venezia dal Medioevo fino ai nostri giorni*, Venice, p. 329.

1855 J. BURCKHARDT, *Le Cicerone*, Paris, 1892, II, p. 267.

1855 G. CAPPELLETTI, *Storia della Chiesa di Venezia*, Venice, IV, p. 332.

1855 A. MAGRINI, *Il Palazzo del museo civico di Vicenza descritto e illustrato*, Vicenza, p. 70.

1856 P. SELVATICO, *Storia estetico-critica delle arti del disegno*, Venice, II, p. 818.

1858 L. CICOGNARA - A. DIEDO - G. SELVA, *Le Fabbriche e i monumenti cospicui di Venezia ... con copiose note ed aggiunte di Francesco Zanotto*, Venice, II, p. 105.

1869 G. B. Lorenzi, *Monumenti per servire alla storia del Palazzo Ducale*, Venice, p. 281.

1876 G. Tassini, *Iscrizioni dell'ex chiesa, convento e confraternita della Carità di Venezia*, Venice, p. 357.

1880 C. Boito, *Terzo centenario di Andrea Palladio. Discorso letto nell'aula del civico museo*, Vicenza.

1880 L. Ferrari, *Palladio e Venezia*, Venice.

1887 Goethe, *Tagebücher, Goethes Warke*, ed. Sophie von Sachsen, pt. 3, vol. I, Weimar, 1887, vol. I.

1893 P. Paoletti, *L'architettura e la scultura del Rinascimento in Venezia*, Venice, II, pp. 271-272.

1907 L. Pearsall Smith, *The Life and Letters of Sir Henry Wotton*, Oxford, I, p. 196.

1909 L. Venturi, *La Compagnia della Calza*, Venice, pp. 69, 112, 117, 156.

1915 G. Tassini, *Curiosità veneziane*, Venice, p. 132.

1924 G. Fogolari, *La Chiesa di Santa Maria della Carità di Venezia*, Venice.

1934 E. Bassi, "L'architetto Francesco Lazzari," in *Rivista di Venezia*, June.

1936 E. Bassi, *Giannantonio Selva architetto veneziano*, Padua.

1940 A. Venturi, *Storia dell'arte italiana*, 11, pt. III, Milan, p. 359.

1941 E. Bassi, *La Regia Accademia di Belle Arti di Venezia*, Florence.

1941 H. Pée, *Die Palastbauten des Andrea Palladio*, Würzburg, pp. 93-98.

1942-1943 G. Vasari, *Le Vite dei più eccellenti pittori, scultori e architetti*, ed. C. L. Ragghianti, Milan-Rome, V, pp. 618-619.

1943 A. Dalla Pozza, *Palladio*, Vicenza.

1943 N. Pevsner, *An Outline of European Architecture*, London.

1944 R. Wittkower, "Principles of Palladio's Architecture," *Journal of the Warburg and Courtauld Institutes*, VIII, p. 102.

1945 R. Wittkower, "Principles of Palladio's Architecture," *Journal of the Warburg and Courtauld Institutes*, VIII, p. 68.

1947 E. Bassi, "Il Ripristino di un ambiente palladiano all'Accademia di Venezia," in *Arte Veneta*, Venice, p. 142.

1948 R. Pane, *Andrea Palladio*, Turin.

1949 G. Fiocco, "L'esposizione dei disegni di Andrea Palladio a Vicenza," in *Arte Veneta*, Venice, p. 184.

1954 V. Moschini, *Canaletto*, Milan, p. 36.

1954 R. Wittkower, "Giacomo Leoni's Edition of Palladio's *Quattro Libri dell'Architettura*," in *Arte Veneta*, Venice, p. 310.

1955 S. Moschini-Marconi, *Gallerie dell'Accademia di Venezia*, Rome, p. xi.

1955 N. Pevsner, "Palladio and Europe," in *Venezia e l'Europa*, Venice, p. 81.

1955 R. Pane, "Andrea Palladio e l'interpretazione dell'architettura rinascimentale," in *Venezia e l'Europa*, Venice, p. 408.

1958 *La Civiltà veneziana del Rinascimento*, Venice, p. 233.

1959 F. Franco, "La piccola e grande urbanistica del Palladio," in *Bollettino del Centro Internazionale di Studi di Architettura Andrea Palladio*, Vicenza, I, p. 19.

1959 G.G. Zorzi, *I Disegni delle antichità di Andrea Palladio*, Vicenza.

1959 B. Zevi, *Palladio*, Paris, II, in *Les Architectes célèbres*, p. 78.

1960 *Enciclopedia dello spettacolo* (voce Palladio), Florence-Rome, p. 1531.

1960 R. Pane, "Le Chiese di Venezia e le ultime opere vicentine," in *Bollettino del Centro Internazionale di Studi di Architettura Andrea Palladio*, Vicenza, II, p. 65.

1960 C. Brandi, "Perché Palladio non è neoclassico," in *Bollettino del Centro Internazionale di Studi di Architettura Andrea Palladio*, Vicenza, II, p. 9.

1961 R. Pane, *Andrea Palladio*, Turin.

1962 W. G. Constable, *Canaletto*, Oxford, II, p. 404.

1962 R. Wittkower, *Architectural Principles in the Age of Humanism*, London (3rd ed.).

1963 B. Zevi, *Palladio*, in *Enciclopedia Universale dell'Arte*, Venice, X, colonna 443.

1964 G.G. Zorzi, *Le Opere pubbliche e i palazzi privati di Andrea Palladio*, Vicenza, p. 11.

1965 A. Chastel, "Palladio et l'éscalier," in *Bollettino del Centro Internazionale di Studi di Architettura Andrea Palladio*, Vicenza, VII, pt. I, p. 11.

1966 J. S. Ackermann, *Palladio*, Harmondsworth.

1966 G. De Angelis d'Ossat, "I Sangallo e Palladio," in *Bollettino del Centro Internazionale di Studi di Architettura Andrea Palladio*, Vicenza, VIII, pt. II, p. 43.

1966 L. Puppi, *Palladio*, Florence.

1966 B. Zevi, "Palladio," in *Encyclopedia of World Art*, XI, cols. 59-81.

1966 G. G. Zorzi, *Le Chiese e i ponti di Andrea Palladio*, Vicenza, p. 45.

1967 N. Ivanoff, *Palladio*, Milan.

1968 G. G. Zorzi, *Le Ville e i teatri di Andrea Palladio*, Vicenza, p. 277.

1968 E. Battisti, "Le tendenze all'unità verso la metà del Cinquecento," in *Bollettino del Centro Internazionale di Studi di Architettura Andrea Palladio*, Vicenza, X, p. 127.

1968 R. Wittkower, "Il baluastro rinascimentale e il Palladio," in *Bollettino del Centro Internazionale di Studi di Architettura Andrea Palladio*, Vicenza, X, p. 332.

INDEX OF PERSONS AND PLACES

Names of persons are given in small capital letters, names of places in italics. Numbers in italics indicate pages with illustrations.

ACKERMAN JAMES S., *35*, 115, 116, 154
AGOSTINO, master stonecutter, 145
AGOSTINO, prior of the Carità, 146
ALEMAGNE (D'), GIOVANNI, 21
ALEXANDRE III, pope, 22
ALLEGRI ANTONIO, called CORREGGIO, 56
ANGARANO GIACOMO, 23, 114
"Antigono", 133, 134, 135
ANTOLINI GIOVANNI, 76, 77, 138
ANTONIO DI ZUANE, mason, 140
ANTONIO DI GASPARE, stonecutter, 140, 142
Aquileia, 23
AQUILINA MARCELLO, student of architecture, 151
ARETINO PIETRO, 25, 31, 134
ARNALDI VINCENZO, 133
ASTORI (di) STEFANO quondam ZUANE, notary, 140
ATHENA, 129
AUGUSTINE, saint, *18*, 53
Augustinian canons, 138

Baalbek, 103
BARBARI (DE') JACOPO, 14, 22, 24, 31, 101
BARBARIGO AGOSTINO, *procuratori*, 22
BARBARIGO, family, 22
BARBARIGO GREGORIO, prior of the Carità, 22
BARBARIGO MARCO, doge, 22
BARBARO DANIELE, 23, 29, 31, 35, 36, *67*, 112, *117*, 128, 129
BARBARO MARC'ANTONIO, 28
Bassano
  Museo Civico, 125
BASSI ELENA, 154
BASTIAN (kiln-workman), 137, 140
BATTISTI EUGENIO, 29, 154
BEAUHARNAIS (DE), EUGÈNE, Viceroy of Italy, 138

BEMBO PIETRO, 23
BERCHET FEDERICO, 111
BERNINI GIAN LORENZO, 112
BERTOTTI SCAMOZZI OTTAVIO, 52, 60, *69*, *73*, 105, 106, 153
BISSONE (da), ANTONIO, stonecutter, 41, 42, 138, 140, 142
BOITO CAMILLO, 79, 111
BONZI (BONSA), family, 14, 139
BONZI (BOZZA), NICOLÒ, 139
BORSATO, GIUSEPPE, 109, 116, *122*, *123*
BORTOLO DI DOMENICO, stonecutter, 141
BRAMANTE DONATO, 31, 59, 103, 115, 128
BRANDI CESARE, 154
BRIAMONTE, See GAMBELLO
BUONARROTI MICHELANGELO, 21, 114, 115
BURCKHARDT JACOB, 111, 153
BURLINGTON RICHARD (LORD), 102

CAGNA GIROLAMO, 139, 151
CALIARI CARLETTO, 21, 52, 53
CALIARI BENEDETTO, *18*, 21, 130
CALIARI PAOLO called VERONESE, 58
CANALETTO ANTONIO, *17*, 21, 95, 102, 103, 116, *118*, 125, 131
CANOVA ANTONIO, 109
CAPPELLETTI GIUSEPPE, 137, 153
Carità (allegory), 56
CARLEVARIJS LUCA, 22, *118*
CASPENIO ENEA, notary, 139
CASTER STEFANO, barge-master, 140
CERVI ENNIO, student of architecture, 151
CHASTEL ANDRÉ, 114
CICOGNA EMANUELE, 150
CICOGNARA LEOPOLDO, *69*, *72*, *73*, 77, 108, 153

CIRILLI GUIDO, 79, 138
CODUSSI MAURO, 22
COLE HOPPUS, 102
COMBATTI GAETANO, *20*, 76, 79, 153
Compagnia della Calza, 40, 133, 134
Compagnia degli Accesi, 133, 134
Compagnia dei Sempiterni, 134
CONDULMER GABRIELE, 13
Confratelli della Carità, 14, 21, 53
Congregazione dei Canonici Lateranensi, 13, 29
CONSTABLE W. C., 154
CONTARINI, family, 133
CORNARO ALVISE, 23
CORNER FILIPPO, 137
CORNER FLAMINIO, 153
CORNER GIROLAMO, 16, 137, 140
CORNER PIETRO, 16, 21, 137, 140
CORONELLI VINCENZO, 80, 101, 102, 103, 104, *119*, 131
CORREGGIO, See ANTONIO ALLEGRI

DALLA POZZA ANTONIO, 154
DANDOLO ANTONIO, 16, 137, 140
DANDOLO GEROLAMO, 137, 140
DA MONTE ANTONIO, See PIGATTI ANTONIO
DA PONTE NICOLÒ, doge, 41
DE ANGELIS D'OSSAT GUGLIELMO, 114, 154
DE CRISTIN ZANANTONIO, See ZANANTONIO D. C.
DE GRASSI FULVIO, student of architecture, 151
DELLA ROVERE FRANCESCO, 134
DE LOGU GIUSEPPE, 80
DE PORTI ISEPPO, 31
Dessau, 107
DIEDO ANTONIO, *69*, *72*, *73*, 107, 153
DOGLIONI NICOLA, 76, 153
DONI ANTON FRANCESCO, 21, 153

ELIA (de), BATTISTA, mason, 147
England, 84, 131
EUGENIUS IV, pope, *See* CONDULMER GABRIELE

FAPANNI, FRANCESCO, 79, 150
FERRARI LUIGI, 154
FIOCCO GIUSEPPE, 154
Florence, 131, 153, 154
FOGOLARI GINO, 13, 22, 154
FONTEBASSO FRANCESCO, 103
FOSSATI GIORGIO, 102
FRANCESCO (don), padre della Carità, 147
FRANCESCO (di), INNOCENZO, mason, 142
FRANCO FAUSTO, 113, 154

GALLICCIOLLI GIAMBATTISTA, 153
GAMBELLO BRIAMONTE, 65, 148
GAMBELLO VITTORE, 65, 104, 148
GAZZANIGA (da), STEFANO DI GIOVANNI, stonecutter, 140
Gazzetta Veneta, 138
Giudici del Piovego, 15, 138, 146
Giudici del Proprio, 53, 138, 146
GOETHE WOLFGANG, 62, 105, 106, 107, 111, 113, 116, 127, 131, 154
GOZZI (abbot), 75, 104, 134, 135
GRADENIGO PIETRO, 134, 150
GRANDO (del) ANTONIO, *proto* of the Ufficio del Proprio, 142
Greenwich, Queen's House, 59, *98*
GUASCHI (or GUASCO, de) ANDREA, public magistrate, 146
GUBERNI PIETRO, 23

Harmondsworth, 154
HERCULES, 129
HYRCANIAN, king of Gerusalem, 133, 134

ILLUMINATO DA PADOVA, abbot, 142
INNOCENZO DI FRANCESCO LOMBARDO, mason, 142
Italy, 39, 138
IVANOFF NICOLA, 116, 154

Jerusalem, 133, 134
JONES INIGO, 40, 41, 47, 55, 59, 84, *98*, 131, 135, 138, 142, 153

Lateran canons, 13, 16, 18, 29, 31, 39, 40, 53, 76, 77, 104, 127, 129, 130, 138, 139, 140, 141, 142, 146, 147, 149, 151
LAZZARI-WCHOWICH FRANCESCO, 42, 52, 55, 58, *60*, 76, 77, 79, 85, 103, 108, 110, 111, 138, 153
LENARDA ALESSANDRO, student of architecture, 151
LEONI GIACOMO, *48*, 59, *68*, 84, 101, 102, 103, 153
Lombardo Veneto (kingdom of), 76
London, 84, 102, 153, 154
  British Museum, 117
  National Gallery, 17, 22
  RIBA, *49*, 103
LONGHENA BALDASSARE, 59, *99*, 112
LORENZI GIAN BATTISTA, 22, 154

MACCARUCCI BERNARDINO, 76
Magdalene, 35
Magistrato al Piovego, 15
MAGRINI ANTONIO, 22, 40, 54, 58, 110, 139, 153
Malo
  Villa Muzzani alla Pisa, 115
« Mandragola, La », 133
MANSUETI GIOVANNI, 22
MANTEGNA ANDREA, 65
Mantua, 153
MARCÒ (da) ANTONIO, *See* PALEARI A.
MARCÒ (da) ANTONIO, « Murer de San Zorzi », *See* PALEARI A.
MARCOLINI GEROLAMO, priest from Treviso, 140
Marcote, 39
MARTINELLI DOMENICO, 153
Maser, church at, 130
MASSARI GIORGIO, 76, 77, 80, 130
MARZOCCO GIACOMO, mason, 142
MEMMO ANZOLO, 16, 141
MEMMO, family, 15, 139
MERLO PIETRO, *16*, 101, 153
Milan, 154
MILIZIA FRANCESCO, 57, 105, 153
MOCENIGO, family, 16
Mogliano Veneto
  Vila Smith, 117
Montagnana
  Villa Pisani, 31, 111
MOSCHINI GIANNANTONIO, 75, 77, 109, *121*, 153
MOSCHINI MARCONI SANDRA, 81, 154
MOSCHINI VITTORIO, 102, 154
MUCCI ALESSANDRO, 69, 71, 105, 153
MUGNON, 105
MURER ANTONIO, *See* PALEARI A.
MUTTONI FRANCESCO, 58, *68*, 69, 70, 102, 103, 134, 153

NAPOLEON BONAPARTE, 109
Naples
  Temple of Castor and Pollux, 65
NARDI GILBERTO, student of architecture, 151

Ossero, pietra di, 128
Ovado, 140
Oxford
  Worcester College, 84, 153, 154

Padua, 106, 134, 153
PALEARI ANTONIO, *capomastro*, 39, 40, 41, 52, 81, 140
PALEARI GIAN BATTISTA, 52
PALEARI ZANANTONIO, *See* PALEARI ANTONIO
PALLADIO MARC'ANTONIO, 23
Palmyra, 103
PANE ROBERTO, 58, 64, 113, 154
PAOLETTI PIETRO, 16, 65, 137, 154
Paris, 153, 154
Parma
  Convento di San Paolo, Camera della Badessa, 56
PASOTTI AGOSTINO, Kiln-workman, 137, 140
PASOTTI ALVISE, quondam ZUANNE, kiln-workman, 137, 140
PASOTTI ISEPPO, kiln-workman, 137, 140
PASOTTI ZUANNE, kiln-workman, 137, 140
PAUL III, pope, 22
PEARSALL SMITH L., 154
PÉE HERBERT, 112, 154
PELLEGRINI GIOV. ANTONIO, 103
PENNOTTO GABRIELE, 22, 153
PERISSINI MARCO, 79, 153
PERSEPHONE, 129
PERUZZI OTTAVIO, public magistrate, 146
PEVSNER NIKOLAUS, 154
PICART B., 102
PICCIO GIUSEPPE, bursar of the Accademia, 79
PIGATTI ANTONIO, 133
Piove di Sacco
  Contrà San Nicolò, 140
PISONI ANDREA, 139, 151
PISONI GEROLAMO, 139, 151
Pola
  Arena, 116, 129
POLLAIOLO (ANTONIO DEL), 65
Pompeii, 110
PORTO GIUSEPPE, 114
PRIULI GIAN FRANCESCO, 23
PRIULI GIROLAMO, doge, 23
PRIULI LORENZO, doge, 23
Provveditori all'Arsenale, 134
PUPPI LIONELLO, 115, 154

QUARENGHI GIACOMO, 108, 109, 153
QUARENGHI GIULIO, 108, 153
QUATREMÈRE DE QUINCY ANTOINE-CRYSOSTOME, 111, 153

RAGGHIANTI CARLO LUDOVICO, 154
Ravenna, 137
   Santa Maria in Porto, 13
RENI (DI) GEROLAMO, notary, 140
RICCI SEBASTIANO, 103
Rome, 16, 23, 31, 103, 109, 129, 137, 153, 154
   Belvedere, 59
   Chiesa di Santa Maria della Pace, 31
   Colosseum, 113, 114, 115, 116, 129, 133
   Crypta Balbi, 65
   Imperial palaces, 31
   Ospedale di Santo Spirito, 109
   Palazzo Farnese, 31, 59, 115
   Theater of Pompey, portico, 65
   Theater of Marcellus, 113, 115, 116
   Temple of Fortuna Virilis, 56
   Temple of Vesta, 56
ROMANO GIULIO, 31
ROVERE (DELLA) FRANCESCO MARIA, See DELLA ROVERE F.
Rovigno, pietra di, 128
RUSCONI GIANNANTONIO, 125, 134
Russia, 108

St. Petersburg, 108
   Anichov Bridge, 108
   Imperial Palace, 108
SANMICHELI MICHELE, 111, 128, 129, 130
SANGALLO (family), 21, 154
SANGALLO ANTONIO (the younger), 49, 114, 115
SANGALLO GIULIANO, 58
SANSOVINO FRANCESCO, 65, 116, 128, 130, 131, 133, 134, 135, 138, 147, 153
SANSOVINO GIACOMO, 21, 65, 83, 111, 128, 129, 130, 131, 133, 135, 137
SARDI GIUSEPPE, 59, 99
SCAMOZZI VINCENZO, 41, *97*, 135
SCATTOLIN ANGELO, 150
Scolari della Carità, see Confratelli della Carità
SELVA GIANNANTONIO, 52, 58, *69*, *72*, *73*, 76, 77, 78, 79, 104, 107, 108, 109, 110, 111, 131, 133, 134, 138, 153, 154

SELVATICO ESTENSE PIETRO, 79, 110, 111, *124*, 153
Senigaglia, 22
SERLIO SEBASTIANO, 57, 153
SILVESTRINI GIOVANNI, 105
SMITH JOSEPH, 84, 86, 104, 125
SOLIANO BENEDETTO, notary, 142
SOLIAN BONIFACIO, quondam MATHIO, notary, 140

"Talanta", 134
TASSINI GIUSEPPE, 65, 134, 154
TEMANZA TOMMASO, 25, 52, 55, 57, 58, 75, 76, 83, 104, 105, 107, 111, 131, 134, 135, 147, 153
TESTAGROSSA GEROLAMO, stonecutter, 41, 138, 140, 142
Theater of the Compagnia della Calza, 40, 133, 135
THIENE OTTAVIO, 31
Ticino, 39
TITIAN, see VECELLIO
Tivoli
   Temple of Vesta, 35, *50*, 56, 104, 148
Treviso, 140
TRISSINO GIANGIORGIO, 23, 31, 111

UGHI LUDOVICO, 75, 153
Urbino
   Palazzo Ducale, 129

VALDAGNINO, see VAVASSORI ZUAN ANDREA
VASARI GIORGIO, 83, 84, 129, 131, 133, 134, 137, 153, 154
VAVASSORI ZUAN ANDREA, 15
VECELLIO TIZIANO, 21
Veneto, 108
VENEZIA (DA) DON PAOLO, 140
Venice
   Academia di Belle Arti, 20, 76, 77, 78, 79, 80, 104, 108, 109, 115, 125, 138, 150, 151, 154
      Archivio, 138, 150
      Nuova Pinacoteca, 77, 78, 79
      Pinacoteca, 53, 76
      Sale Nuovissime, 79
   Archivio di Stato, 23, 24, 31, 41, *42*, *43*, *44*, *45*, *46*, 134, 136, 139, 150
   Biblioteca Marciana, 81, 150
   Biblioteca Correr, 54, 125, 135, 147, 150
   Ca' d'Oro, 65
   Calle del Dose, 15, 24, 33, 40, 42, 52, 53, 63, 77, 80, 101, 103, 104, 107, 136, 138, 141, 146

   Calle Pisani, 96
   Campo della Carità, 21, 52, 102, 104
   Canale di Sant'Agnese, see Rio di S. Agnese
   Canale di S. Trovaso, 15, 139
   Canale della Giudecca, 5
   Canal Grande, 13, 14, 21, 24, 40, 42, 59, 63, 100, 104, 125, 134
   Cannaregio, 134, 150
   Carampane, 25, *96*
   Casa Bonza, 15, 139
   Chiesa dei Frari, see di Santa Maria Gloriosa dei Frari
   Chiesa dei Santi Apostoli, 125, 140, 142
   Chiesa del Redentore, 22, 63, 108
   Chiesa di San Francesco della Vigna, 40
   Chiesa di San Gervaso e Protasio, 139
   Chiesa di San Giacomo di Rialto, 21
   Chiesa di San Giorgio Maggiore, 23, 40, 64, 112
   Chiesa di San Nicolò dei Mendicoli, 21
   Chiesa di San Nicolò di Castello, 78
   Chiesa di San Pietro di Castello, 23
   Chiesa di Sant'Agnese, 139
   Chiesa di Santa Maria della Carità, 13, 17, 18, 22, 24, 28, 41, 53, 62, 78, *85*, *86*, 87, 101, 105, 106, 116, 127, 128, 129, 134, 135, 136, 138, 139, 143, 147, 149, 154
      Barco, 51, 134
      Campanile, 76
      Choir, 42, 144
   Chiesa di Santa Maria della Salute, 53
   Chiesa di Santa Maria Gloriosa dei Frari, 76
   Chiesa di Santa Maria Maddalena, 76, 149
   Chiesa di San Trovaso, see San Gervaso e Protasio
   Chiesa di San Vitale, 140, 142
   Convento dei Crociferi, 133
   Convento dei Domenicani, 76
   Convento dei Frari, 76
   Convento dei Gesuati, 76, 80, 130
   Convento della Carità,
      Abbot's room, 51, 78, 134, 144, 145
      Ante-sacristy, 51, 63, 134
      Atrium, 24, 25, 26, 28, 29, 40, 41, 42, 46, 52, 62, 75,

80, 81, 84, 101, 102, 105, 107, 109, 110, 112, 113, 114, 115, 116, 125, 127, 128, 129, 130, 131, 134, 135, 136, 137, 138, 140, 143, 144, 145, 147, 149
Bakery, 24, 28, 141
Barbaria, 24, 51, 145
Camera del fuoco, 24, 135, 141
Cavana, 24
Cellar, 24, 28, 31, 52, 141
Cells, 51, 79, 80, 101, 113, 127, 129, 145
Chapter hall (large), 24, 31, 52, 113, 136
Chapter hall (small), 136
Cistern, 31, 145
Clock, 145
Cloister, 15, 24, 28, 29, 31, 33, 40, 51, 62, *68*, *69*, *71*, *73*, 75, 79, 86, 90, 91, 92, 101, 103, 105, 109, 110, 113, 114, 115, 116, 119, 120, 121, 122, 129, 134, 136, 138, 141, 143, 144, 145, 148, 149
Dormitory, 24, 51, 78, 80, 86, 90, 136, 141, 144
Farm, 141
Garden (Giardino), 28, 129
Garden (Orto), 24, 31, 129
Granary, *33*, 141
Guest rooms, 24, 28, 51, 55, 63, 78, 79, 89, 94, 95, 101, 127, 130, 134, 136, 144, 145
Impluvium, 24, 41, 62, 75, 105, 127
Kitchen, 24, 28, 52, 135, 141
Library, 24, 141
Mezzanine level, 24, 40, 79, 141
Peristyle, *see* cloister
Refectory, 24, 28, 29, 31, 42, 52, 53, 62, 75, 76, 77, 80, 83, 103, 105, 109, 125, 127, 129, 136, 138, 141, 146
Sacristan's room, 24, 141
Sacristy, 24, 28, 31, 42, 51, 52, 55, 63, 76, 104, 107, 108, 110, 111, 113, 128, 130, 135, 136, 141, 143, 145, 147, 148
Sala capitolare, 24, 94
Stairs (main), 24, 136, 141
Stairs (oval), 28, 29, 37, 39, 42, 47, 48, 51, 59, 62, 73, 79, 80, 88, 89, 100, 101, 104, 106, 107, 114, 116, 125, 127, 128, 129, 130, 134, 135, 138, 143, 145, 147, 148

Stairs (small), 89, 144
Storeroom, 24, 141
Studietto, *53*, 101, 107, 146
Tablinum, 24, 28, 29, *33*, *35*, 51, *55*, 62, 68, 70, 73, 75, 78, 79, 80, 89, 94, 100, 101, 105, 107, 109, 110, 111, 116, 123, 124, 125, 127, 128, 130, 138
Terrace, 43, 55, 75, 86, 102, 104, 109, 125, 127, 129, 138
Vestibule, 24
Vineyard, 29, 53, 76, 77, 80
Wardrobe, 24
Washhouse, 24, 28, 141
Woodstore, 28, 141
Convento della Madonna dell'Orto, 128
Convento dei Gesuati, 130
Convento dello Spirito Santo, 128
Convento di San Giorgio Maggiore, 31
  Cellar, 31
  Cloister, 31, 115, 127
  Kitchen, 31
  Refectory, 31, 39, 40
  Wine-cellar, 31
Convento di San Michele, 128
Convento di San Salvatore, 128
Convento di Sant'Apollonia, 14, 127
Convento di Santo Stefano, 128
Convento di San Zaccaria, 128
Fondaco dei Tedeschi, 128
Fondaco dei Turchi, 111
Fondamenta delle Zattere, 76, 130
Galleria dell'Accademia, *18*, 21, 53, 78, 79, 107, 108, 115, 138, 150, 151
Giardini Pubblici, 77
Libreria Marciana, *see* Biblioteca Marciana
Museo Correr, 54, 65, 81, 109, 125, 135
Ospedale della Carità, *see* Scuola della Carità
Ospedaletto, 59, 100, 130
Palazzetto Smith ai Santi Apostoli, 102
Palazzo Corner, 21, 128, 134
Palazzo Ducale, 21, 23, 63, 130, 134
  Sala del Maggior Consiglio, 22
  Sala delle Quattro Porte, 52
  Scala d'Oro, 21
  Ufficio del Sale, 23
Palazzo Dolfin, 128, 133, 135
Palazzo Nani, 111
Palazzo Treves de' Bonfili, 111
Ponte del Dose, 42, 101
Rialto, 133

Rio della Carità, 13, 14, 21, 78, 127
Rio di Sant'Agnese, 13, 14, 15, *19*, 21, 29, 40, 42, 51, 52, 53, 63, 64, 76, 77, 79, 87, 101, 104, 105, *119*, 127, 136, 137, 138, 139, 140, 145, 146
Rio di San Trovaso, *see* Canale di San Trovaso
Rio terra' Foscarini, 13, 79
Scuola dei Battuti, 13
Scuola della Carità, 13, *52*, *53*, 76, 77, 78, 79, 96, 97, 104, 108, 127, 138, 139, 141, 146
  Albergo, 79
  Courtyard, 24, 31, 53, 62, 73, 77, 78, 79, 96, 97
  Hospice, 24, 31, 53, 79, 96, 139, 140, 146
Scuola della Misericordia, 78
Scuola di San Marco, 76
Soprintendenza alle Gallerie, 80, 138
Soprintendenza ai Monumenti, 80, 138
Teatro degli Accesi, 133
Zecca, 77, 128
VENTURI ADOLFO, 111, 154
VENTURI LIONELLO, 135, 154
Venus, 35
VERONESE PAOLO, *see* CALIARI
Vicenza, 21, 23, 24, 35, 106, 112, 114, 133, 134, 140, 153, 154
  Basilica, 23, 58, 116
  Biblioteca Comunale, 135
  Centro di Architettura A. Palladio, 112, 139
  Loggia del Capitaniato, 116
  Museo Civico, 151
  Palazzo Angarano, 23, 24, 114, 128
  Palazzo Barbaran, 40
  Palazzo Chiericati, 23, 62, 116
  Palazzo De' Porti, 31, 114, 116
  Palazzo Thiene, 31, 49, 57, 58, 112
  Palazzo Trissino, 31
VIERO TEODORO, 75, 153
VISENTINI ANTONIO, 53, 57, 75, 102, 103, 104, 125, *118*, *120*, *121*, 131, 147, 151
VITRUVIUS MARCO VISPANIUS, 23, 29, 105, 110, 111, 114, 115, 129, 148, 153
VITTORIA ANDREA, 23
VITTURI ANTONIO, fu Andrea, 15, 139
VIVARINI ANTONIO, 21

WARE ISAAC, *68*, *72*, 102, 153
Windsor
  Windsor Castle, 102

Wittkower Rudolf, 42, 102, 113, 154
Wotton Henry, 55, 84, 131, 135, 153, 154

Zago (del) Domenico, stonecutter, 142
Zago (del) Pasqualin, stonecutter, 140, 142
Zannantonio de Cristin, mason, 140, 142
Zanotto Francesco, 108, 153
Zavatin Gasparo, ship master, 140
Zenoni Vincenzo, chancellor of the Accademia, 79
Zeus, 58
Zevi Bruno, 114, 154
Ziani Sebastiano, 22
Zoppa Giuseppe, 150
Zoretto Cesare, *capomastro*, 146
Zorzi Giangiorgio, 23, 40, 54, 58, 65, 103, 114, 134, 142, 154
Zuccheri Federico, 133, 134
Zucchi Francesco, 103

ILLUSTRATIONS IN THE TEXT

    I   JACOPO DE' BARBARI, *Monastery and Church of the Carità* (from the plan of 1500)

    II   ZUAN ANDREA VAVASSORI, called VADAGNINO, *Monastery and Church of the Carità* (from the plan of 1517)

    III   PIETRO MERLO, *The Area of the Convento della Carità* (from the plan of 1696)

    IV   CANALETTO, *Santa Maria della Carità*. London, The National Gallery

    V   BENEDETTO CALIARI, *St. Augustine Giving the Rule of the Lateran Canons*. Altarpiece executed for the sacristy of the Church of the Carità. Venice, Gallerie

    VI   *The rio terra' Sant'Agnese on November 4, 1966*. From *Venezia fino a quando?*, 1967

    VII   *Convento della Carità adapted for use by the Accademia*. Engraving by Combatti (1847)

    VIII   ANDREA PALLADIO, *The casa dei Romani*. From *I Quattro Libri dell'Architettura*, 1570, II, vii, p. 34

    IX   ANDREA PALLADIO, *Tuscan atrium, in small-scale representation*. From *I Quattro Libri dell'Architettura*, 1570, II, iv, p. 25

    X   ANDREA PALLADIO, *Tuscan atrium, in large-scale representation*. From *I Quattro Libri dell'Architettura*, 1570, II, iv, p. 26

    XI   ANDREA PALLADIO, *Convento della Carità: plan and section*. From *I Quattro Libri dell'architettura*, 1570, II, vii, p. 30

    XII   ANDREA PALLADIO, *Convento della Carità: atrium, in large-scale representation*. From *I Quattro Libri dell'Architettura*, 1570, II, vi, p. 31

    XIII   ANDREA PALLADIO, *Convento della Carità: atrium and cloister, in large-scale representation*. Photomontage from *I Quattro Libri dell'Architettura*, 1570, II, vi, pp. 31-32

    XIV   ANDREA PALLADIO, *Convento della Carità: cloister, in large-scale representation*. From *I Quattro Libri dell'Architettura*, 1570, II, vi, p. 32

    XV   ANDREA PALLADIO, *" Delle scale."* From *I Quattro Libri dell'Architettura*, 1570, I, xxviii, p. 63. The example indicated with the letter " F " is the oval stair in the Convento della Carità

    XVI   *The Atrium of the Convento della Carità with the Project for Rebuilding the Terrace* (anonymous watercolor drawing). Venice, Archivio di Stato

    XVII   ANDREA PALLADIO, *Project for reconstructing the Convento della Carità: plan of the ground floor*. Venice, Archivio di Stato

    XVIII   ANDREA PALLADIO, *Legend illustrating the project for reconstruction* (detail of the fig. XVII). Venice, Archivio di Stato

    XIX   ANDREA PALLADIO, *Project for reconstructing the Convento della Carità: plan of the second floor*. Venice, Archivio di Stato

    XX   *Palladio's receipt for payment by the canons for the project of reconstructing the Convento della Carità and for beginning the work* (June 1, 1562). Venice, Archivio di Stato

    XXI-XXII   *Instructions to Palladio for rebuilding " quadri nell'atrio " at the Convento della Carità*. From the " Sommario delle scritture " of 1569 and 1570. Venice, Archivio di Stato

    XXIII   INIGO JONES, *Sketch of the stairs in the Convento della Carità* (in the copy of Palladio's treatise belonging to Jones)

    XXIV   *Anonymous designs for two doors proposed for the Convento della Carità*. Venice, Archivio di Stato

    XXV   GIACOMO LEONI, *The stairs in the Convento della Carità (at left)*. From *The Architecture of A. Palladio in Four Books*, 1721, II, pl. XL

    XXVI   ANDREA PALLADIO, *Autograph design for the Palazzo of M. A. Thiene in Vicenza: detail of the façade along the via S. Stefano*. London, RIBA, XVII, 10

    XXVII   ANTONIO DA SANGALLO THE YOUNGER, *Project for the courtyard of the Palazzo Farnese in Rome*. Florence, Uffizi, Gabinetto dei Disegni, 627 A

XXVIII   ANDREA PALLADIO, *Temple of Vesta at Tivoli: details*. Vicenza, Museo Civico, D 4^v

XXIX   *Comparison of the preliminary project and the project in the treatise for the ground floor of the Convento della Carità*

XXX   *Comparison of the preliminary project and the project in the treatise for the second floor of the Convento della Carità*

XXXI   *Plan of the ground floor of the complex of the Convento della Carità (present condition) with the design in the Quattro Libri, containing indications of the parts that exist, those destroyed in the fire, and those destroyed by Lazzari, superimposed*

XXXII   *Convento della Carità: plan of the east wing of the second floor derived from the design in the Quattro Libri, with indications of the extant parts and of those destroyed in the fire*

XXXIII   *Convento della Carità: plan of the east wing of the third floor derived from the designs in the Quattro Libri, with indications of the extant part and of that destroyed in the fire*

XXXIV   *Convento della Carità: the east wing of the ground floor (still extant) as it was built and used during the architect's lifetime*

XXXV   DANIELE BARBARO, The *Casa dei Romani*. From *I Dieci Libri dell'Architettura di M.V. Vitruvio...*, 1556, VI, p. 167

XXXVI   ANDREA PALLADIO, *The casa dei Greci*. From *I Quattro Libri dell'Architettura*, 1570, II, XI, p. 44

XXXVII   ANDREA PALLADIO, *L'atrio di quattro colonne*. From *I Quattro Libri dell'Architettura*, 1570, II, V, p. 28

XXXVIII   ANDREA PALLADIO, *Sala di quattro colonne*. From *I Quattro Libri dell'Architettura*, 1570, II, VIII, p. 37

XXXIX   ANDREA PALLADIO, *Plan and section of the Convento della Carità with the proper orientation*. From *I Quattro Libri dell'Architettura*, 1570, II, VI

XL   GIACOMO LEONI, *Plan and section of the Convento della Carità*. From the *Architecture of A. Palladio in Four Books*, 1721, II, pl. XXII

XLI   ISAAC WARE, *Plan and section of the Convento della Carità*. From *The Four Books of Andrea Palladio's Architecture*, 1738, II, pl. XX

XLII   FRANCESCO MUTTONI, *Section and plan of the Convento della Carità*. From *Architettura di Andrea Palladio Vicentino*, I, pt. I, 1740, pls. III-IV

XLIII   FRANCESCO MUTTONI, *Section and plan of the Convento della Carità*. From *Architettura di Andrea Palladio Vicentino*, V, 1744, pl. XXI

XLIV   OTTAVIO BERTOTTI SCAMOZZI, *Plan and section of the Convento della Carità*. From *Le Fabbriche e i Disegni di Andrea Palladio*, IV, 1783, pls. XXIV, XXVI

XLV   ALESSANDRO MUCCI, *Plan and section of the Convento della Carità*. From *I Quattro Libri dell'Architettura di Andrea Palladio*, 1791, II, p. 55

XLVI   CICOGNARA, DIEDO, SELVA, *Section and plan of the Convento della Carità*. From *Le Fabbriche e i monumenti cospicui di Venezia...*, 1858, pls. 207, 211

XLVII   ISAAC WARE, *Cloister of the Convento della Carità, in large-scale representation*. From *The Four Books of Andrea Palladio's Architecture*, 1738, II, pl. XXII

XLVIII   ISAAC WARE, *Atrium of the Convento della Carità, in large-scale representation*. From *The Four Books of Andrea Palladio's Architecture*, 1738, II, pl. XXI

IL   FRANCESCO MUTTONI, *Cloister of the Convento della Carità, in large-scale representation*. From *Architettura di Andrea Palladio Vicentino*, I, pt. I, 1740, pl. VI

L   FRANCESCO MUTTONI, *Tablinum and cloister of the Convento della Carità*. From *Architettura di Andrea Palladio Vicentino*, I, pt. I, 1740, pl. V

LI   FRANCESCO MUTTONI, *Cloister in the Convento della Carità, in large-scale representation*. From *Architettura di Andrea Palladio Vicentino*, V, 1744, pl. XXIII

LII   FRANCESCO MUTTONI, *Atrium in the Convento della Carità, in large-scale representation*. From *Architettura di Andrea Palladio Vicentino*, V, 1744, pl. XXII

LIII   ALESSANDRO MUCCI, *Cloister of the Convento della Carità, in large-scale representation*. From *I Quattro Libri dell'Architettura di Andrea Palladio*, 1791, II, p. 59

LIV   ALESSANDRO MUCCI, *Atrium of the Convento della Carità, in large-scale representation*. From *I Quattro Libri dell'Architettura di Andrea Palladio*, 1791, II, p. 57

LV   CICOGNARA, DIEDO, SELVA, *Parts of the orders of the Convento della Carità*. From *Le Fabbriche e i monumenti cospicui di Venezia...*, 1858, II, pl. 210

LVI   CICOGNARA, DIEDO, SELVA, *Parts of the orders of the Convento della Carità*. From *Le Fabbriche e i monumenti cospicui di Venezia*, 1858, II, pl. 209

LVII	Cicognara, Diedo, Selva, *Section and plan of the tablinum of the Convento della Carità*. From *Le Fabbriche e i monumenti cospici di Venezia*, 1858, II, pl. 208
LVIII	Ottavio Bertotti Scamozzi, *Section of the atrium of the Convento della Carità*. From *Le Fabbriche e i Disegni di Andrea Palladio*, IV, 1783, pl. XXV
LIX	Cicognara, Diedo, Selva, *Peristyle of the Convento della Carità after the nineteenth-century restoration*. From *Le Fabbriche e i monumenti cospicui di Venezia...*, 1858, II, pl. 212
LX	*Convento della Carità: detail from the Ionic loggia on the second floor*
LXI	*Convento della Carità and apses of the church: details*
LXII	*Convento della Carità: façades facing the former atrium and cloister in the interior of the monastery; the terrace next to the former dormitory is visible along the former atrium at center left*
LXIII	*Convento della Carità: the space of the former atrium at its junction with the church*
LXIV	*Convento della Carità: the flank along the rio terra' Sant'Agnese; on the left the nineteenth-century addition is discernible in the variation in the exposure of the eaves*
LXV	*Convento della Carità: arch of the cavana, closed in the nineteenth century: interior view*
LXVI	*Convento della Carità: details in brick from the terrace that encircled the "impluvium"*
LXVII	*Convento della Carità: stone slab wtih a medieval inscription, reused in oval stairs*
LXVIII	*Convento della Carità: stone slab with a medieval relief, reused in the oval stairs*
LXIX	*Convento della Carità, attic: in the foreground, the covering of the oval stairs; in the distance, the covering in wood and cane of one of the cells*
LXX	*Convento della Carità, ground floor: traces of a stair between the tablinum and the guests' rooms, indicated in the plan in the* Quattro Libri *and destroyed in the nineteenth century*
LXXI	*Convento della Carità: covering in cane of the corridor on the third floor, discovered during restorations (1970); traces are visible of the groin in the area where it turned the corner to the peristyle (destroyed in the nineteenth century)*
LXXII	*Convento della Carità: covering in cane of the cells uncovered during restorations (1970)*
LXXIII	*Convento della Carità: corridor on the third floor (formerly containing dormitories), during restorations (1970)*
LXXIV	*Convento della Carità, arcade: traces of the groin that turned the corner to the left-hand return arch, destroyed in the nineteenth century*
LXXV	*Convento della Carità: vault in one of the cells after the restorations of 1970-71*
LXXVI	*Convento della Carità: traces of a balcony formerly extant at the end of the corridor on the third floor; closed in the nineteenth-century modifications*
LXXVII	*Convento della Carità: arcade in the cloister*
LXXVIII	*Convento della Carità: ambulatory between the atrium and the medieval portion of the monastery after the reconstruction following the fire of 1630*
LXXIX	*Convento della Carità: traces of the window between the tablinum and the atrium, closed in the nineteenth century*
LXXX	*Convento della Carità: traces of the window between the atrium and the chapter hall*
LXXXI	*Convento della Carità: traces of the archway between the space of the "cavana" and the guests' rooms, closed in the nineteenth century*
LXXXII	*Convento della Carità: flank of the medieval buttressed structure*
LXXXIII	*Convento della Carità: guests' rooms on the ground floor; the cavity in the wall results from restorations (1958)*
LXXXIV	*Convento della Carità, ground floor: Doric portico; nineteenth-century doorway and traces of the window that opened into the "cavana" (the window is visible in the painting by Canaletto)*
LXXXV	*Flank of the Nuova Pinacoteca, constructed with a volume analogous to that of the refectory envisaged for the Convento della Carità*
LXXXVI	*Scuola and Convento della Carità: common courtyard with the well and the entrance to the hospice of the scuola*
LXXXVII	*The courtyard of the Carampane, Venice*
LXXXVIII	Vincenzo Scamozzi, *Scuola della Carità, courtyard: entrance portal to the scuola*
LXXXIX	*Scuola della Carità, courtyard: fifteenth-century loggia*
XC	Inigo Jones, *The Tulip Staircase in the Queen's House, Greenwich (1616-29)*
XCI	G. Sardi, B. Longhena, *Oval stair in the Ospedaletto, Venice (1664-66)*
XCII	*Convento della Carità, oval staircase: window and jamb toward the Grand Canal*

XCIII *Convento della Carità: door between the* tablinum *and the stair hall under the oval stairs*
XCIV *Convento della Carità: five steps of the oval staircase, covered in the nineteenth century, and now restored (1968)*
XCV DANIELE BARBARO, *Elevation of the Latin theater.* From I Dieci Libri dell'Architettura di M.V. Vitruvio tradutti..., 1556, V, p. 152
XCVI ANTONIO VISENTINI, *The Chiesa della Carità (etching after Canaletto)*
XCVII LUCA CARLEVARIJS, *The Chiesa and the Scuola della Carità: between the two, the entrance to the monastery and the scuola (etching after Canaletto)*
XCVIII VINCENZO CORONELLI, *The Convento della Carità toward the rio di Sant'Agnese.* Venice, Museo Correr
IC VINCENZO CORONELLI, *View of the cloister of the Carità.* Venice, Museo Correr
C ANTONIO VISENTINI (?), *Façade of the cloister of the Carità.* London, RIBA
CI ANTONIO VISENTINI (?), *Elevation and section of the cloister of the Carità.* Florence, Soprintendenza alle Gallerie, 3510A
CII ANTONIO VISENTINI (?), *Elevation and section of the cloister of the Carità.* London, RIBA, XIII, 2
CIII GIANNANTONIO MOSCHINI, *Atrium and cloister of the Convento della Carità in 1828.* From Nuova Guida di Venezia, 1847
CIV GIUSEPPE BORSATO (?), *The cloister of the Convento della Carità (imaginary reconstruction).* Venice, Accademia di Belle Arti
CV GIUSEPPE BORSATO (?), *The tablinum of the Convento della Carità (imaginary reconstruction).* Venice, Accademia di Belle Arti
CVI PIETRO SELVATICO, *The tablinum of the Convento della Carità.* From Sulla Architettura e sulla scultura in Venezia dal Medioevo fino ai nostri giorni, 1847, p. 329

PLATES

1. Venice. The Convento della Carità: aerial view from the west
2. Venice. The Convento della Carità: at the top, the church and monastery of the Gesuati; aerial view from the north
3. Venice. The Convento della Carità: aerial view from the southeast
4. Convento della Carità: view down the rio terra' Sant'Agnese toward the Grand Canal
5. The apse of the Church of Santa Maria della Carità and the monastery looking toward the canale della Giudecca
6. Convento della Carità: water gate and *cavana* on the rio terra' Sant'Agnese
7. Convento della Carità: the *cavana* on the rio di Sant'Agnese, closed when the canal was filled in
8. Convento della Carità: peristyle wing
9. Convento della Carità: peristyle wing
10. Convento della Carità, peristyle: details of the Ionic and Corinthian orders
11. Convento della Carità, peristyle: details of the Doric order
12. Convento della Carità, peristyle: the Doric arcade
13. Convento della Carità, peristyle: an arch of the Doric arcade
14. Convento della Carità, peristyle: Doric capital and Ionic frieze
15. Convento della Carità, peristyle: engaged column, Doric capital, and details of the lateral arches
16. Convento della Carità, peristyle: monogram of the monastery and date of construction in the Ionic frieze
17. Convento della Carità, peristyle: sequence of the orders
18. Convento della Carità, peristyle: second and third orders and the corner bays
19. Convento della Carità, peristyle: Ionic order and the nineteenth-century corner bay
20. Convento della Carità, peristyle: frieze and intercolumniation of the second story
21. Convento della Carità, peristyle: Doric arcade, Ionic loggia, and the Corinthian floor with the dormitories
22. Convento della Carità, peristyle: Corinthian order and the coping of the Ionic loggia
23. Convento della Carità, peristyle: Ionic capital and Corinthian base resting on two layers of bricks
24. Convento della Carità, peristyle: Corinthian pilaster between two dormitory windows
25. Convento della Carità, peristyle: soffit of the Ionic cornice (terra cotta)
26. Convento della Carità, peristyle: soffit of the Doric cornice (terra cotta)
27. Convento della Carità, peristyle: Corinthian coping stone
28. Convento della Carità, façade along the rio terra' Sant'Agnese: Doric frieze
29. Convento della Carità, peristyle: Doric base
30. Convento della Carità, peristyle: Ionic base and coping of the Doric order
31. Convento della Carità: Ionic loggia
32. Convento della Carità: doorway in the Ionic loggia
33. Convento della Carità, tablinum: exedra that contained a door for entering the ante-sacristy and church
34. Convento della Carità, tablinum: door giving access to the oval stair
35. Convento della Carità, tablinum: door opening into the guests' rooms; on the right, a nineteenth-century door
36. Convento della Carità, tablinum: exedra that contained the altar with the altarpiece by Carletto Caliari
37. Convento della Carità, tablinum: wall with windows facing the rio terra' Sant'Agnese
38. Convento della Carità, tablinum: nineteenth-century door with steps that rise from the sixteenth-century level to the present one
39. Convento della Carità, tablinum: section of frieze added in the nineteenth century to the original one when the then extant window was closed

40 Convento della Carità, tablinum: stucco Doric frieze around the exedrae and the present-day entrance portal (photomontage)
41-42 Convento della Carità, tablinum: frieze of the exedrae, above the niches and columns
43 Convento della Carità, tablinum: frieze and capital with the column and Doric pilaster (the marble revetment of the pilaster was added in 1948)
44 Convento della Carità, tablinum: capital and Doric cornice
45 Convento della Carità, tablinum: wall toward the atrium
46 Convento della Carità, tablinum: Doric column and niche
47 Convento della Carità, tablinum: base of a column
48 Convento della Carità: oval stair from the bottom
49 Convento della Carità, stair: steps between two niches and the window on the rio Sant'Agnese cut by a stair landing
50 Convento della Carità, stair: oblique view of the steps above the doorway into the sacristy
51 Convento della Carità, stair: steps between two windows facing the Grand Canal
52 Convento della Carità, stair: helicoidal form of the steps
53 Convento della Carità, stair: termination, with the entrance to the dormitory, the niches one above the other, and the access door to a room above an apse of the church
54 Convento della Carità: the oval stairs from above
55 Convento della Carità: the vault in the oval stair hall
56 Convento della Carità, stair: monogram of the monastery in the center of the vault

COLOR PLATES:

a CANALETTO: *The Courtyard of the Convento della Carità.* Windsor Castle, Royal Collections
b Convento della Carità: peristyle
c Convento della Carità: peristyle
d Nineteenth-century watercolor with the design of the sacristy pavement in the Convento della Carità. Venice, Biblioteca dell'Accademia di Belle Arti

SCALE DRAWINGS

The scale drawings were executed under the direction of Dott. Arch. Gilda d'Agaro, with the collaboration of Dott. Arch. Vittoria Pelzel Pallucchini, Dott. Arch. Pietro Pelzel, and Dott. Arch. Andrzej Pereswiet-Sołtan.

- *a* Convento della Carità: general plan of the area
- *b* Convento della Carità: general plan of the present-day state
- *c* Convento della Carità: plan of the ground floor
- *d* Convento della Carità: plan of the second floor
- *e* Convento della Carità: plan of the third floor
- *f* Convento della Carità: façade toward the rio terra' Sant'Agnese
- *g* Convento della Carità: façade of the courtyard and sections of the tablinum and stairs
- *h* Convento della Carità: plan of the tablinum and stairs
- *i* Convento della Carità: transverse section of the tablinum
- *j* Convento della Carità: plan and section of the stairs

PLATES

1 - Venice. The Convento della Carità: aerial view from the west

2 - Venice. The Convento della Carità: at the top, the church and monastery of the Gesuati; aerial view from the north

3 - Venice. The Convento della Carità: aerial view from the southeast

4 - Convento della Carità: view down the rio terra' Sant'Agnese toward the Grand Canal

5 - The apse of the Church of Santa Maria della Carità and the monastery looking toward the canale della Giudecca

6 - Convento della Carità: water gate and *cavana* on the rio terra' Sant'Agnese

7 - Convento della Carità: the *cavana* on the rio di Sant'Agnese, closed when the canal was filled in

8 - Convento della Carità: peristyle wing

9 - Convento della Carità: peristyle wing

10 - Convento della Carità, peristyle: details of the Ionic and Corinthian orders

11 - Convento della Carità, peristyle: details of the Doric order

12 - Convento della Carità, peristyle: the Doric arcade

13 - Convento della Carità, peristyle: an arch of the Doric arcade

14 - Convento della Carità, peristyle: Doric capital and Ionic frieze

15 - Convento della Carità, peristyle: engaged column, Doric capital, and details of the lateral arches

16 - Convento della Carità, peristyle: monogram of the monastery and date of construction in the Ionic frieze

17 - Convento della Carità, peristyle: sequence of the orders

18 - Convento della Carità, peristyle: second and third orders and the corner bays

19 - Convento della Carità, peristyle: Ionic order and the nineteenth-century corner bay

20 - Convento della Carità, peristyle: frieze and intercolumniation of the second story

21 - Convento della Carità, peristyle: Doric arcade, Ionic loggia, and the Corinthian floor with the dormitories

22 - Convento della Carità, peristyle: Corinthian order and the coping of the Ionic loggia

23 - Convento della Carità, peristyle: Ionic capital and Corinthian base resting on two layers of bricks

24 - Convento della Carità, peristyle: Corinthian pilaster between two dormitory windows

25 - Convento della Carità, peristyle: soffit of the Ionic cornice (terra cotta)

26 - Convento della Carità, peristyle: soffit of the Doric cornice (terra cotta)

27 - Convento della Carità, peristyle: Corinthian coping stone

28 - Convento della Carità, façade along the rio terra' Sant'Agnese: Doric frieze

29 - Convento della Carità, peristyle: Doric base

30 - Convento della Carità, peristyle: Ionic base and coping of the Doric order

31 - Convento della Carità: Ionic loggia

32 - Convento della Carità: doorway in the Ionic loggia

33 - Convento della Carità, tablinum: exedra that contained a door for entering the ante-sacristy and church

34 - Convento della Carità, tablinum: door giving access to the oval stair

35 - Convento della Carità, tablinum: door opening into the guests' rooms; on the right, a nineteenth-century door

36 - Convento della Carità, tablinum: exedra that contained the altar with the altarpiece by Carletto Caliari

37 - Convento della Carità, tablinum: wall with windows facing the rio terra' Sant'Agnese

38 - Convento della Carità, tablinum: nineteenth-century door with steps that rise from the sixteenth-century level to the present one

39 - Convento della Carità, tablinum: section of frieze added in the nineteenth century to the original one when the then extant window was closed

40 - Convento della Carità, tablinum: stucco Doric frieze around the exedrae and the present-day entrance portal (photomontage)

41-42 - Convento della Carità, tablinum: frieze of the exedrae, above the niches and columns

43 - Convento della Carità, tablinum: frieze and capital with the column and Doric pilaster
(the marble revetment of the pilaster was added in 1948)

44 - Convento della Carità, tablinum: capital and Doric cornice

45 - Convento della Carità, tablinum: wall toward the atrium

46 - Convento della Carità, tablinum: Doric column and niche

47 - Convento della Carità, tablinum: base of a column

48 - Convento della Carità: oval stair from the bottom

49 - Convento della Carità, stair: steps between two niches and the window on the rio Sant'Agnese cut by a stair landing

50 - Convento della Carità, stair: oblique view of the steps above the doorway into the sacristy

51 - Convento della Carità, stair: steps between two windows facing the Grand Canal

52 - Convento della Carità, stair: helicoidal form of the steps

53 - Convento della Carità, stair: termination, with the entrance to the dormitory, the niches one above the other, and the access door to a room above an apse of the church

54 - Convento della Carità: the oval stairs from above

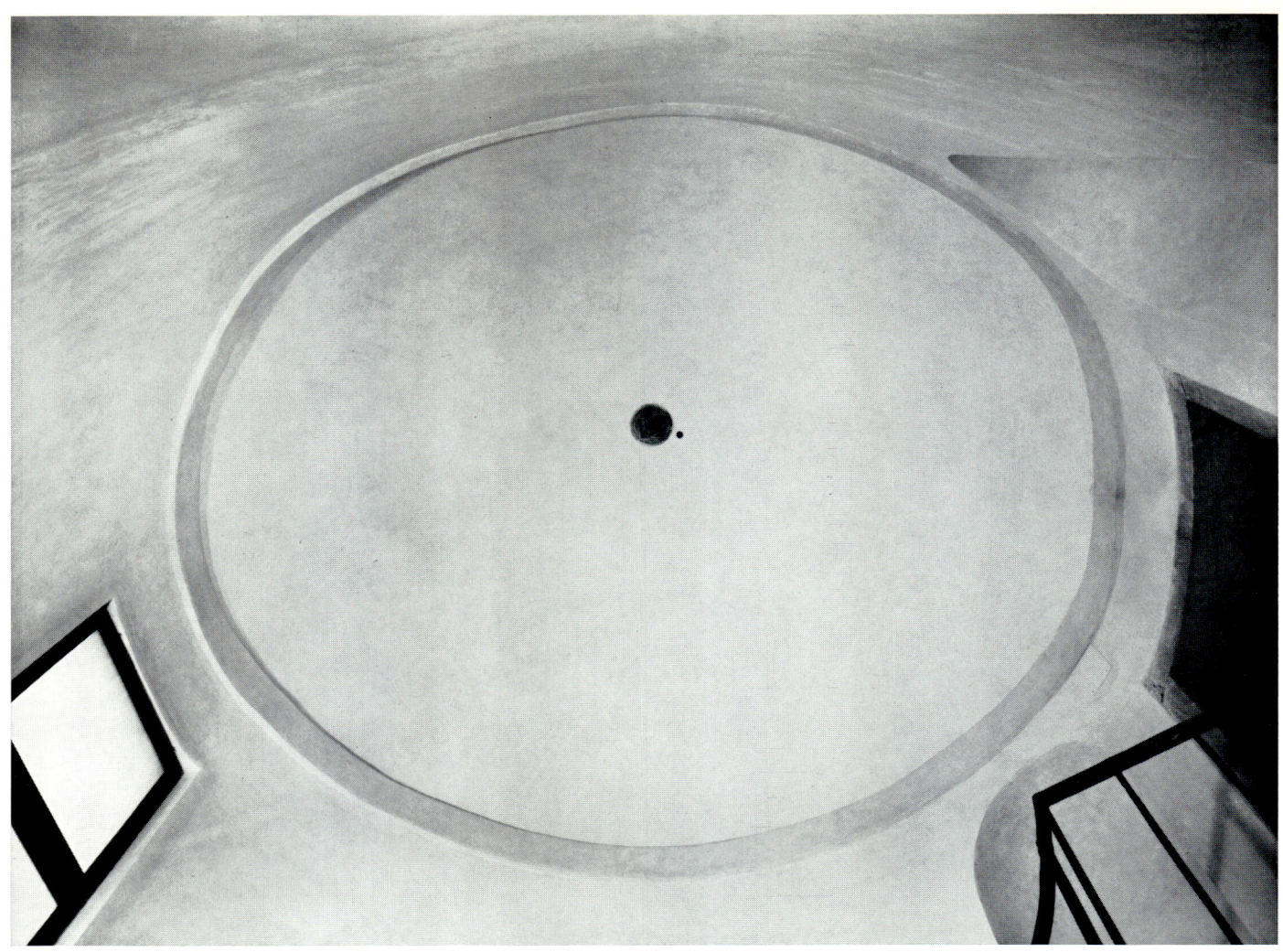
55 - Convento della Carità, the vault in the oval stair hall

56 - Convento della Carità, stair: monogram of the monastery in the center of the vault

SCALE DRAWINGS

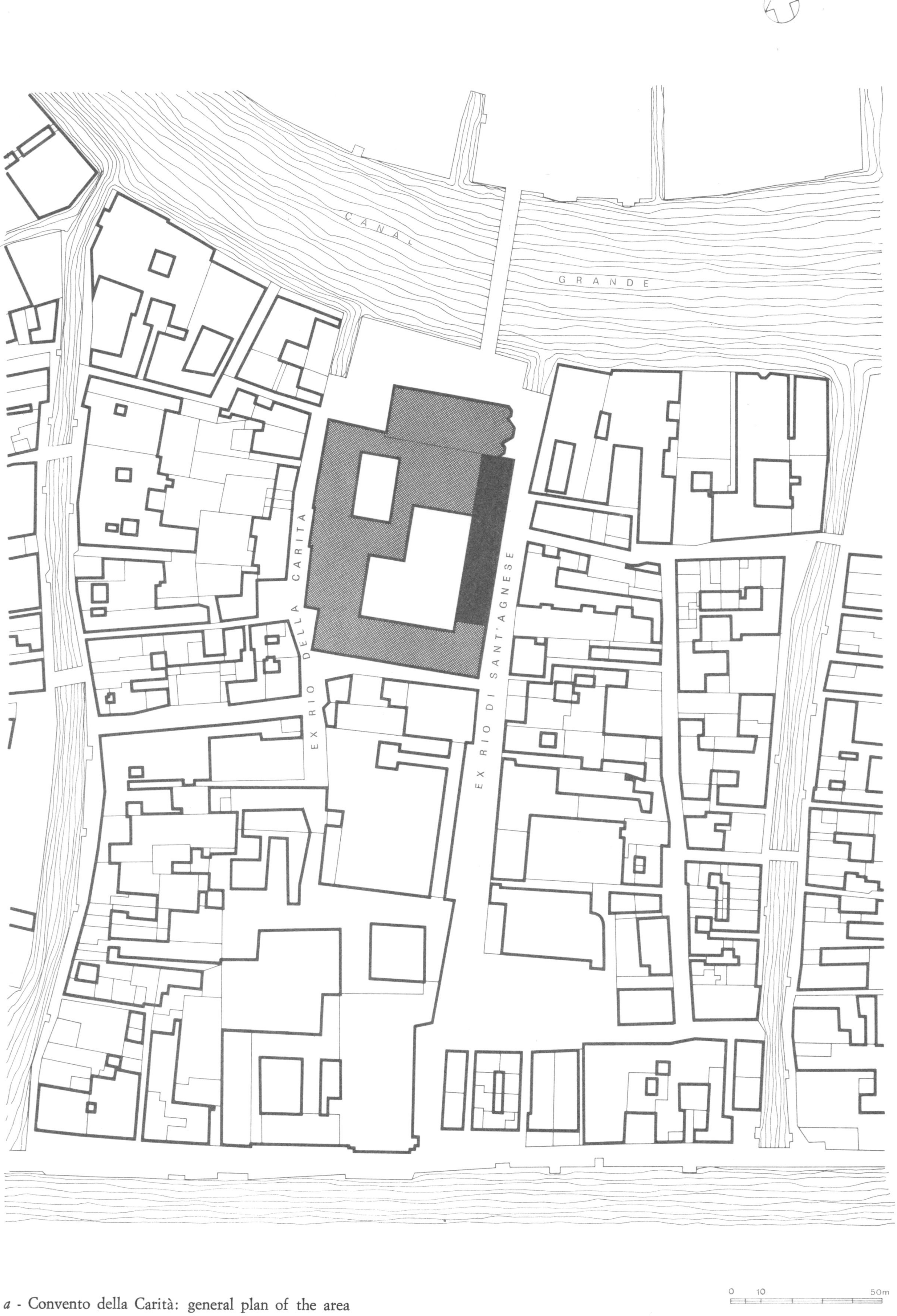

a - Convento della Carità: general plan of the area

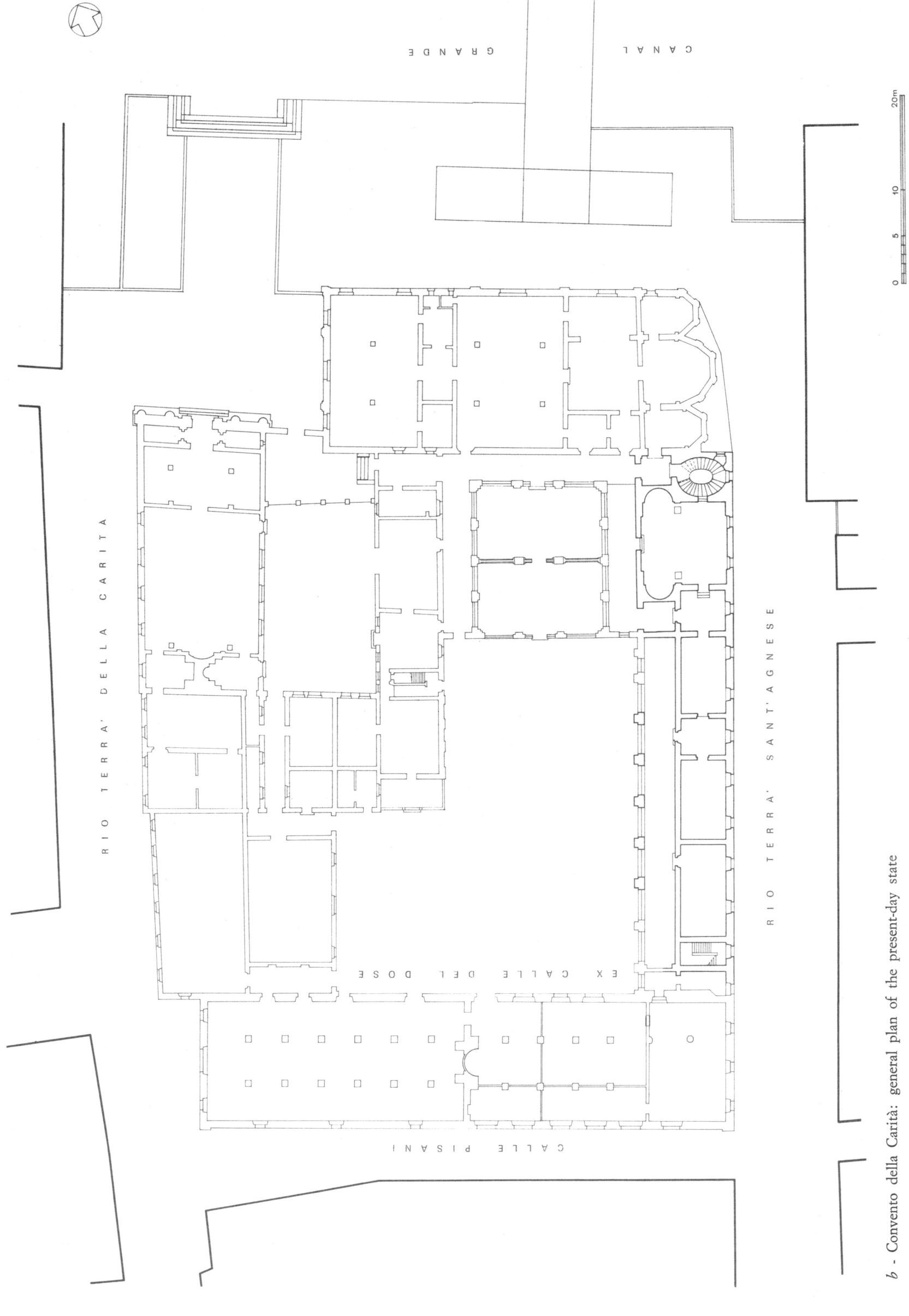

b - Convento della Carità: general plan of the present-day state

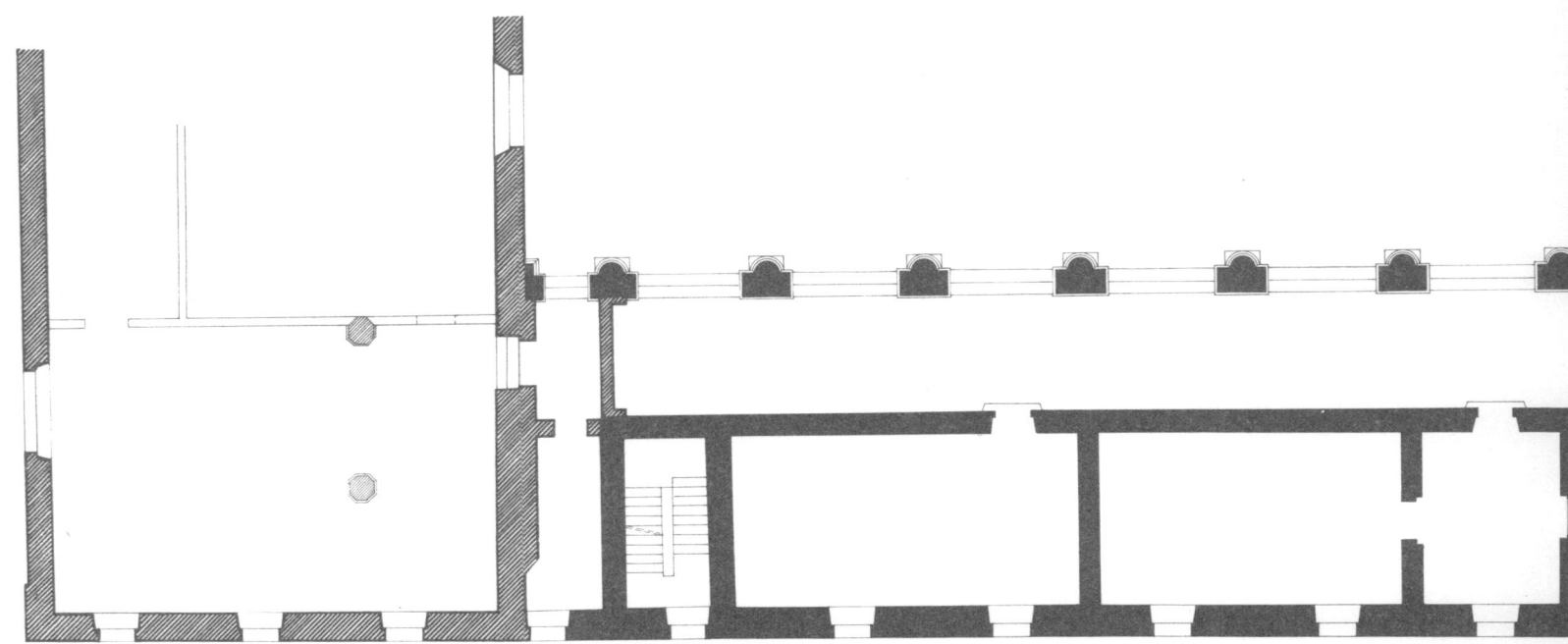

c - Convento della Carità: plan of the ground floor

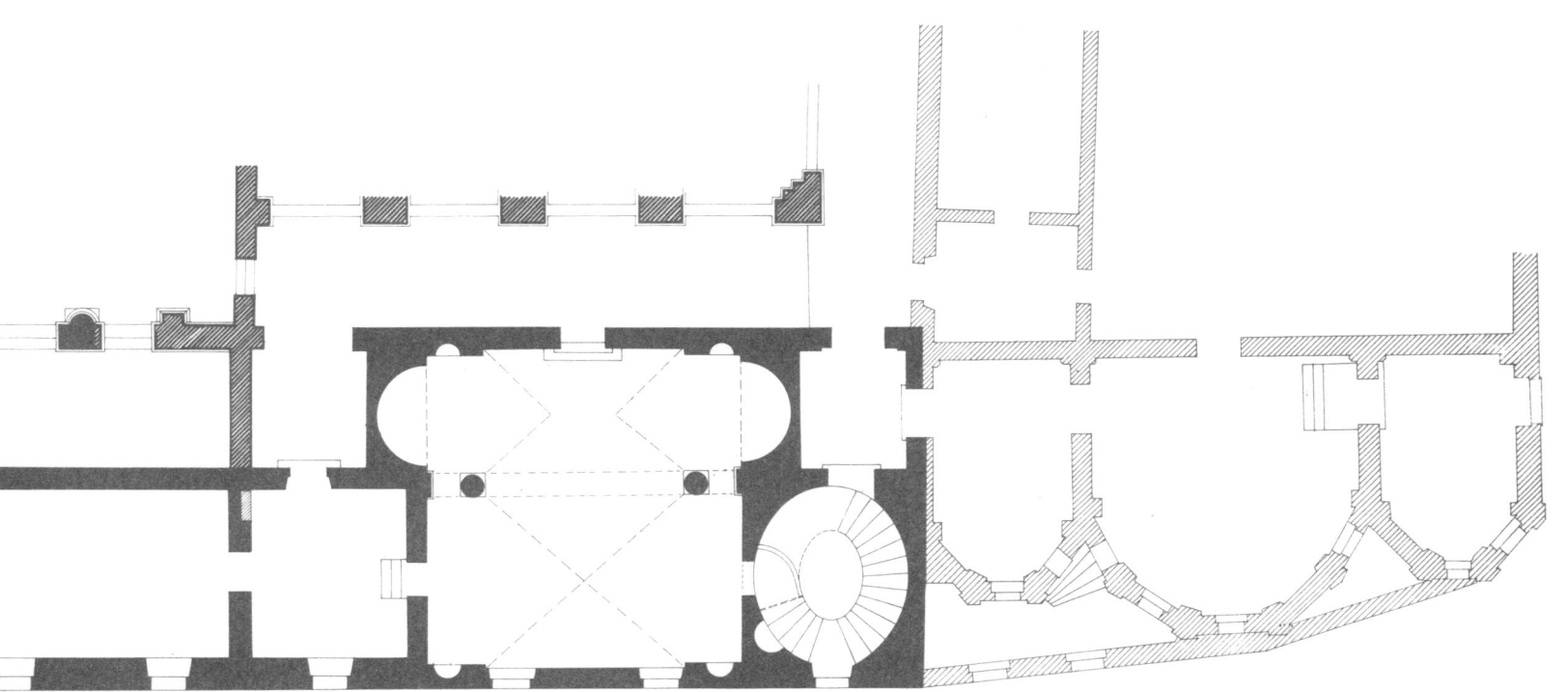

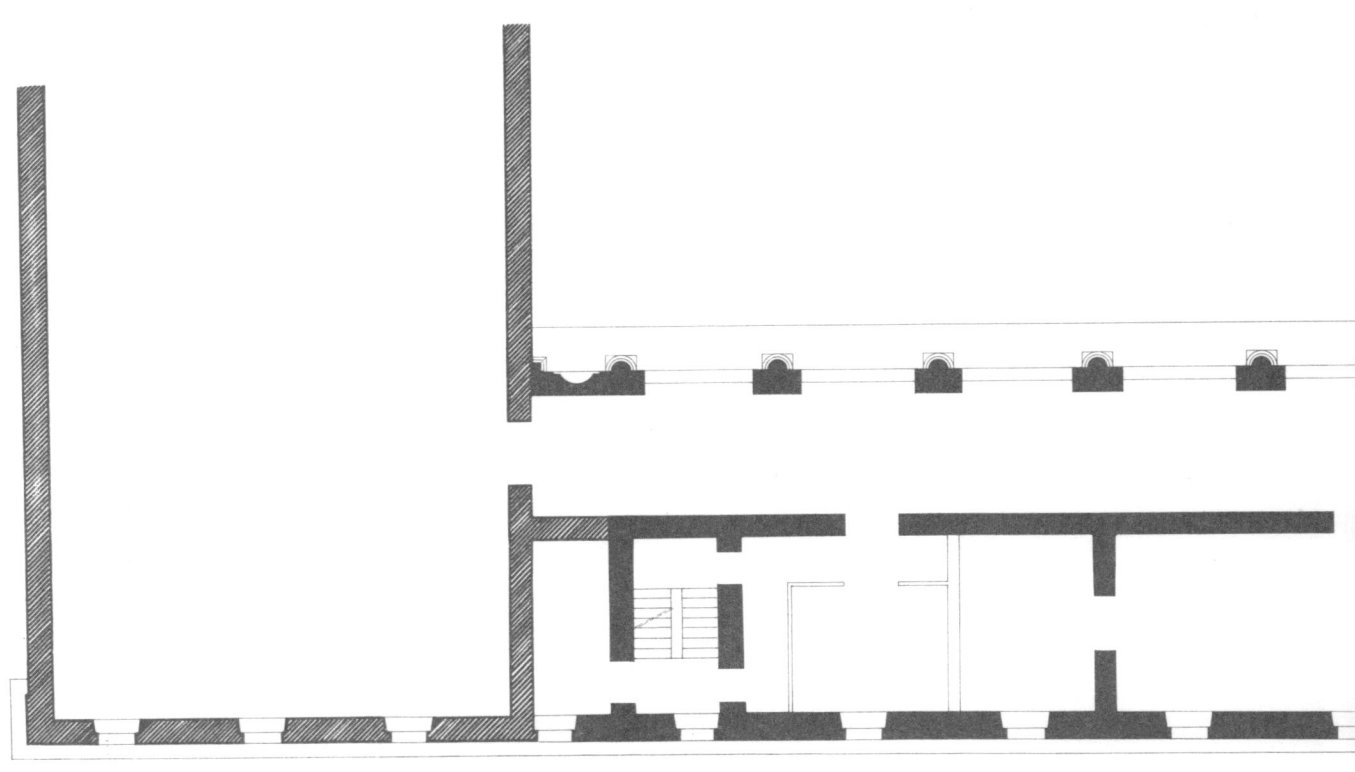

d - Convento della Carità: plan of the second floor

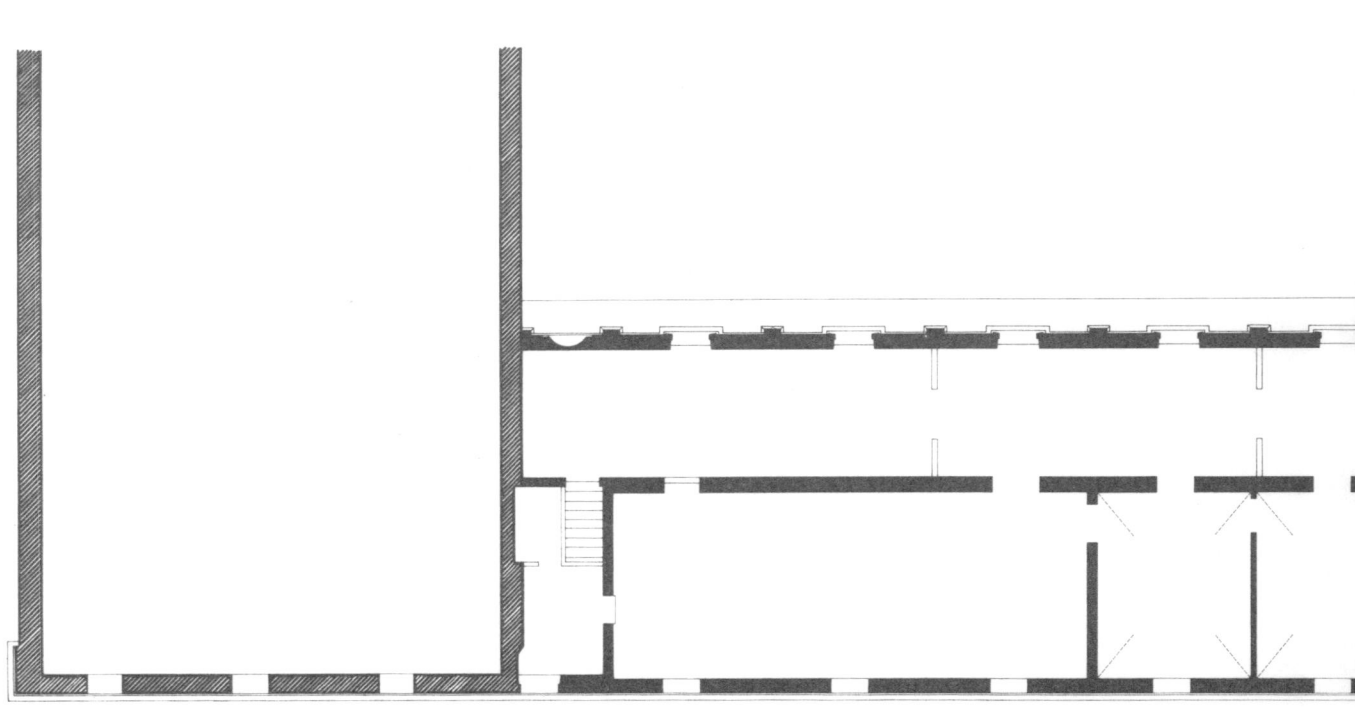

e - Convento della Carità: plan of the third floor

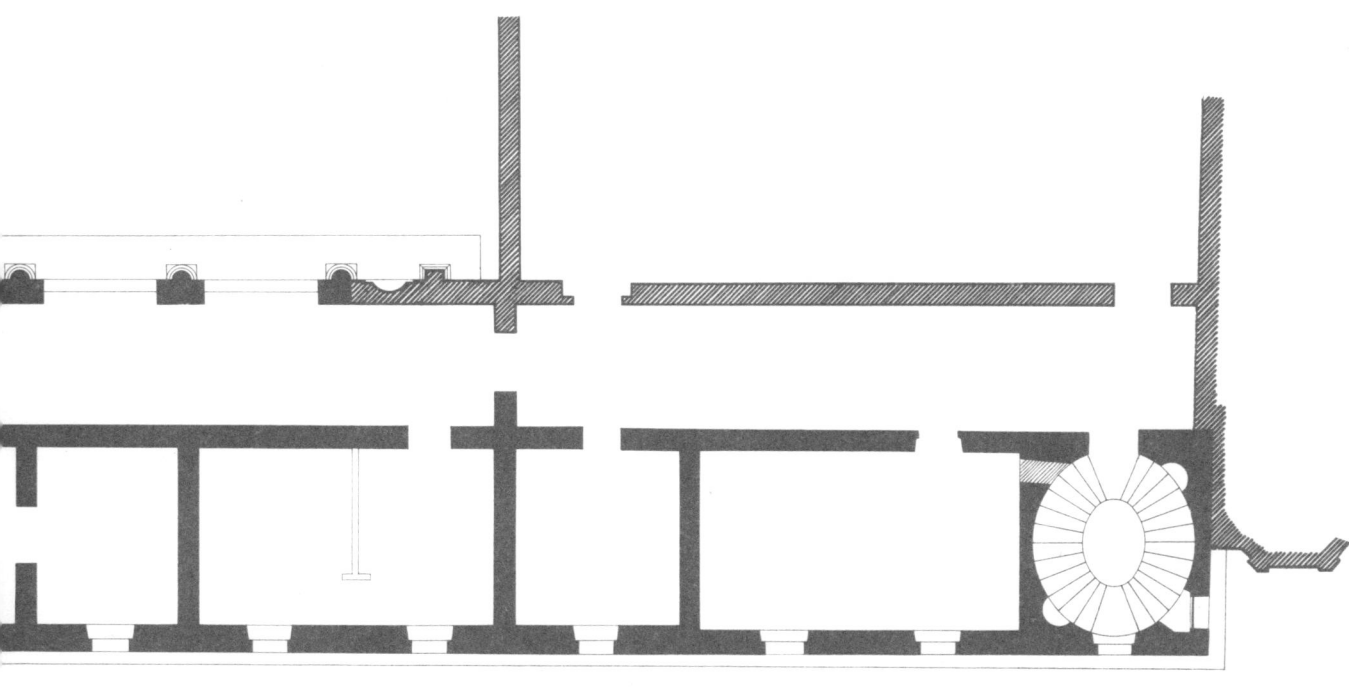

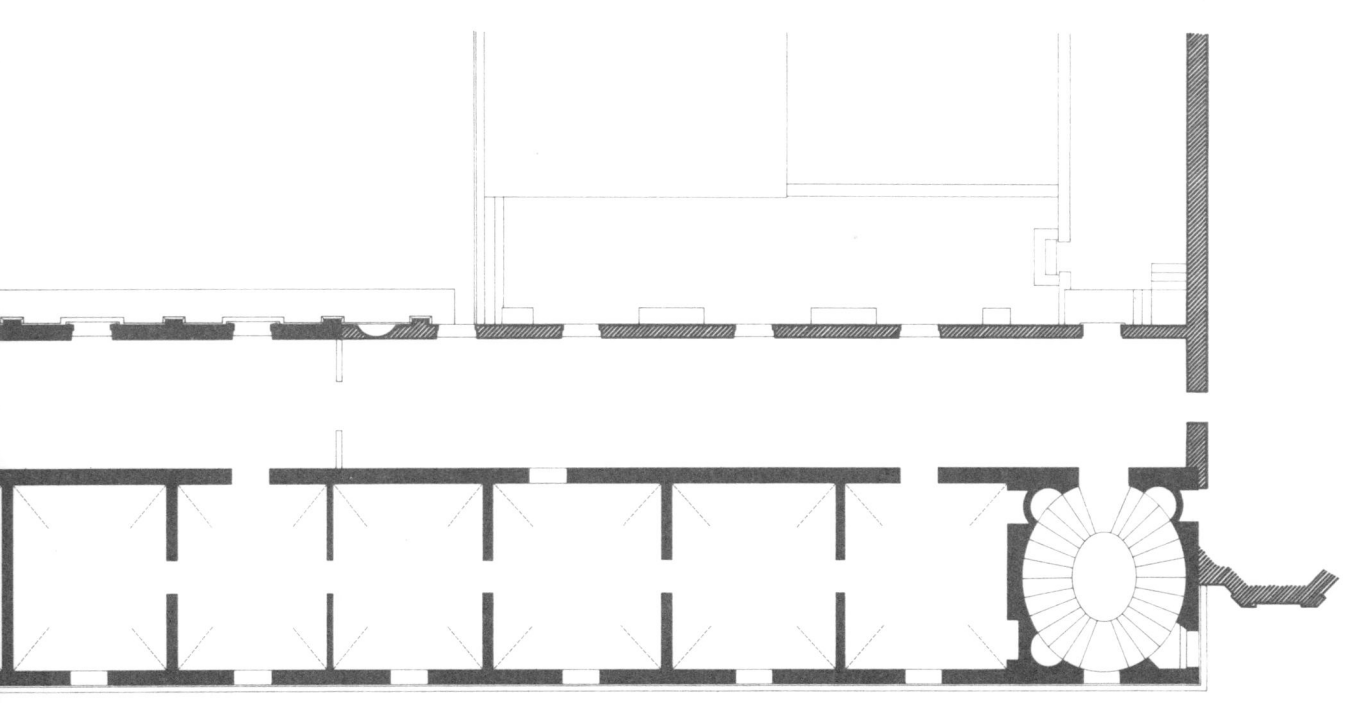

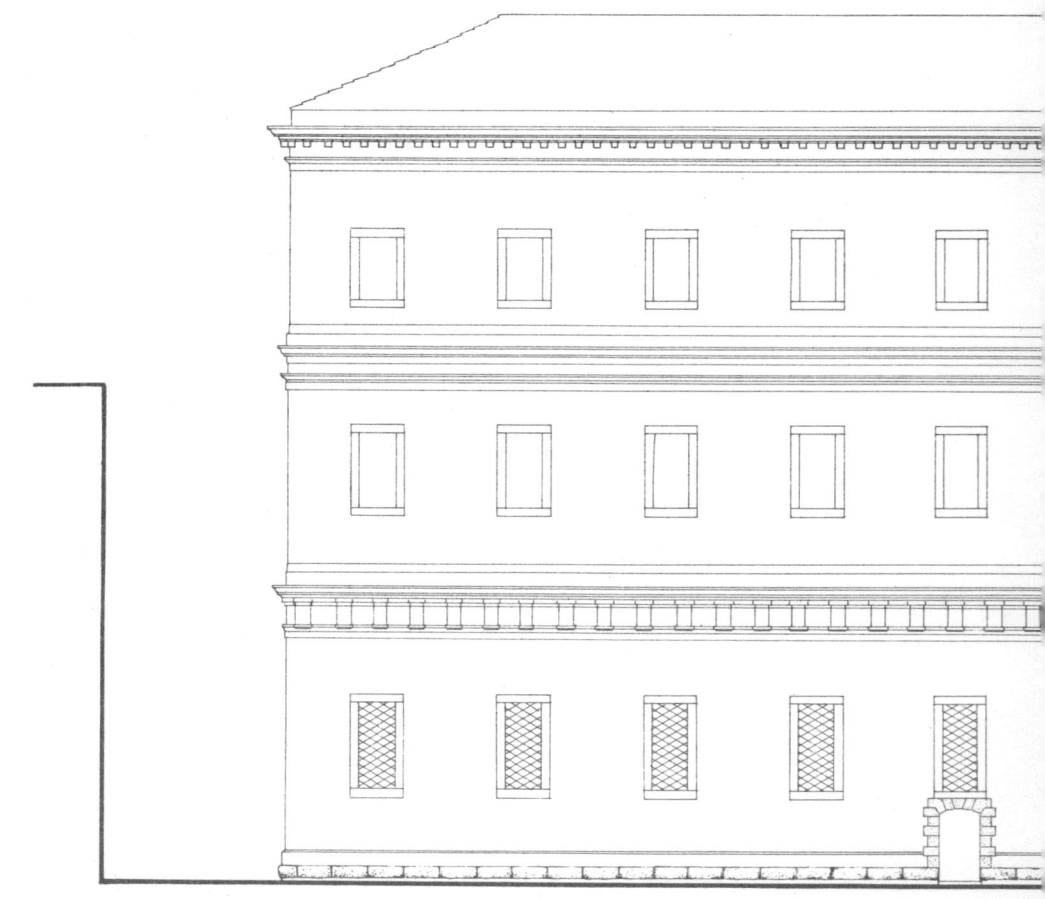

f - Convento della Carità: façade toward the rio terra' Sant'Agnese

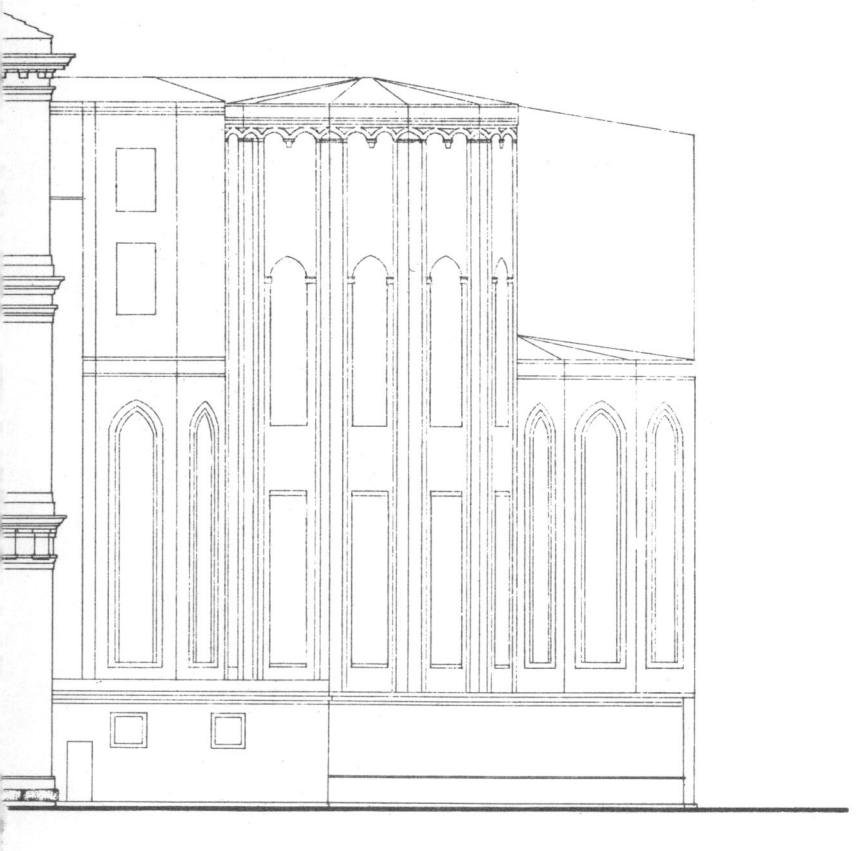

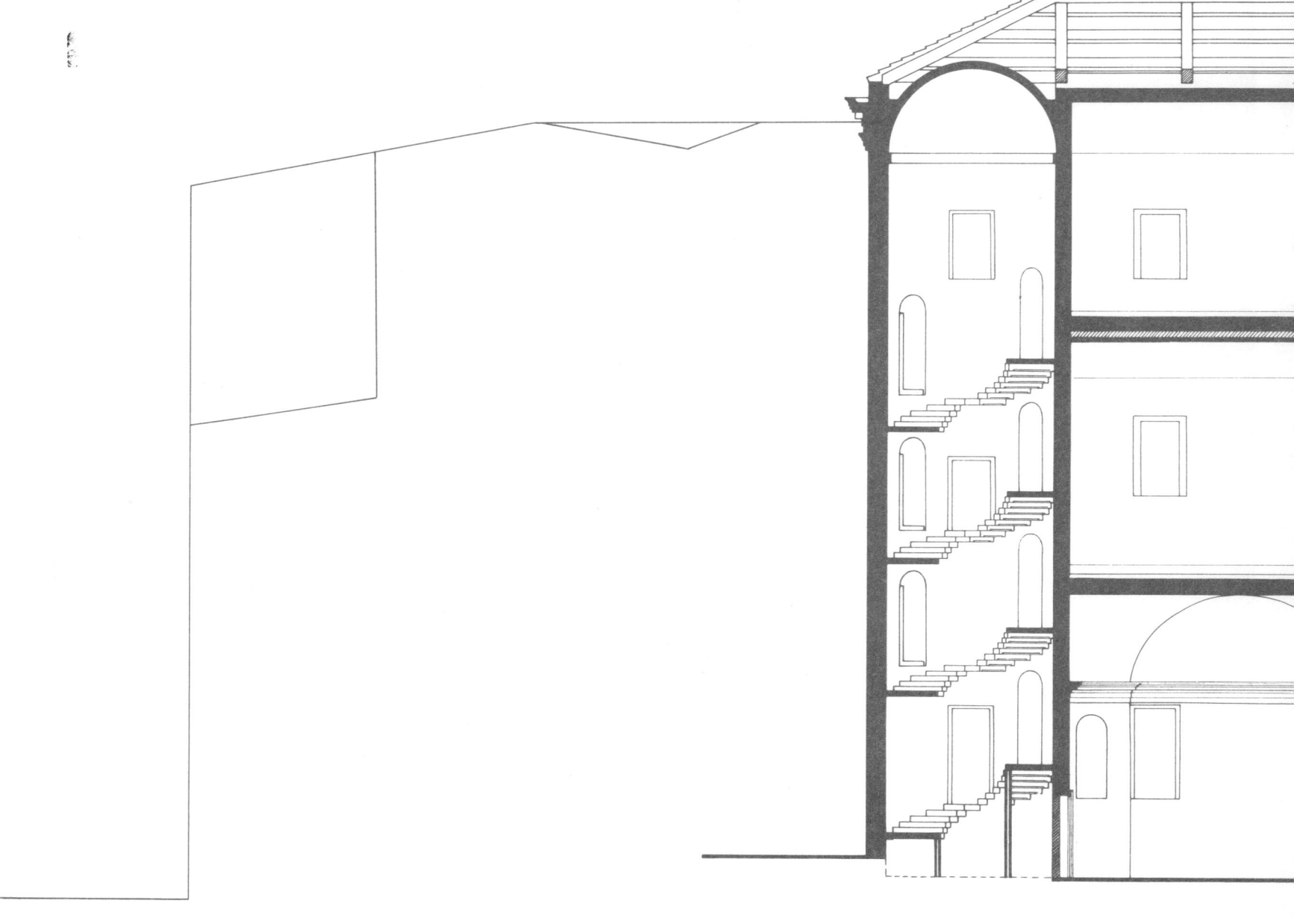

g - Convento della Carità: façade of the courtyard and sections of the tablinum and stairs

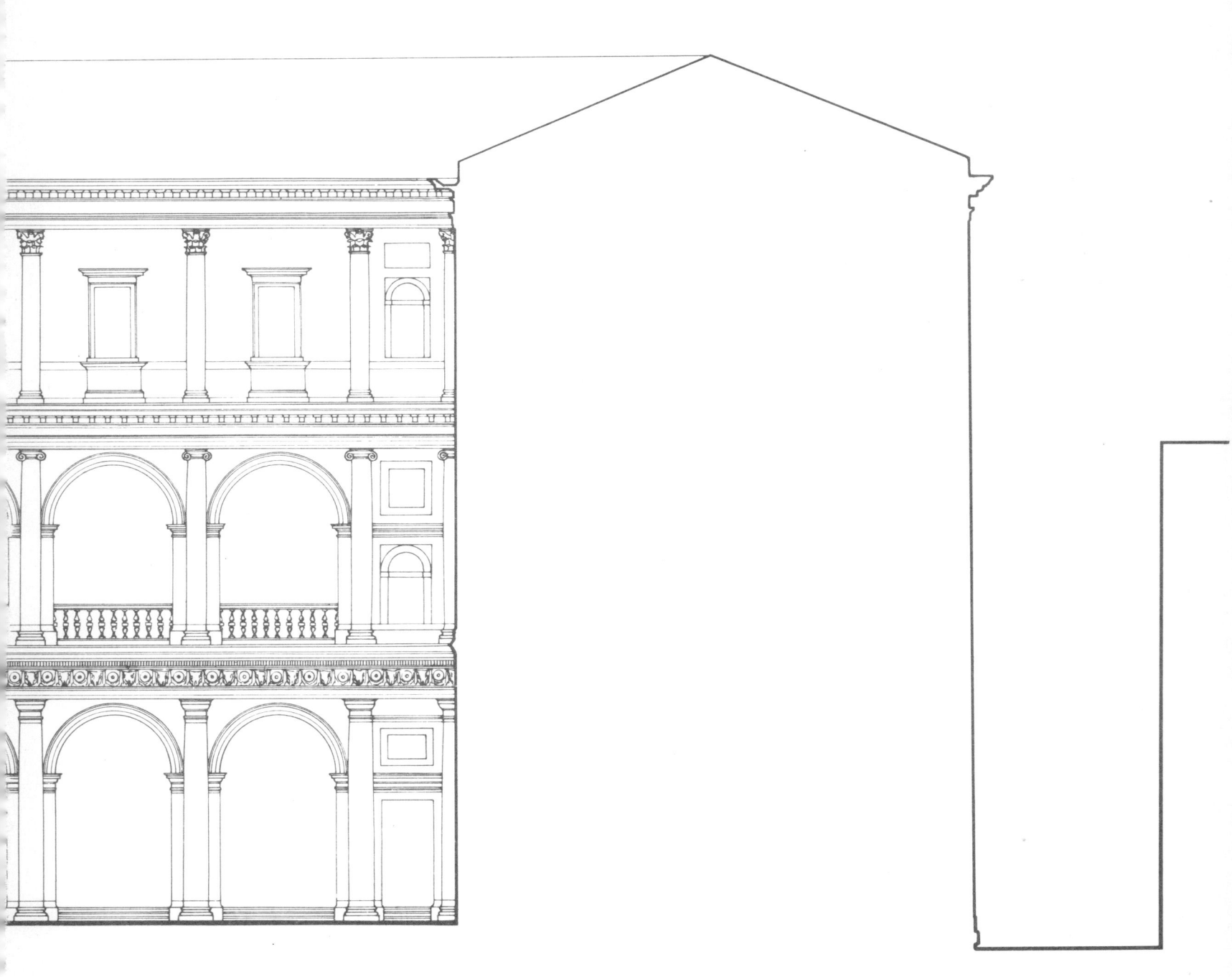

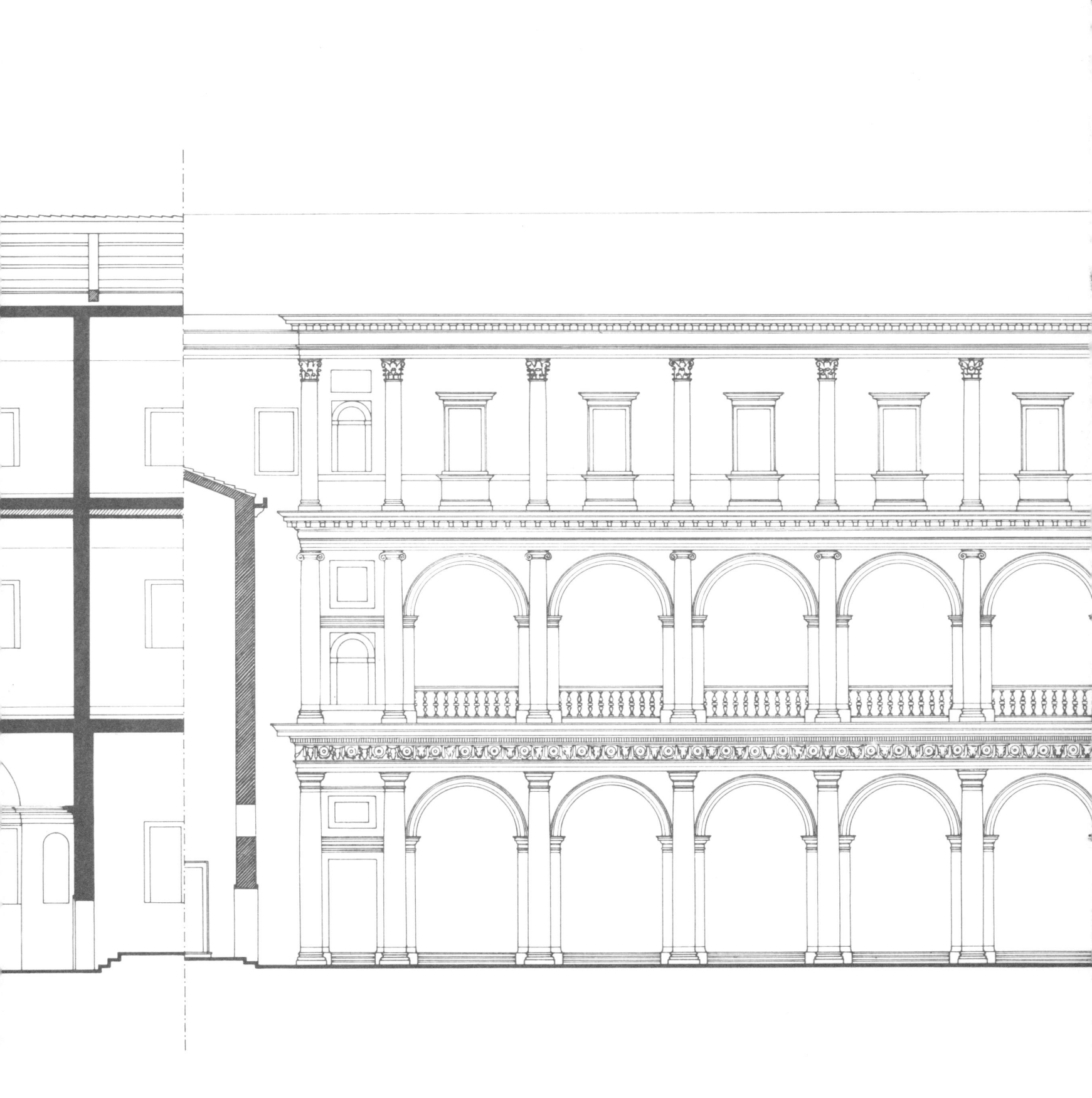

b - Convento della Carità: plan of the tablinum and stairs

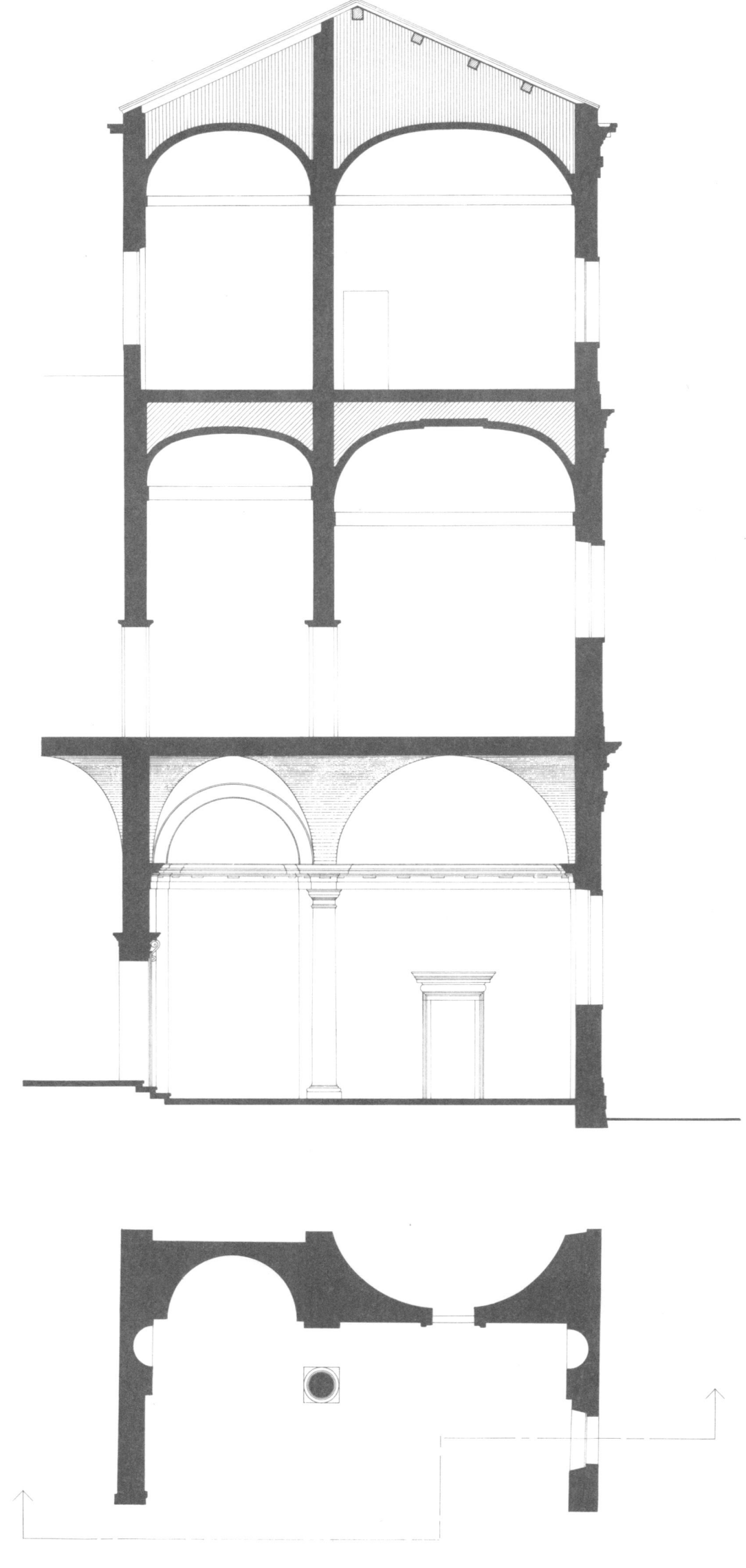

i - Convento della Carità: transverse section of the tablinum

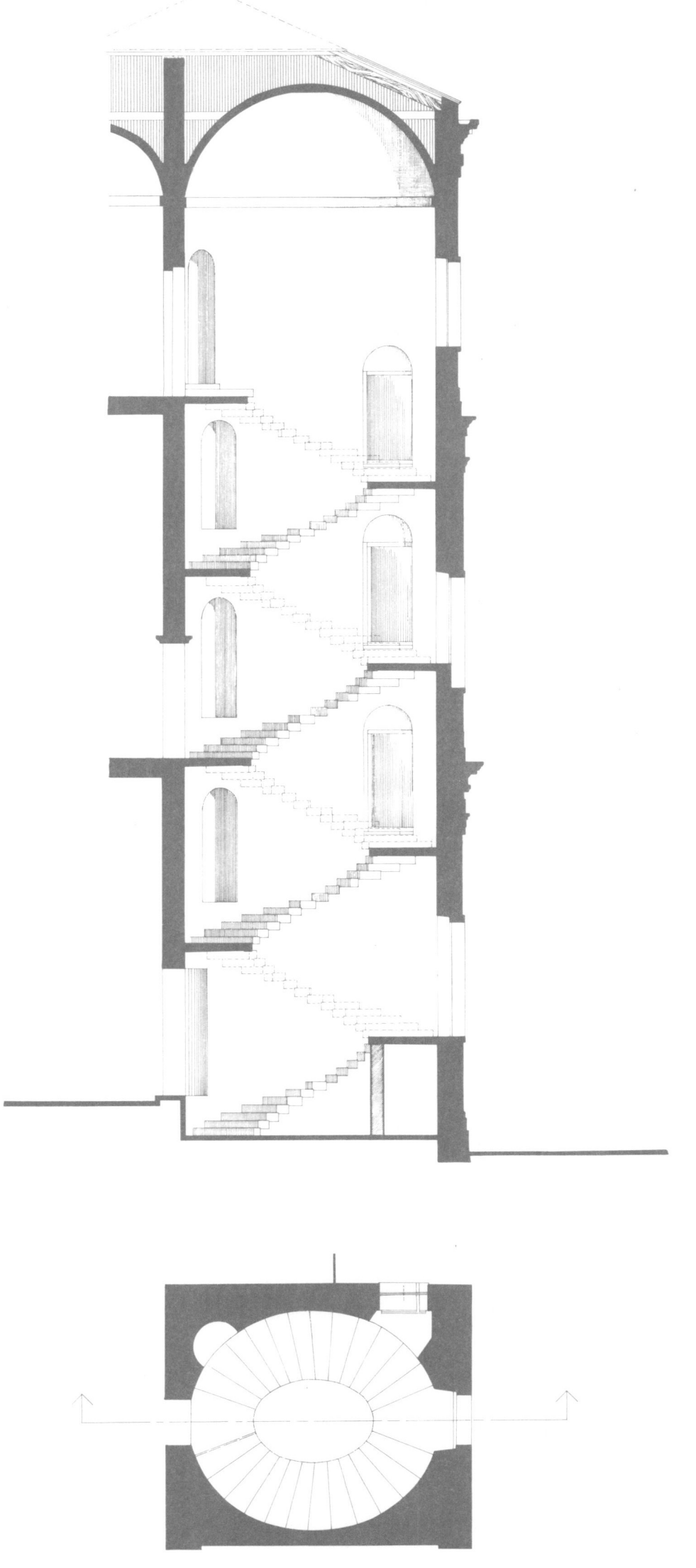

j - Convento della Carità: plan and section of the stairs

PRINTED BY O.T.V. STOCCHIERO S.p.A., VICENZA, IN GARAMOND TYPE USING PAPERALBA (TEXT) AND RUSTICUS (DRAWINGS) FROM CARTIERA VENTURA AND LARIUS (ILLUSTRATIONS) FROM CARTIERA BURGO. THE PLATES WERE PRINTED BY A. MONTICELLI, PADUA. THE DRAWINGS WERE PRINTED BY FOTOTECNICA AND VAJENTI, VICENZA. BINDING BY LAGHETTO & C. S. A.S., VICENZA.

PHOTOGRAPHIC CREDITS: ALINARI, FLORENCE: V; ARCHIVIO DI STATO, VENICE: XVI-XXII, XXIV; ARCHIVIO MARSILIO EDITORI, PADUA: VI; BORLUI, VENICE: 1, 3; CINECOLORFOTO, VICENZA: XLII, IL, L, LVII; C.I.S.A., VICENZA: VIII-XII, XIV, XXV, XXXV, XXXVI, XXXIX-XLI, XLIII-XLVIII, LIII-LVII, LIX; FERRUZZI, VENICE: 2; G.F.S.G., FLORENCE: CI; GIACOMELLI, VENICE: I-III; LORD CHAMBERLAIN'S OFFICE, LONDON: *a* (*copyright reserved*); MUSEO CIVICO, VICENZA: XXVIII; MUSEO CORRER, VENICE: XCVIII-IC; R.I.B.A., LONDON: XXVI, C. CII; ROSSI, VENICE: b - c, LXI, LXIII-LXV, LXVII-LXX, LXXVIII, LXXIX, LXXXI-LXXXIII, LXXXV, LXXXVI, LXXXVIII, LXXXIX, XCII, XCIV, 4, 5, 7-20, 28-33, 35, 36, 47, 48, 50, 54-56; THE NATIONAL GALLERY, LONDON: IV (*reproduced by courtesy of The Trustees of the National Gallery*); TOFFOLETTI, VENICE *d*, VI, VII, XIII, XXIII, LX, LXII, LXVI, LXXI-LXXVII, LXXX, LXXXIV, LXXXVII, XCI, XCIII, XCV-XCVII, CIII-CVI, 6, 21-27, 34, 37-46, 49, 51-53; UFFIZI, GABINETTO DEI DISEGNI, FLORENCE: XXVII; VAJENTI, VICENZA: XV, XXXVII, XXXVIII.

THE NEGATIVES FOR PHOTOS FROM ROSSI, VENICE, ARE HELD BY THE C.I.S.A.